How to Buy Everything for Your Wedding on eBay . . . and Save a Fortune!

Other books by Dennis L. Prince

How to Sell Anything on eBay . . . and Make a Fortune!

Unleashing the Power of eBay

How to Sell Anything on eBay . . . and Make a Fortune! Organizer

With Lynn Dralle

*How to Sell Antiques and Collectibles
on eBay . . . and Make a Fortune!*

With William M. Meyer

*How to Sell Music, Collectibles, and Instruments
on eBay . . . and Make a Fortune!*

How to Buy Everything for Your Wedding on eBay . . . and Save a Fortune!

Dennis L. Prince
Sarah Manongdo
Dan Joya

McGraw-Hill

New York   Chicago   San Francisco
Lisbon   London   Madrid   Mexico City   Milan
New Delhi   San Juan   Seoul   Singapore

The **McGraw·Hill** Companies

1 2 3 4 5 6 7 8 9 0   DOC/DOC   098765

ISBN 0-07-145541-8

This publication is designed to provide accurate and authoritative information in regard to the subject matter covered. It is sold with the understanding that the publisher is not engaged in rendering legal, accounting, or other professional service. If legal advice or other expert assistance is required, the services of a competent professional person should be sought.
>   —From a declaration of principles jointly adopted by a committee of the
>   American Bar Association and a committee of publishers.

McGraw-Hill books are available at special quantity discounts to use as premiums and sales promotions, or for use in corporate training programs. For more information, please write to the Director of Special Sales, Professional Publishing, McGraw-Hill, Two Penn Plaza, New York, NY 10121-2298. Or contact your local bookstore.

 This book is printed on recycled, acid-free paper containing a minimum of 50% recycled, de-inked fiber.

Library of Congress Cataloging-in-Publication Data

Prince, Dennis L.
  How to buy everything for your wedding on eBay—and save a fortune! / Dennis L. Prince, Dan Joya, Sarah Manongdo.
     p. cm.
  Includes index.
  ISBN 0-07-145541-8 (alk. paper)
  1. Weddings—Planning. 2. Internet auctions. 3. eBay (Firm) I. Joya, Dan. II. Manongdo, Sarah. III. Title.
  HQ745.P75 2005
  395.2'2—dc22
                              2005000244

We jointly dedicate this book to aspiring eBay brides and grooms everywhere, as well as to their families. Have fun planning your eBay wedding, and never be afraid to dream, because dreams do come true.

FROM SARAH

*My dedication goes to my parents, Ernesto and Leticia Manongdo;
my older brothers, Mark and Bryan; my cousins Andrew and Viola
and their kids; my aunts Tita Mel, Tita Beth, and their families;
all my family in the Philippines; my posse Jenny Mui, Kim Solis,
Kathy Chang, and Isabel Collins; and my good friends Faye Tumang,
Eliza Moe, and Dien Le, for their support and love. Last but not least,
I dedicate this book to my best friend, fiancé, and coauthor,
"Ranger Dan," the one who can make me laugh for life
and who makes every day an adventure.
I love you, Bunny!*

FROM DAN

*I dedicate this book to my parents, Norberto and Violeta Joya; my
grandmother Magdalena Fernandez; my aunt Teresita Corcuera and her
loving family; my aunt and uncle Josephine and Ed Fernandez and their loving
families; my cousins JoCezar ("JC") Fernandez, Ishmael Joya, and
Noel Figueroa; my myriad of Joya relatives; my friends John Moe,
Victor Dixon, Cory Dolley, Stephan Zaniolo, Bill Messner, Debjit Sarkar,
Matt Lehan, and Jim ("Aviam") Ancmon; and my two dogs Rags and
Dodger, for their love, friendship, and support. A special thanks
and dedication to Sarah, the soon-to-be Mrs. Joya—my coauthor,
my partner in crime, my Rubber Ducky, and my love.*

FROM DENNIS

For my wife, Diane—you are the "find" of a lifetime.

Contents

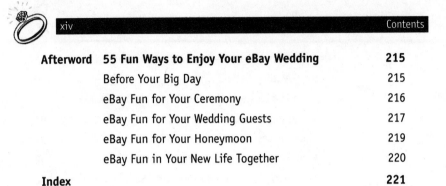

Acknowledgments

From Dennis L. Prince

The truth is that any good book that one person writes is made better by the team with which he or she works. Certainly, my case is no exception, and it's my duty—no, it's my pleasure—to extend my sincerest thanks to those with whom I've worked to bring this book to completion.

Of course, I begin with my coauthors, Sarah Manongdo and Dan Joya. It's been my privilege to have had the opportunity to work and write with you as you have chronicled the excitement of planning and preparing for your wedding—eBay style—which has reminded me of the joy of my own wedding some 18 years ago. I toast the two of you and wish you the best of life together.

Next, at McGraw-Hill, I give my deepest thanks and ask Donya Dickerson, acquisition editor, to stand for a well-deserved round of applause. She has the innate vision, enthusiasm, and terrific timing to bring a new title like this to publication without ever missing a step or overlooking a crucial detail. Donya, you're the best, and I'm always happy to be in your "wedding party." Rounding out the McGraw-Hill team in attendance are the wonderful Mary Glen, Anthony Sarchiapone, Brian Boucher, and the entire sales and marketing team. Thanks to all of you for sharing this unique experience with us.

And, last but not least, thanks to every bride, groom, and attendant who ever recognized eBay as a place where beautiful lives together can begin. For all those mentioned in this book and everyone else we've talked to, we raise our glasses to you for playing such a pivotal role in helping couples host their own celebrations in exciting eBay style. And for those of you who are readying your own joyous celebrations, get ready to enjoy the experience of a lifetime.

From Sarah Manongdo and Dan Joya

We'd like to thank our coauthor, Dennis Prince, for giving us the opportunity to tell our story and share in this wonderful and exciting project, and for inspiring us to work hard and, at the same time, have fun. We'd also like to thank our editor, Donya Dickerson, for her hard work and patient guidance during the writing of this book. Last but not least, we'd like to thank the more than seven dozen eBay wedding sellers who participated and enthusiastically supported us in this adventure. We wouldn't have been able to do it without you!

How to Buy Everything for Your Wedding on eBay . . . and Save a Fortune!

PART 1

THE NEW WAY TO PLAN YOUR WEDDING . . . AND SAVE A FORTUNE!

1

Getting Started and Getting Ready to Save a Fortune!

Congratulations on your upcoming wedding! It's a very exciting time for you, your fiancé, and your family. Almost as exciting is the fact that shopping for your wedding items on eBay is fun and cost-effective. Before you can begin your wedding shopping and saving at eBay, though, you'll first need to register. Nope, not the kind of "registering" you do to help your wedding guests pick out gifts for you (that comes later). You need to become a registered eBay user to make the most of all the site has to offer in preparation for your big day.

Registration is the key to your success at eBay; by registering, not only will you clearly identify who you are (and thereby indicate your intention to do good business), but you'll gain access to thousands of sellers who have exactly what you need to make your wedding a success. And through eBay, these sellers have all identified themselves—this should give you the confidence to bid and buy until you have everything you need for the wedding of your dreams. Registration takes only a few minutes, and once it's completed, you're ready to begin your shopping adventure.

eBay TIP: Of course, if you're already a registered eBay user and have used the site in the past to buy or sell, feel free to skip this section (but don't forget to read the part of this chapter that discusses online payment sites that will make your eBay shopping experience easier yet).

REGISTERING AT eBAY

Starting at eBay's home page, look for either the set of three blue buttons just below the "What are you looking for?" search window or the text link "register" above the toolbar at the top of the page. Use either the pushbutton or the link to begin your registration (see the illustration in Figure 1-1).

Next, click on the "register now" button or the "register" text link and jump to the initial registration screen, pictured in Figure 1-2. In the first part of this registration screen, enter your name, address, and phone number(s). This information will be stored by eBay and can be provided to other users to help them contact you. Don't worry; eBay isn't in the practice of distributing this information freely, but, in an effort to ensure safe trading, it does make the information available (upon legitimate request from registered users only) to smooth out any issues related to a transaction.

When you have the first half of the screen filled out, scroll down to the second half (pictured in Figure 1-3), enter your e-mail address, and establish your user ID and password. Providing a valid e-mail address here is critical in completing the registration process, as eBay will send a confirming message to that address, giving you a critical bit of information that you'll need to retrieve for the final step in registering.

Figure 1-1 Use either the "register now" button or the "register" text link to get started at eBay.

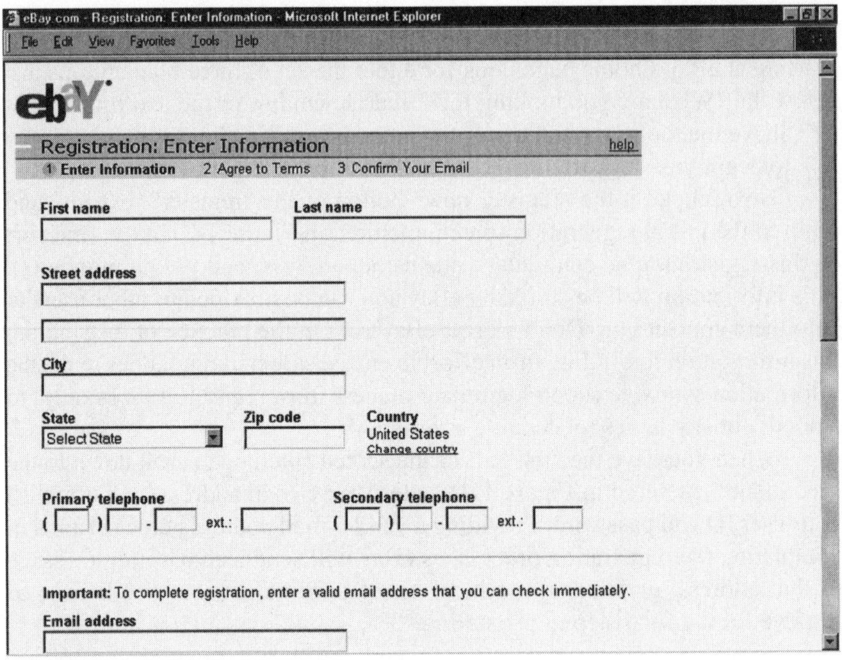

---

eBay.com - Registration: Enter Information - Microsoft Internet Explorer

File   Edit   View   Favorites   Tools   Help

eb Y®

Registration: Enter Information   help

1 Enter Information   2 Agree to Terms   3 Confirm Your Email

First name

Last name

Street address

City

State

Select State

Zip code

Country
United States
Change country

Primary telephone
( ) - ext.:

Secondary telephone
( ) - ext.:

Important: To complete registration, enter a valid email address that you can check immediately.

Email address

Figure 1-2 Begin the registration process by providing your personal information.

---

eBay TIP: Your eBay user ID is more than just a catchy screen name—it's also a form of privacy protection. At one time, eBay used your e-mail address as a user ID; then along came the "harvesters": individuals and customized "bots" (automated programs) that would collect all the e-mail addresses they could find and use them for addressing unsolicited e-mail messages, annoying sales pitches, and other forms of spam. In response, eBay implemented the user ID, which allows users to protect their e-mail addresses from prying eyes.

Once you've filled out the rest of this information, click on the "Continue" button to move forward in the registration process. Be advised, eBay checks to ensure that the user ID you've chosen isn't already being used by someone else. If it is, you'll see a screen like that pictured in Figure 1-4, and you'll need to make another selection. You can elect to have eBay help you determine a different ID (as noted on the left-hand portion of the screen), or you can directly enter a new ID of your own (using the right-hand portion of the screen). Click on the "Create Another User ID" button to validate your new selection.

eBay.com - Registration: Enter Information - Microsoft Internet Explorer

File   Edit   View   Favorites   Tools   Help

Important: To complete registration, enter a valid email address that you can check immediately.

Email address

Re-enter email address

Create your eBay User ID

Example: rose789 (Don't use your email address)
Your User ID identifies you to other eBay users.

Create password

6 character minimum
Enter a password that's easy for you to remember, but hard for others to guess. **See tips.**

Re-enter password

Secret question   **Secret answer**

Pick a suggested question...

You will be asked for the answer to your secret question if you forget your password.

Date of birth

–Month–   –Day–   Year

Continue >

Figure 1-3 The second part of the initial registration screen requires your e-mail address and the creation of your user ID and password.

If the user ID you've selected is valid, your next step in the registration process is to confirm your acceptance of the site's User Agreement and Privacy Policy (as shown in Figure 1-5). Please read the text in both scrollable windows carefully so that you understand the terms on which you'll be expected to conduct yourself and to what degree eBay will bear any responsibility for your actions and transactions.

While there's nothing in eBay's user agreement that truly has "teeth," you need to recognize that eBay stands by its assertion that it is a venue only and cannot be held liable for your actions or the actions of others while transacting on the site. Again, there's nothing dangerous here, and if you apply the safe trading methods presented throughout this book, you'll find that trading on eBay can be quite safe indeed. So, if you agree to the terms, indicate as much by clicking on the "I Agree To These Terms" button at the bottom of the page. Oh, and don't forget to click on the checkboxes indicating that you're of legal age (no youngsters allowed) and that you understand that you can change your notification preferences at a later time. If you disagree with all of this, click the little "I decline" text link; of course, you won't be able to use the site to prepare for your wedding should you choose this option.

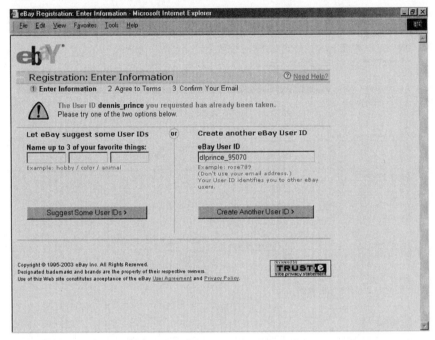

Figure 1-4 If the user ID you chose has already been taken, this screen will help you select another.

If you've agreed to the terms and processed the user agreement screen, you'll see another screen, shown in Figure 1-6, instructing you to check your e-mail for a special message that holds the final key to eBay registration. The message you'll receive, as pictured in Figure 1-7, provides an active link, labeled "Confirm eBay Registration," that confirms communication with the e-mail address you've provided. Click on the link and you'll soon be taken to the eBay site, where you'll be greeted by the screen pictured in Figure 1-8.

Armed with your active user ID, you're ready to set out on your quest for great wedding deals along the path to saving a fortune on your bridal needs at eBay. By the way, you might have seen the popup window, also pictured in Figure 1-8, where eBay is curious to learn a bit more about you. Answer only if you want to; this information isn't required in order to proceed into the site. For the moment, though, congratulations; you're a bona fide eBay community member.

EASING INTO ONLINE PAYMENT

Registering to become an eBay buyer is free and easy. Before you start shopping, though, think about how you'll *pay* for your purchases. That's right; you'll be dealing with sellers from across the nation and around the world, and

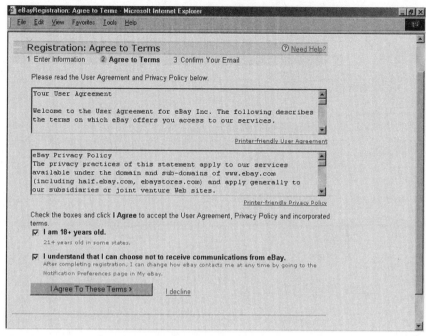

Figure 1-5 No one likes to read small print, but it's in your best interest to fully understand eBay's registration agreement before you sign up.

you need to be sure that you can pay for your purchases quickly and safely to ensure that everything you buy for you wedding arrives in plenty of time. And though you've probably considered the traditional payment methods—money orders, cashier's checks, personal checks, and cash—paying online (especially when you're planning a time-constrained event like a wedding) does require you to become familiar and adept with other types of payment solutions. No problem, though, because online payment is fast, easy, and convenient.

Why Online Payment Makes a Difference

Experienced bidders and other online buyers have found online payment to be the fastest and arguably the easiest method of paying for a variety of goods quickly, at eBay and other venues. It's as easy as sending an e-mail message, as online payments are effected in a few simple steps:

1. The buyer establishes an account with an online payment provider.
2. The seller, who also has an active online payment account, indicates the user ID to which payment is to be forwarded (separate from an eBay user ID).

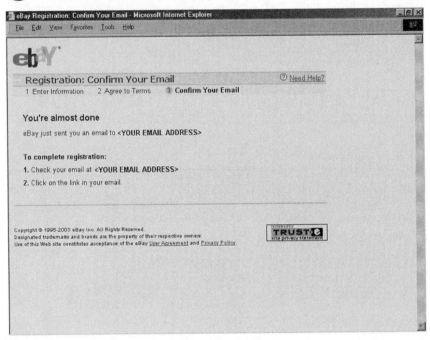

Figure 1-6 You're almost finished! This screen instructs you to check your e-mail for the final steps of registration.

3. The buyer posts the agreed-upon payment amount and is provided verification of the seller's account that will receive funds.
4. Payment is posted to the seller's account and deducted from the buyer's account, with a notification of the transaction being provided to both parties via e-mail.

Thanks to online payment services, an auction transaction can be completed in a matter of minutes (literally), with many buyers and sellers indicating that they've been able to close the post-auction deal in less than 30 minutes.

But is time of such importance in completing an online transaction? Couldn't you just send your money through traditional snail mail? Actually, as previously mentioned, traditional payment methods work just as well for online purchases, but you may find that fast online payment simply makes sense and offers a truly integrated approach to selecting, purchasing, and paying for goods, all made possible from your home computer. And the best part is that most online payment services enable both you and the seller you are working with to transact your business using your credit card. Sites like Pay-Pal allow sellers to accept online credit card payments without the cost and

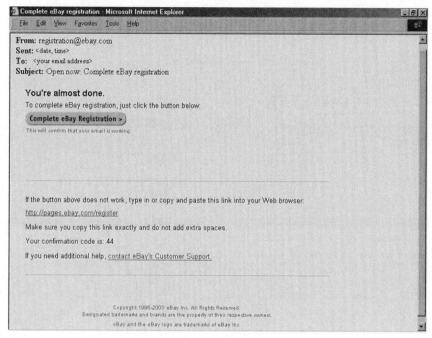

Figure 1-7 A confirmation e-mail from eBay contains the link to complete your registration.

complexity of establishing a traditional merchant account. Likewise, you as a buyer are able to make your purchases with your credit card and are no longer limited to funds in a checking or saving account alone. For everyone involved, then, online payment serves as another convenient option in shopping online to take advantage of great bargains.

Taking Steps to Make Online Payment Safe

To folks who are new to shopping and paying for purchases online, the thought of conducting online electronic funds transfers can be quite mysterious and even a little scary. However, take comfort in the fact that online payment services have quickly evolved into a secure and increasingly preferred method of managing payment transactions at eBay and other online shopping destinations. There are several different online payment sites available for use today, and each has implemented appropriate customer safeguards and protections to thwart any unauthorized or otherwise illicit account tampering.

Likewise, your financial institution is also capable of handling online payment. Most credit card issuers and personal bank account managers offer protections to their customers should something go amiss during an online transaction.

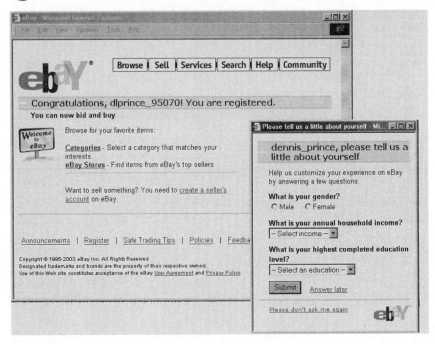

Figure 1-8 Congratulations and welcome to eBay. Your registration is complete.

Check with your issuer and other financial institutions to be clear about their safeguards and your responsibilities as an account owner. The bottom line, though, is that millions of online transactions are completed every day, with the vast majority being completed as easily as those at your local department store.

Introducing PayPal.com

By and large, PayPal.com is the biggest player in the online payment arena. Like eBay itself, PayPal arrived on the scene early (October 1999) and gained fast brand and service recognition. Many other sites have come and gone, but PayPal has stood fast. The site, boasting a registered user base of more than 16 million, was so successful that it even supplanted eBay's former Billpoint payment site. In an about-face, eBay acquired PayPal for $1.5 billion in October 2002, making it a truly integrated tool in the eBay experience. PayPal is free for buyers and charges a small sales commission to sellers, which is deducted from the amount of payment received. Registration and account activation can be accomplished in a matter of minutes. Business and Premiere accounts are available to sellers at a monthly fee; they provide access to automated e-mail tools, an invoicing system, inventory management, and more. PayPal also allows you to purchase goods from 39 different countries. Imagine purchasing your dream wedding gown from such exotic places such as Italy or Australia, at great savings and with the ease of purchasing an item in your hometown.

Getting registered as a buyer at PayPal is actually easier than registering at eBay. Begin by visiting PayPal's home page at http://www.paypal.com (see Figure 1-9) and click on the "Sign Up" text link near the top.

In the next screen, you decide if you want to create a personal account (typically used by folks who intend to operate only on an individual basis, whether buying or selling) or a business account (for budding businesspersons who plan to conduct significant sales volumes utilizing PayPal).

eBay TIP: If you'll only be buying and thus using PayPal exclusively to send funds (a free service, by the way), the personal account without the Premier upgrade will suit you fine. However, if you think you might sell some items on eBay after the wedding's over (or at any point along the way when you discover the great fortunes you can make on

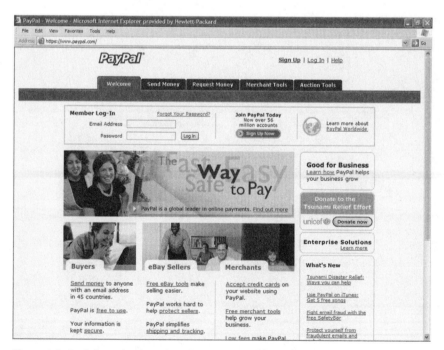

Figure 1-9 PayPal may be the only online payment site you'll ever need.

eBay), then you should consider establishing a Premier account to allow you, too, to receive credit card payments from folks who buy the items that you may soon be selling.

Choose the appropriate account type for your needs, specify your country, and click on the "Continue" pushbutton (see Figure 1-10).

On the succeeding registration page, fill out the form as prompted. If you'll be creating a Premier account, enable the "Yes" selection where appropriate so that you can proceed to complete a credit card registration page (Figure 1-11). Otherwise, if yours will be a non-Premier account, simply click on the "Sign Up" button once you've completed the form.

Credit Card/Account Safety

If you wish to *receive* credit card payments for items you'll be selling, you need to provide your own valid credit card information. This allows PayPal to identify you and verify your identity prior to granting you payment receipt privileges. All sellers who receive credit card payments via PayPal have had to provide this critical identifying information.

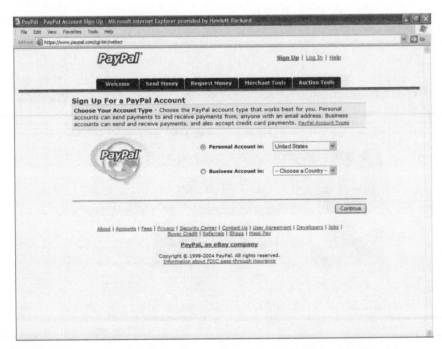

Figure 1-10 Choose the account type you want and proceed to the registration page.

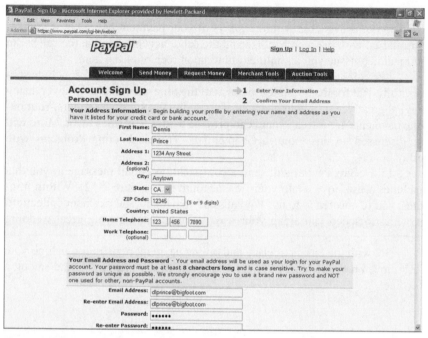

Figure 1-11 If you elected to create a Premier account, you'll need to provide credit card information in this secure screen.

eBay TIP: Some sellers are uncomfortable with the potential exposure that results from providing credit card information to a Web site (you'll need to provide both credit card and personal bank account information if you decide to become a seller on eBay). Though it's unlikely ever to happen, if you fear your credit card information could be retrieved and used illicitly, open a separate credit card account and establish a low maximum charge limit ($3,000 or less) to give you added protection. Also, check with the card issuer to be clear on its policies and its protections against credit card fraud.

If you would like to keep track of your wedding purchases and online payments, consider opening a credit card or checking account exclusively for your wedding purchases. Consistently choose this credit card or checking account as the "source of funds" when paying with PayPal. That way, you can track (via your credit card or bank statement) the dollar amounts you are spending on eBay wedding items and the dates of your purchases.

Another bonus when you use PayPal is the ease with which a seller can issue you a refund. A seller who for some reason is unable to deliver the wedding items you purchased can issue you an instant refund via your PayPal account (this option is available within 30 days of your payment date). Or, if you are unsatisfied with the merchandise and the seller accepts returns, the seller can immediately issue you an online refund upon receipt of the item.

About 99 percent of the time, your eBay transactions will conclude successfully. But for the possible 1 percent of the time when things go awry, using PayPal greatly assists your chances of resolving disputes with sellers. Your online payments are traceable and can provide evidence in your favor. More will be discussed on this topic in Chapter 10, "Troubleshooting Problems with eBay Sellers."

Like eBay, PayPal will send a confirmation e-mail message to you that includes a link to activate your new account (see Figure 1-12). Within minutes, you're now ready to use PayPal's easy payment (and payment collection) services to speed you along your way to finding and buying great wedding bargains.

So, with the basics of eBay and online payment registration behind you, let's move on to the basics of planning a beautiful wedding . . . and saving a fortune!

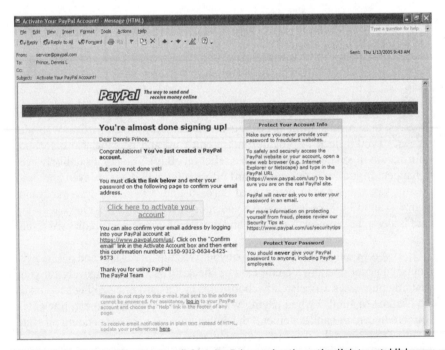

Figure 1-12 The confirmation e-mail from PayPal contains the active link to establish your account.

2

The Basics of Planning a Wedding

With your eBay and online payment service registrations behind you, it's time to turn to the more traditional matters of actually planning your wedding. If your wedding is a year or more away, you may think you have plenty of time to get everything planned and put together for your big day, but time has a way of flying when you're having fun planning your wedding (and are extremely busy with school, a day job, or whatever else was keeping you well occupied prior to your engagement).

This chapter will help you keep your focus and establish a sound, sensible, and thorough method of planning to ensure that everything will be just as you dream it when the joyous event finally arrives. Here you'll read about the many *non-eBay* aspects of planning a beautiful wedding (and saving a fortune) and get information that will help you retain your sanity and reserve your energy for the wedding day itself.

ESTABLISHING A PLANNING CALENDAR

It's generally easier to plan your wedding and keep track of your progress if you create a calendar of events and to-dos. To help keep you on track, we've created a general timeline and countdown to the big day (you can personalize and customize this calendar as you see fit). All the different tasks are in list format first, then we discuss them in more detail later in the chapter. First off, though, you need to get comfortable with what a useful wedding plan will look like at each major time milestone leading to the ceremony and beyond.

Timely Tasks Twelve Months or More Before Your Wedding

Sometimes it's best to break up a plan into smaller, time-dependent segments to keep you from becoming overwhelmed and to make sure that you address the most time-sensitive matters first. We'll begin by looking at what you should be doing a full year before your wedding date:

- ❑ Choose the date and time for your wedding and rehearsal.
- ❑ Decide how formal or informal your wedding and reception will be.
- ❑ Choose your color schemes. One color and multiple-color combinations are both fine.
- ❑ Review your budget. Consult pertinent parties (for example, your parents) about the appropriate distribution of the budget funds.
- ❑ Select ceremony and reception sites.
- ❑ Make an appointment with your officiant to inquire about premarital requirements.
- ❑ Plan the guest list to get an approximate head count.
- ❑ Choose your wedding party (bridesmaids, groomsmen/ushers).
- ❑ Research possible honeymoon locations.
- ❑ Interview wedding coordinators (if you are using one).
- ❑ Shop for your wedding gown and veil.
- ❑ Book the musicians for your ceremony and reception.
- ❑ Interview photographers, videographers, caterers, and florists.

Timely Tasks Nine to Twelve Months Before Your Wedding

- ❑ Place an engagement announcement in the newspaper.
- ❑ Select dresses for your bridesmaids.
- ❑ Start shopping for attire for the guys.
- ❑ Book the caterer, photographer, and videographer.
- ❑ Decide on a florist (if you aren't getting all your flowers on eBay) and choose floral arrangements.
- ❑ Register for gifts at bridal registries.
- ❑ Choose transportation for the ceremony, reception, and anything else in between.

Timely Tasks Six to Nine Months Before Your Wedding

- ❑ Finalize your wedding gown and bridal accessories purchases. Arrange for alterations if needed.
- ❑ Help mothers choose and coordinate their wedding outfits.
- ❑ Reserve any rental equipment (if you are having an at-home reception or at a site that does not provide furnishings).
- ❑ Select your baker and order your wedding cake. Add a groom's cake for whimsy.
- ❑ Select your wedding lingerie for your trousseau.
- ❑ Choose your wedding stationery: invitations, envelopes, and thank-you cards.
- ❑ Look up accommodations for out-of-town guests.

- ❑ Plan the rehearsal dinner with the host (usually the parents of the groom).
- ❑ Research the requirements for obtaining a marriage license.
- ❑ Pick out and purchase wedding favors.
- ❑ Confirm honeymoon reservations. Compile the necessary travel documents (passports, visas, government-issued identification).
- ❑ Finalize your guest list.

Timely Tasks Three to Four Months Before Your Wedding

- ❑ Choose the ceremony music.
- ❑ Discuss reception music with your DJ or band.
- ❑ Consult the caterer regarding menu details.
- ❑ Confirm accommodations for out-of-town guests.
- ❑ Finalize purchases of wedding rings and arrange for engraving.
- ❑ Visit officiant and review vows, readings, and hymns.
- ❑ Select and reserve men's wedding attire.
- ❑ Address invitations and announcements.

Timely Tasks Two Months Before Your Wedding

- ❑ Mail your wedding invitations.
- ❑ Plan a trial run with your hairstyle, veil, and makeup.
- ❑ Arrange your hair appointment for your wedding day.
- ❑ Confirm ceremony details.
- ❑ Finalize rehearsal and dinner plans.
- ❑ Make and print out maps to ceremony and reception sites.
- ❑ Complete the proper documents for changing your maiden name to your married name, if indeed you will be doing so.

Timely Tasks One Month Before Your Wedding

- ❑ Obtain your marriage license.
- ❑ Pick up wedding rings and check the engraving.
- ❑ Confirm details with the caterer, florist, entertainers, and officiant.
- ❑ Send wedding announcement and photograph to the newspapers.
- ❑ Schedule final dress fittings for you and your attendants.
- ❑ Purchase gifts for attendants, flower girl, ring bearer, fiancé, parents, and other special guests (family and friends).
- ❑ Plan pre-wedding party for attendants.

Timely Tasks Two Weeks Before Your Wedding

- ❑ Confirm rehearsal dinner plans.
- ❑ Research gown, bouquet, and/or cake preservation.
- ❑ Contact guests who did not RSVP to your wedding invitations.
- ❑ Arrange seating plan and write out the place cards.

❑ Break in wedding shoes while at home.
❑ Meet photographer and videographer and submit list of important names and requested shots.
❑ Have your wedding gown pressed or dry cleaned professionally.

Timely Tasks One Week Before Your Wedding

❑ Pick up your wedding dress from the cleaners.
❑ Give your bridesmaids a pre-wedding get-together.
❑ Pack your stuff for the honeymoon.
❑ Call your travel agent and confirm your itinerary. Purchase foreign currency in advance.
❑ Write out your toast for the rehearsal dinner and/or wedding reception.
❑ Make an appointment to have a relaxing facial and other beauty treats for yourself and/or your mom, bridesmaids, and so on.
❑ Confirm transportation details.
❑ Finalize the guest count with the caterer.
❑ Review any last-minute details and unpaid balances with your vendors.

Final Tasks One Day Before Your Wedding

❑ Schedule a manicure and pedicure (for you and your mom).
❑ Go for a relaxing walk or jog or a massage.
❑ Greet out-of-town guests.
❑ Attend the rehearsal and dinner.
❑ Get a good night's sleep. Congratulations!

Your Organizer to Guide You through Your Wedding Day

It's here! This list is the one you'll want to tape to your bedroom or bathroom mirror, letting it guide you to and through your ceremony instead of those fluttering butterflies in your stomach. With a list like this to lead you, you'll be less anxious about forgetting anything and better able to enjoy all that this special day has to offer.

❑ Get up early and have a nice relaxing bath or shower (you can, of course, purchase bath oils on eBay).
❑ Eat a light but nutritious breakfast.
❑ Go to your hair and makeup appointments on time.
❑ Have your mom or attendants help you with your dress and veil.
❑ Get out the bouquets and get ready to pose at home with your family and attendants for the photographer.
❑ Leave for the ceremony site 10 minutes earlier than you originally planned. You're on your way. Enjoy!

And there you have it: your wedding plan. Naturally, you'll add or subtract to-dos to suit your particular ceremony and personal tastes. Nonetheless, develop a plan similar to this and stick to it to make sure you're never running late when tackling the various tasks. Plus, if you keep a list like this, you'll always see a clear path of progress and you'll quickly quell any fears or doubts that you're forgetting something.

eBay TIP: Since you're going to be shopping for your wedding items on eBay, you have the advantage of purchasing goods well in advance (even a year or more is fine, if you have adequate storage space). There's no need to make a hefty down payment on your dress at the bridal salon and then be forced to wait months for its delivery. If you purchase a gown and/or other wedding items on eBay, your merchandise will be on its way to you as soon as your payment clears, usually in as little as a week. Shopping on eBay not only saves you time, but also saves you money—two commodities that most brides have precious little of during the hectic days of wedding planning.

SETTING A WEDDING BUDGET . . .
AND STICKING TO IT

Once you have your wedding plan in front of you, the next step is to set a wedding budget, and then stick to it like glue. The wedding budget determines the reception sites you can afford, the vendors you can hire, the number of guests you can invite, and so on. Sit down with your fiancé and other pertinent parties whom you have earlier determined will contribute to the wedding budget. Unless you plan on having a reception at home, the biggest percentage of the wedding budget usually goes for the wedding reception and catering. Don't forget to allot funds for a honeymoon—some newlyweds are unpleasantly surprised when they have forgotten to place the honeymoon in their budget.

Here is an example of an allotment of wedding funds for a wedding for 100 guests in a major city in the United States during the peak wedding months (May through August):

Reception/catering	$8,000	29%
Rings (wedding bands and engagement rings)	$4,000	15%
Honeymoon	$3,000	11%
Photography	$3,000	11%
Videography	$2,000	7%
Flowers	$2,000	7%
Wedding apparel (gown, alterations, tuxedo rentals)	$1,500	6%

Reception music (DJ, band)	$1,000	4%
Miscellaneous (gifts, favors, marriage license)	$1,000	4%
Cake	$500	2%
Transportation	$500	2%
Invitations	$250	1%
Ceremony music	$200	1%
Donation to church/ceremony site	$200	1%
TOTAL	$27,150	100%

Naturally, you can personalize this list to suit your, your fiancé's, and your family's priorities. Perhaps you want to spend a little bit more on the honeymoon, and so you scale back on the photography. Or perhaps you would like to splurge a little bit on the wedding rings, and so you cut down your guest list to accommodate your decision. The following sections in this chapter will help you do just that.

Now, before you panic at the total we've just provided, recognize that this table chart doesn't take into account the substantial savings you can realize by shopping through eBay (50 to 90 percent off retail, remember). Chapter 8 helps you find all the best ways to locate and save on the items for your wedding and how to include those special "extras" that you may fear you can't afford. For now, though, let's keep the plan itself in the forefront of your mind.

Identifying Sources of Financing for Your Wedding

If you're a bride and groom on a tight budget, it's helpful to visualize the different sources of funds that will be available for your wedding. These sources could include one or both of your saving accounts, stocks, bonds, and other monetary sources. If your parents are going to contribute to your wedding fund, determine the amount they are willing to give you (as well as the concessions you must make in acquiescing to their "suggestions" about your wedding). Don't be afraid to be a creative entrepreneur. Make a goal of building your wedding fund via other means, such as having garage sales, taking on extra work, or selling on eBay!

eBay TIP: Here's Sarah's eBay bride success story: After Dan and I got engaged and started determining how to pay for the wedding, I gave myself a goal of being extra hardworking when it came to selling stuff on eBay. I would then take my "eBay earnings" and purchase wedding items on (you guessed it) eBay. So I wasn't really spending any money when it came right down to it. I was "recycling" my stuff—selling items to happy bidders on eBay, and taking those earnings to purchase my wedding items. Thanks to eBay, the majority of my wedding items were purchased without my spending an extra dime or taking money out of my student loan. It worked for me, and it can work for you, too.

PLANNING A BEAUTIFUL CEREMONY ON A BUDGET

As outlined earlier, the first step in planning your wedding is picking a date. It could be a date special to the two of you, like the anniversary of your first date, a special holiday, or perhaps one exact year from the date of the marriage proposal.

eBay TIP: Keep in mind that most brides in the United States pick the peak wedding months (May to August) or holidays (Valentine's Day, Christmas, Memorial Day, and New Year's) to get married. Most wedding expenses are higher during these times than at other times because of the law of supply and demand: Wedding sites and vendors simply have more bridal business at that time, and thus they can increase their rates or hike up their minimums, since there are a lot more brides competing for their business.

After you pick a wedding date, you need to find a ceremony site that has your date available. Most ceremonies are performed in religious surroundings (churches, temples, and so on), while others are performed outdoors, on the beach, or at someone's home. Here is a list, along with some easy tips on how to decrease these ceremony expenses—some by simply shopping on eBay.

- *Ceremony site fee.* This fee can range from nothing (if you hold the ceremony at home) to a modest fee for a public place like a park or beach or at the courthouse. If you will have your ceremony at your church, a donation (usually of a specified amount) will suffice.
- *Officiant fee/donation to the church.* This fee varies with the officiant and religious affiliation.
- *Fee for ceremony musicians.* You can hire professional musicians to play during your ceremony. To save money, hire a soloist (like a pianist, violinist, organist, or harpist) instead of several musicians. Use your church organist if he or she is available—he or she knows the layout of the church and what music is appropriate for your ceremony. Consider hiring student musicians—they usually charge less than professional musicians. If you have a talented friend or close family member, consider asking that person to participate in your ceremony as a musician, as a wedding gift to you. Ask early, to give the person plenty of time to prepare. Most people you ask would feel honored and would love to help you out in this way.

- *Fee for the cantor.* The same goes for the cantor. Usually a specified fee is paid to the cantor that your church or religious hall provides. However, if you have a talented friend or relative who usually performs this role for his or her congregation, consider asking that person to be an important part of your ceremony as a wedding gift to you.
- *Ceremony decorations and flowers.* These include pew bows, unity candles, aisle runners, altar floral arrangements, and other decorations. You can purchase these on eBay for great savings; make sure to read Chapter 8 on the best way to go about doing so.
- *Personal flowers (bouquets, corsages, boutonnieres).* When it comes to flowers for the wedding party and special guests, eBay again is the way to go for finding them at significant savings from retail price. Both silk and live flowers are available on eBay. If you want to save even more money and you have a talent for flower arranging, consider purchasing flowers from eBay in bulk lots and creating your bouquets and wedding flowers yourself.
- *Ceremony programs.* These are also available on eBay at prices much lower than those of the local printers. There are professionally printed programs as well as blank, do-it-yourself programs on eBay.
- *Photography.* Wedding photography is the one aspect that most brides (and past brides) insist be done professionally. There is no "retake" for your wedding day, and so we highly recommend that you select a professional to perform this service. Ask for recommendations from recently married family members and friends. Attend bridal shows to obtain brochures from several local photographers at one time. Visit several photography studios to view samples of photographers' work as well as comprehensive price lists.

  Get "special deals" in writing when a studio offers those deals verbally during its sales pitch. One studio may offer low prices for wedding album packages but charge high prices for reprints. Another studio might offer customized personalization and more input from you when it is putting together your wedding album, but then charge you accordingly. Some photographers may include negatives in your package, while the rest may keep your negatives as part of their property until you "earn" them by ordering enough pictures.

  Wedding photographers either charge by the hour or charge a flat fee for unlimited time with you on your wedding day. Determine how early and how late you would like to have photography services, and take that into account when perusing price differences between the photography packages being offered. You may be better off paying a flat fee for unlimited time from your photographer, instead of originally paying for eight hours of photography and then getting charged overtime fees later on.

Determine whether you want traditional photography, photo-journalistic-style (more candid) photography, or a mixture of both. Ascertain what your priorities are: Do you prefer a customized album over free proofs? Would you like wedding picture enlargements instead of an engagement portrait option? What you decide you would like will help narrow down your choice of studio as well as photography package deals.

Look for and book your wedding photographer early—you can lock in this year's prices for next year's wedding. The most popular and/or affordable photographers are usually booked a year or more in advance. Book extra early if your wedding falls in a peak wedding month (May through August). Ask for any special discounts that could apply to your wedding date: Friday, Sunday, or weekday discounts may apply, as well as a discount if you book a videographer from the same company. Negotiate with the studio for any changes you want to make in its wedding packages. Consider the location of the studio and estimate the distance between the studio and your ceremony site/reception site (some studios charge extra if they have to travel long distances). Insist on meeting your photographer at least a month before your wedding, so that he or she will get to know you and the style of photography you prefer. Get your contract in writing, and put your deposit on a credit card.

eBay TIP: There is a growing trend of photographers advertising their wedding services on eBay (see Figure 2-1). Type in the keywords *wedding photog** and you will see some photographers auctioning off their services on eBay (with location restrictions—for example, "Wedding Photographer for Washington DC area"). As with any item or service listed on eBay, check the seller's feedback and sales history carefully—make sure the photographer is a professional one. Ask for phone numbers of references, and check out the seller's official Web site if there is one. You might just end up with a steal for your wedding photography—from eBay!

- *Videography.* Most of the how-to-shop and how-to-save tips for photography apply to videography as well. Some photography studios also offer videography services. Ask if there are any discounts for booking these two services from the same studio. Sift through the videography services price list and prioritize what you think you need versus what are just pricey options—for example, a second unmanned camera at the ceremony may cost an additional $200, or a DVD (instead of VHS) version of your wedding video may set you back another couple of

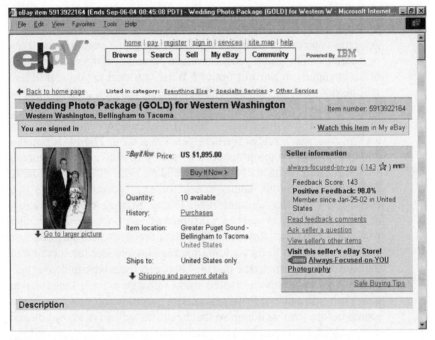

Figure 2-1 You can find wedding photography services at a steal on eBay.

hundred dollars. Ask to see several samples of a videographer's work. Select and book your videographer early, much the same as your photographer. Get all details of the contract in writing, and put your deposit on, of course, a credit card.

- *Transportation.* The wedding limousine is the quintessential and classy mode of transportation for the bride and groom. Look through bridal magazines, on the Internet (http://www.limos.com is a good place to retrieve price quotes for limo companies in most major cities), and in the Yellow Pages for ads for limo companies. Some of the best deals are from companies that place smaller, less flashy ads—they are paying less for advertisements, and they pass on the savings to you. Smaller companies may also offer more personalized customer service—you can talk to the owner, for example, instead of just the manager of a large company. Look for companies that own their own limousines—they are likely to maintain their cars better than companies that lease their limousines from others. Search for local limousine companies; the closer the company is to your home, ceremony site, and reception site, the less likely it is that you'll have to pay extra for mileage or overtime charges. Carefully read the packages the companies offer as well as what vehicles they have available. Consider renting the limo for one or two hours instead of the more common three- to four-hour bridal packages if all you really want is a nice ride to the reception.

If possible, visit the limo company and see the cars for yourself—nothing beats a personal inspection. A limo company might even offer to drop by your residence during one of its runs so that you can inspect the vehicle yourself. Get the license number of the car you like written into the contract to avoid substitution of cars on your big day. Also look into alternative forms of transportation (SUV limousines, trolleys, limo buses)—some of them are more affordable than you might think, and they can hold more passengers than regular stretch limousines, giving you more "ride" for your wedding dollar.

Find out whether the limo company starts the clock when the limo leaves the company parking lot or when the limo actually arrives at the bride's home—you'd be surprised at the "overtime" charges that may appear on your bill later on. Book early to lock in this year's prices and to avoid competing with prom-goers if your wedding is set to happen during prom season. Pay your deposit with a credit card. And, of course, if you don't have the room in your budget to hire a limousine, don't overlook the transportation resources you already have: Ask friends and family to help you coordinate wedding transportation using their own cars. If someone you know has a fancy car or roomy SUV, ask that person to do you the honor of transporting you from the church to the reception as a wedding gift to you.

PLANNING AN ELEGANT RECEPTION WITHOUT BREAKING THE BANK

The reception and catering are likely to be your biggest wedding expenses by far. The good news is that the cost is largely under your control—the site you pick, the date and time of your reception, the number of guests you invite, and the type of food you choose to serve. Here are some easy money-saving tips to help you plan your reception.

Reception Site

There are many types of reception sites you can choose from: hotels, country clubs, your church's hall, your home, restaurants, public parks, and so on. The fees can range from nothing (your home) to an hourly fee to rent a reception site. Here's a breakdown of some of the most common reception site options, the pros and cons of each, and our advice on each to help you in your decision making.

Hotels

- *Pros:* Most hotels include a convenient in-house caterer, discount room rates for your wedding guests, and complimentary extras like a honeymoon suite for the newlyweds. Their all-inclusive wedding packages may include the room rental, linens, silverware, food, beverages, alcohol, table centerpieces, wedding cake, hors d'oeuvres, and other items that would cost a lot more if purchased separately.
- *Cons:* You may get a limited menu to pick from, as well as the possibility of sharing the space with another wedding at the same time (if the hotel has more than one ballroom). A minimum dollar amount (without taxes added on) is usually required for your event, regardless of how many guests show up. High sales taxes (9 to 10 percent in major cities) and mandatory gratuities (20 percent) quickly add up on the bill.
- *Our advice:* Make appointments to visit several local hotels personally and speak to the catering manager of each. Prioritize what you really want in a reception (for example, an affordable menu or a big dance floor) and let the catering manager know what you are looking for. Give the hotel an honest estimate of your budget and negotiate whatever items in its wedding packages you would like to change. Once you fall in love with a place, book early (especially if your wedding is during peak season) and get all details in writing. Specify that the contract should include the exact ballroom you want, in case a business convention comes along and the hotel is tempted to bump you into a smaller ballroom to make room for the conference.

Country Clubs

- *Pros:* Great views, possibly an in-house caterer, luxurious surroundings.
- *Cons:* The country club may require membership before you can hold an event there. Prices are not necessarily lower than those of hotels that can offer the same (if not more) amenities.
- *Our advice:* If your heart is set on having your reception at the country club, research the requirements for booking one. Compare and contrast the cost and service of a country club with that of a hotel.

Church Hall or Cathedral

- *Pros:* Convenient for wedding guests (it's located right next to the church where the ceremony takes place) as well as affordable (fees range from zero to a modest donation).

- *Cons:* Your own caterer is most likely required, as is rental equipment (chairs, tables, linens, silverware, portable dance floor), and this can jack up the price pretty fast.
- *Our advice:* If you hire an outside caterer, look for one that can also offer you rental equipment, so that you don't have to coordinate two vendors instead of one. If you are having a smaller, more intimate wedding, consider having family members and friends help you cater your own wedding.

Your Home

- *Pros:* If it's at your house, the reception will be held at a place that is already special to you. Also, there is no site rental fee to worry about. You are already familiar with the layout of the place, as well as the number of people it can hold. You will have fond memories of your wedding ceremony and/or reception if it is held at your own home.
- *Cons:* You will have to hire a rental company and a caterer (unless you cater the wedding yourselves).
- *Our advice:* Again, research caterers that can also provide you with equipment rentals, so as to avoid having to book two vendors instead of one. Also consider asking family and friends to help you cater your own wedding as a wedding gift. Consider having the ceremony at your home as well—it means more convenience and less traveling for your guests. Don't forget to make arrangements with nearby hotels for your guests' accommodations—they still need a place to stay after the festivities are over.

Public Parks

- *Pros:* Public parks have beautiful views and are ideal for outdoor weddings during the spring and summer months. You may have to donate a small fee for use of the park.
- *Cons:* As above, rental equipment and catering companies are required.
- *Our advice:* Outdoor weddings depend on the weather; make sure you have a contingency plan in case it rains (i.e., rent a sturdy and spacious weatherproof tent from the rental company, or have an alternative indoor location for the reception).

Restaurants

- *Pros:* Restaurant cuisine generally tastes better than wedding food served at other places. A nice restaurant may be able to provide you with a private room or space for your wedding reception. Explore the restaurants' bridal packages if they have any; these may be similar to the all-inclusive packages at hotels.

- *Cons:* There are no hotel amenities, discounted hotel rates, or changing rooms for your guests—you have to seek out accommodations at nearby hotels.
- *Our advice:* If a particular restaurant has special meaning for both of you, research that site as a possibility. Most restaurants have minimums to meet for special events (such as a minimum number of guests), especially on Saturdays of popular wedding months—be aware of the fine print. Negotiate the menu carefully with the head chef or catering manager. Ask for perks for your guests, such as discounted or free parking (especially if the restaurant is in a popular area like the downtown area of a major city).

Reception Date and Time

As the reception date depends on your ceremony date, you will have to make a firm decision about your ceremony date and then stick to it. Remember that Saturdays are the most popular days for weddings, and that as a result, reception sites give discounts for non-Saturday weddings. Read the fine print, though—most sites consider the Sunday of a three-day holiday as a "Saturday." If your heart is set on a Saturday wedding and you still need to cut costs, consider decreasing the number of guests you invite or rethinking the menu.

Menu

Ask anyone who has been to a wedding what they remember most, and the most common answer is "the food." Therefore, the wedding menu is a big deal and must be given considerable thought. Read through your reception site or caterer's menu offerings and packages carefully. Usually there is a price difference between entrees (seafood is more expensive than beef, which is more expensive than chicken) and types of meal service (a sit-down dinner is usually more expensive than a buffet). There is also a higher cost associated with offering guests a choice of entrée, unless you are fortunate enough to find a hotel or caterer that does not charge extra for entrée choices. All-inclusive packages can be a great time- and money-saver if the items cost more a la carte.

If you are trying to save money, our advice is to consider having a lunch reception instead of a dinner reception. The price difference (multiplied by the number of guests) may mean substantial savings for you. Consider a buffet-type meal instead of a sit-down dinner, but make sure you have enough stations and servers set up so that your guests won't be in line too long.

Always ask the caterer of your site for a taste test of the menu items offered at weddings. The reason? The food won't be such a bargain if you opt to shop by mere price alone, and then at the wedding you find that the food is mediocre at best. Make careful decisions about the menu after several taste tests at different locations—the quality of the food may be a major factor in your decision to book a particular site or caterer. You might also end up thinking that the prime rib is worth the money, and that you need to scale down the floral budget to make room for it.

Adult guests are charged the full price per head, but you can negotiate lower prices for guests under 21 (they won't drink alcohol) and children under 12 (they usually receive the children's meal). Ask for discounted rates for meals for your DJ, photographer(s), and videographer(s)—they won't need to eat prime rib either, but it would be nice for them to have sustenance while they are hard at work for you.

Beverages

The bar tab usually takes up a substantial amount of the catering bill. The debate still rages about having an open bar or a cash bar (with a cash bar, guests pay for each alcoholic drink). The open bar is more etiquette-friendly than the cash bar, and there are ways to save money here. Instead of having an open bar during the entire reception, have an open bar only at certain times (during cocktail hour and after dessert is cleared away) and have only wine served during dinner. Use champagne sparingly—save it for the champagne toast. Have a well-meaning friend or family member (or a courteous bartender) spread the word about what time the bar opens and closes, so that your guests will be aware of when drinks are and aren't being served.

If you want to provide your own liquor, let the bride beware: Some reception sites penalize you if you want to do this by charging exorbitant "corking" fees that will eat up the savings you made when you purchased your liquor elsewhere. If serving alcohol puts your wedding budget over the top, consider serving only "house" brands (instead of fancy and more expensive "call" brands) of beer and wine.

To limit alcohol consumption, place a bottle of red and a bottle of white wine on each table—this amount is usually enough for guests to have a taste of each. Or go completely nonalcoholic but have a fun alternative like a punch fountain, a fruit smoothie bar, or Italian ice service for your guests to enjoy. Always make sure there is plenty of water, juice, and soda for guests who don't drink.

Music

For most weddings, the big debate is band versus disc jockey (DJ). If you are on a budget, a DJ is an affordable alternative to a live band. Not only do you have to pay only one person (or two if the DJ has an assistant or emcee), but you can also personalize your reception music by giving the DJ a list of your favorite songs to play and when to play them. The DJ can also act as master of ceremonies and keep the crowd engaged during key moments in your reception. Good DJs get booked early—as much as a year in advance.

Ask your family and recently married friends for recommendations. Visit the DJ's studio personally and read the wedding packages carefully. Determine whether the DJ will be appropriately attired for your event, and if he or she has backup sound equipment and is insured. Don't shop by price alone—ask for references and samples of the DJ's work that were videotaped during previous weddings. Make sure that setup and teardown labor and times are included in your contract, and look for wedding packages that are neither too short (the DJ leaves at 10 p.m. when your guests expected to dance the night away until midnight) nor too long (your guests have all straggled home and the DJ is still around—you'll end up paying too much for the services). Ask your DJ if he or she is familiar with your reception site, and if not, if he or she is willing to visit the site with you.

eBay TIP: Did you know that you can find material on eBay on how to DJ wedding receptions? If you have a talented and musically inclined friend or relative who wants to play a major role in your wedding, consider having that person DJ your wedding. To enhance the person's talent, tell her or him to check out how-to books or CDs offered on eBay (see Figure 2-2).

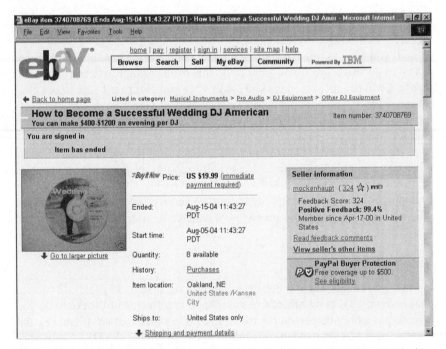

Figure 2-2 Learn how to DJ a wedding reception—find out how through eBay. Use the keyword combination *how to dj wedding*.

Wedding Favors

You can be as creative as you like with your wedding favors, without having to break the bank. The most popular wedding favors include candy, bookmarks, magnets, picture frames, personalized CDs, matchbooks, bubbles, birdseed packets, thank-you scrolls, chocolates, bells, soaps, candles, personalized candy wrappers, and mints. Favors are usually personalized with your names and the wedding date as keepsakes for your big day. Paying retail prices for these could really make a dent in your wedding budget when you think of multiplying the cost per favor times the number of guests you are inviting. Never fear; you can find great bargains on eBay—favors starting at less than $1.00 per favor. Make sure to read Chapter 8 on how to find affordable wedding favors and other wedding necessities on eBay.

Reception Decorations

Check first with your reception site to see what decorations are already included in your wedding package. Some all-inclusive packages at hotels, restaurants, and country clubs may already include reception decorations. If your reception is being held outdoors in a garden in full bloom or in a public park, you may not need to purchase many decorations at all. If you do have to purchase them, keep in mind that the most popular decorations are floral arrangements, candles, place cards, and wedding favors. Before you go and pay retail prices at the stores or at the florists, consider some money-saving options. You can buy everything you need to decorate your reception site at eBay. Read Chapter 8 for full details on how to find these bargains on eBay to save both time and money.

THE FIVE P'S OF CHOOSING YOUR WEDDING VENDORS

Besides the bargains you'll want to find (which are outlined throughout the rest of this book), recognize early that it's essential for you to know how to select your wedding vendors. These are the key people you will look to for assistance in planning and executing your dream wedding. When it comes to this crucial planning phase, a good vendor or seller can keep you on track or even ahead of schedule, whereas a poor seller can throw a monkey wrench into your works. Here are some very important qualities to look for in your wedding vendors, whether at eBay or elsewhere (hint: It's not all about price).

- *Professionalism.* From the initial contact you make with a wedding vendor (whether it be a catering manager, a florist, or a limo service), look for professionalism in the vendor's manner, and observe the way you and other brides are treated in the course of your wedding shopping. Is the vendor courteous, friendly, and informative? Does the vendor seem pushy, or does she or he let you make your decision without rushing you? Does the vendor offer alternatives that you wouldn't have thought of yourself? When dealing on eBay, is the vendor responsive to your e-mail questions, and do his or her eBay listings provide plenty of clear and accurate information to help you in making your shopping decisions?

- *Performance.* Look at the vendor's past performance, and don't be afraid to ask for referrals (on eBay, review the feedback profile). Ask to see portfolios of the vendor's past work (wedding photography/ videography, pictures of floral arrangements, and so on) and present work (ask to visit a reception hall when it's decorated for a wedding or for a taste test of the menu, for example) Wedding vendors that are great at their jobs are more than happy to show off their past and present work—all you have to do is ask. On eBay especially, the better vendors (sellers) are more than eager to share their past successes with you in hopes of convincing you that they can help make your wedding dreams come true.

- *Punctuality.* Weddings are fraught with deadlines and stressful situations. Hence it is vital that your wedding vendors have a good track record of delivering goods and services when they're needed. It simply won't do for the limo to be late, or for your dress alterations to be weeks behind schedule, or for that veil that you won on eBay to be delayed for weeks before being shipped to you. You can gauge your wedding vendors' punctuality by the speed with which they return your calls and e-mail messages as well as through the feedback comments of previous buyers.

- *Price.* The wedding budget needs to be addressed throughout your wedding planning. But don't get too caught up in shopping wedding vendors by price. Instead, shop for *value* and *convenience.* To a busy bride on a budget, time can be just as valuable as money. You also don't want to end up with inferior or mediocre items and services because you pinched pennies here and there. Know a great value when you see one; that is why it is essential to shop for wedding vendors and services as early as possible so that you are able to best compare them.

- *Perks.* Ah, yes, the icing on the cake. This could be the extra "oomph" that makes you decide to pick one wedding vendor (or eBay seller) over another. A perk is a wonderful "extra," above and beyond the usual and customary wedding package, that is added on to your wedding purchases by the vendor to entice you to sign on the dotted line or place that online bid. However, the perk is enticing only if you had a good bridal bargain to begin with. An example would be a photography studio offering a free parents' album ($250 value), or having a custom-designed wedding cake ($400 to $800 value) included in your reception menu free of charge. (Both these perks were given to us by our photographer and reception hall, respectively).

PLANNING A FABULOUS HONEYMOON WITHIN YOUR MEANS

There's nothing more romantic than the first trip you take as husband and wife. Once you've made it to the honeymoon, you can relax and be carefree. To get the honeymoon of your dreams, we offer these three Ds to consider:

- *Destination.* Where do you both want to go? If you and your new spouse both want to go somewhere tropical where you can relax, this decision will be fairly easy to make. However, if one of you wants to go on a ski trip while the other wants to go scuba diving, you have to compromise and choose a place where you can have a variety of activities to select from. Save the ski trip or the scuba-diving adventure for some other vacation in the future.

  Generally speaking, the closer the destination is to your home, the less expensive it will be. But read on to find ways to look for travel bargains that won't limit you geographically as you consider your honeymoon budget. (Hint: One of those ways is the eBay way! Read Chapter 9 to find out about it.)

- *Duration.* How long do you want to go for? Honeymoon packages from travel agents are usually 3, 4, 5, 7, 10, or 14 or more nights. Understandably, the longer you stay, the more you will pay. The most common honeymoon duration is about one week, especially if international travel is involved. That way, you can set aside most of day one for traveling to your destination and most of day seven for going back home and settling in. If you and/or your new spouse work, you may want to coordinate your work schedules to get enough days off to take a honeymoon. Also consider that you may need a few days off before the wedding as well.

- *Date.* When do you want to leave for your honeymoon? Some brides prefer to leave the evening of their wedding day (not advisable unless you are honeymooning very close by, like the next town over). It will probably be more relaxing for you and your spouse to leave the next day, or the day after that. A day of rest after the festivities is critical, since you will probably be exhausted and will not be looking forward to possible flight delays, rush hour traffic, lost luggage, and other little speed bumps on your way to your honeymoon destination. Keep in mind that some honeymoon vacation packages are discounted if you leave on a nontypical travel day, also known as a midweek departure. A Saturday night stay may be required for most vacation packages.

Now that you've looked at the three Ds of picking a honeymoon, here are some easy money-saving tips for booking the honeymoon of your dreams without heading to the poorhouse:

1. Visit your local travel agencies and attend local bridal shows to obtain vacation brochures. An educated consumer is a smart consumer. Read up on how much the honeymoon destination you picked will cost (on average), based on the number of nights you want to stay and your date of departure.

2. Plan ahead and book early to lock in the current prices for your vacation.

3. Search eBay for honeymoon travel bargains. Surprised? You shouldn't be. Verified travel agents from all over the United States are finding that eBay is a great venue for attracting new customers, especially honeymooners on a budget. You can now search for and find a great honeymoon vacation deal from, say, a travel agent in California, even if you live in New York. Read Chapter 9 to see how easy it is to find your honeymoon on eBay.

4. Narrow down your choice of honeymoon vacation destination by making a "wish list" of activities and amenities that you want to have. Examples are water sports (snorkeling, scuba diving) land sports (golf, tennis, horseback riding), spa services (massages, beauty salons), meal services, adults-only restrictions (no children are allowed at some resorts), privacy, proximity to airports and major cities, and travel requirements (some countries require vaccinations before you can travel there). Prioritize which are most important, and compare and contrast honeymoon destinations in terms of the items that are at the top of your list.

5. Get quotes from several travel agents or eBay sellers for the *same* destination, duration, and travel dates. Get offers in writing. Be prepared to do a little bit of negotiating and haggling. Vacation packages are not necessarily set in stone—a good travel agent will be able to accommodate most reasonable requests. Travel agents want your business (and, most importantly, your *repeat* business), and therefore most agencies are willing to beat the lowest quote you received from their competitors.

6. Book the most basic accommodations at the most luxurious resort that you can afford. The most basic room in the poshest resort may still be quite luxurious compared to the rooms at smaller, less expensive resorts. Chances are that if the hotel is not occupied to capacity (most usually operate at around 60 to 70 percent occupancy rate), the manager or front desk may upgrade you to a better room if they find out you are on your honeymoon. Don't be shy about letting

people know you are newlyweds—you will get tons of extra attention lavished on you compared to other vacation-goers. Hey, you
deserve it!

7. If your honeymoon resort offers discounted airfare from charter airlines, consider flying those airlines instead. However, look for flights
with the least number of connecting flights. The time you save with
a direct flight may be well worth the extra money, since a direct
flight lessens the chances of delays in getting to your destination.
Honeymooners are on strict time constraints—seven nights does not
translate to eight nights if you lose a day chasing down your connecting flight.

8. Try an all-inclusive resort in order to have a hassle-free and enjoyable
vacation. There's nothing like feeling stress-free because you don't
have to carry a lot of credit cards, cash, and traveler's checks around
with you—everything is paid up front. To get the most value out of
your all-inclusive vacation, try your best to take advantage of all the
activities, meals, and drinks that the resort provides, and follow
the rules and regulations that the resort may have (such as required
dinner reservations, dress code, and so on). Some all-inclusive resorts
even offer discounts to repeat customers (think anniversaries!) or
discounts at their sister properties (if available). Most all-inclusive
resorts even have a no-tipping policy (although you do have to tip if
you are away from the resort). Consider a smaller resort rather than a
larger, more highly advertised one—you will get more intimate and
personal service from the staff as well as a comparatively lower price
tag for your honeymoon. (Try http://www.couples.com).

9. If you feel that you want to see more than one destination during
your honeymoon, consider booking a cruise. The cruise will be your
"hotel on the water" while you get to enjoy several ports of call at
different regions of a country, or even different countries. A cruise is
one of the best ways to sample and enjoy different places while only
unpacking once.

10. Protect your investment with travel insurance. This relatively modest
fee usually covers emergency cancellations on your part, as well as
lost luggage and mishaps by the resort or travel agency. Travel insurance may even give you a chance to obtain a partial refund if, for
some urgent reason, you are unable to take your vacation. You will
find that it is worth it for the peace of mind that having insurance
will bring.

11. Pay your deposit and balance with a credit card. Credit card companies generally provide additional coverage for travelers—read your
card company's policies on liability coverage as well as your consumer
rights to contest a purchase that is not 100 percent to your satisfaction.

12. If you have any questions whatsoever, don't hesitate to contact your travel agent and/or eBay seller. If you still have difficulty finding the honeymoon of your dreams, your travel agent may be able to custom-design one for you and your budget.

13. Once you've purchased your honeymoon vacation, assess your belongings to see if you need to purchase additional luggage, accessories, and appropriate vacation clothing. You can shop for these on eBay as well—turn to Chapter 9 to find how easy it is to locate bargains for your travel needs.

14. Relax and remember to have fun!

If you've dreaded the prospect and the picayune details of planning your wedding, we hope that this chapter has calmed some of your worries and shown you how effectively you can plan, orchestrate, and enjoy your wedding day and honeymoon without spending a fortune.

A major part of planning is knowing how to find innovative ways, such as using eBay, to save money on your wedding without sacrificing quality. The next chapter zeroes in on the "eBay approach" to an affordably elegant wedding, and how to get the best quality and value for your wedding dollar. Read interviews with seasoned eBay wedding sellers as they give advice to you, the eBay bride.

Be inspired as other eBay brides tell their own success stories on how they saved money using eBay for their wedding.

3

The eBay Approach to an Affordably Elegant Wedding: Lessons from the Power Sellers

---

When you are planning your wedding, your budget becomes both your friend and your foe. The budget you set helps to ensure that you spend your money wisely and keeps you from going into debt before you even begin your new life with your spouse. That same helpful budget also imposes limitations and sometimes seems determined to prevent you from affording the special touches and accoutrements that you and your spouse-to-be so richly deserve. Innovative brides, however, have found that you can eat your wedding cake and have it, too.

Stepping up to the challenge with vigor, brides we've met have found that there are ways to have affordably elegant weddings, to stay well within budget, and to have fun along the way. eBay has become a mainstay for cost-conscious brides and grooms, helping them plan fabulous wedding days, managed and executed within their budgets.

GETTING THE BEST VALUE FOR YOUR WEDDING DOLLAR

Wedding specialist and active eBay seller Carol Ramirez (csmarquis) states succinctly why you should shop for your wedding on eBay: "In a fast-paced world, young women are very busy with careers and school, combined with entry-level salaries and a lot of brides paying for their own weddings. eBay can save a bride-to-be lots of time and money. It's so simple—sit at home at the computer, sign on eBay, and search. Everything needed to do a complete wedding can be done in a very short time." Sage advice, to be certain, but what's the best approach and the best way to get started on your wedding shopping at eBay? Here's how to begin your walk down the aisle to great wedding values, eBay style.

Research, Research, Research

First, research the retail prices of wedding goods and services in your local area. Browse wedding magazine ads for local wedding stores and services to visit. Get a feel for the average cost of each item and service. Then, surf the Internet and browse popular wedding Web sites such as http://www.theknot.com or http://www.weddingchannel.com to get a feel for retail prices in the online realm (and, yes, you will probably find a much better selection and a greater variety of prices online than you may have found locally). Make a record of your findings and keep them handy for ease of comparison shopping.

eBay TIP: Location, location, location; it applies to the prices you'll find for the items you need for your wedding. Different store locations can affect the price of a wedding item or service. For example, a wedding gown purchased from a downtown bridal salon in a major city may carry a heftier price tag than the same wedding gown purchased from a store located in the far suburbs.

With your initial retail facts and findings in hand, now shop eBay to find the same or similar items; you'll most likely find (as we did) that prices are routinely 50 to 90 percent lower than retail. For example, if you find wedding invitations that retail for $300 at the store, chances are you can find the same or similar wedding invitations on eBay for $150 or less.

This is the sort of savings you can expect to find every day at the site. That said, commit to making the "50 percent off retail price" amount your benchmark for savings. That is, if you see a wedding gown that you like that retails for perhaps $900, set your eBay maximum spending value at $450 when you are looking for the same or similar gown at auction. This is by no means an impossible dream; you'll be amazed at how much you can save, day after day, once you see for yourself that shopping for wedding items the eBay way is not only sensible, but also elegant and affordable—even unique.

eBay TIP: Remember, before you bid on or purchase an item on eBay, be sure to calculate the *total cost* for the item by adding the total bid amount (or Buy-It-Now price) to the total shipping and other seller charges, and divide the total cost by the number of items you are receiving. This is the *per-unit cost*. If this amount is less than what you would pay retail at the store, you have a bargain, without a trip to the store and the effort of lugging your purchases home. If the amount is the same or higher than store prices, you may want to consider browsing other sellers who are offering the same or similar items.

Dare to Compare

Yes, it sounds too good to be true; we thought so, too. The facts, however, speak for themselves. Here's an example of how shopping eBay can result in tremendous savings compared to paying retail prices at the stores (check out the totals and see for yourself):

Shopping the Retail Method

Item	Retail Price	Percentage of Total Budget
Reception/Catering	$8,000	29%
Rings (Wedding Bands/Engagement Rings)	$4,000	15%
Honeymoon	$3,000	11%
Photography	$3,000	11%
Videography	$2,000	7%
Flowers	$2,000	7%
Wedding Apparel (Gown/Alterations/Tuxedo Rentals)	$1,500	6%
Reception Music	$1,000	4%
Miscellaneous (Gifts, Favors, Marriage License)	$1,000	4%
Cake	$500	2%
Transportation	$500	2%
Invitations	$250	1%
Ceremony Music	$200	1%
Donation to Church	$200	1%
TOTAL	$27,150	100%

Shopping the eBay Way

Item	Retail Price	Percentage of Total Budget
Reception/Catering	$8,000	41%
Rings (Wedding Bands/Engagement Rings)*	$2,000	10%
Honeymoon*	$1,000	5%

Photography	$3,000	15%
Videography	$2,000	10%
Flowers*	$300	2%
Wedding Apparel (Gown*/Alterations/Tuxedo*)	$300	2%
Reception Music	$1,000	5%
Miscellaneous (Gifts*,Favors*, Marriage License)	$500	3%
Cake	$500	3%
Transportation	$500	3%
Invitations*	$100	1%
Ceremony Music	$200	1%
Donation to Church	$200	1%
TOTAL	$19,600	100%

*Currently available on eBay

Note that we've listed some items in the eBay Way table as being purchased through traditional (local or retail) channels at traditional prices, implying that you'd be securing those items outside of eBay. There are, as we showed in Chapter 2, opportunities to further pare down the cost of items and services not found on eBay. This comparison helps you see that you can mix and match between eBay and retail sources and still save a significant amount of cash. The choice, of course, is yours, and eBay is ready and available to help you customize the way you'll plan for, shop for, and save on your wedding.

eBAY WEDDING SELLERS OFFER ADVICE TO eBAY BRIDES

In the course of researching this book, we've had the pleasure of "meeting" several dozen eBay wedding sellers. Who would be a better source of advice for brides than the sellers who have already helped thousands of brides like you save money on their big day? Most of these sellers are eBay "PowerSellers," a distinction that eBay itself offers to those sellers who generate and maintain a minimum amount of revenue (calculated in the thousands of dollars) on eBay month after month, year after year. We felt much more secure and confident in dealing with these expert wedding sellers, but we were further impressed when we learned that many of these eBay wedding sellers were also eBay brides. We asked them, "What advice do you have for budget-minded brides who want to use eBay?" Here's what they graciously shared.

General eBay Wedding Advice

We began by asking these wedding sellers overall advice for brides and grooms who turn to eBay to plan their wedding and what tips they might have for making it a pleasant and productive experience.

- *Read feedback.* Annette Emelity (chicbridal), an eBay PowerSeller, says that her best advice "is to buy from a seasoned vendor on eBay. If you know you are buying from a PowerSeller with good feedback, you know you will get fair, honest service." Powerseller Karen Mark (daddyskiki) agrees: "Be sure and check out the feedback. If you see any negative feedback, check to see what happened. Unfortunately, you will see most negatives left by new 'eBayers' because they are not familiar with eBay policies on buying or selling. It's worth your time to read about how eBay auctions work."

- *Plan ahead.* Katherine Mercer (unitycandles), an eBay PowerSeller, says, "Wedding items offered on eBay are at the best prices you can possibly find anywhere. I think that planning ahead is the one thing that brides can do who want to minimize cost. By planning ahead, you have the chance to check out the auctions and watch to see what is being offered and what things are selling for. You also eliminate having to ship by more expensive methods."

- *Look for good customer service.* Shannon (duchess101) advises shoppers to "comparison shop and look at sellers' feedback. Don't rule them out if they have a negative, but read the responses and see how the seller handled the negative [feedback]. Then when you have narrowed it down to your favorites, send them e-mails that require an answer to a question. Look at what kind of replies you get, how quickly they respond, etc. This way, you can see what type of customer service you will be getting with the product. If it is a high dollar item like florals, don't be afraid to ask for a reference."

    Lisa Brideau (lilibriluv) agrees, saying, "Brides should definitely be aware of the great advantages of shopping on eBay. Of course you can always find great deals on anything, at any given time . . . but patience can let you save even more money. Patience is definitely a must for super savings. Brides should also know that private sellers [home or small private companies, as opposed to larger businesses] like to interact with the buyers on a more personal level. I personally like to think I make new friends. I like to know they have faith in me and they trust me enough to make their beautiful day an even better one. I get to know my customers' needs, and from there, transactions go great. This is important because this wedding day is such an important day that you can't take it lightly. And the best piece of information I could share with you and every bride-to-be is that most private sellers can and should be able to find a way to work around all kinds of budgets. As long as both parties keep an open mind about it, they should both come to an understanding in terms of price versus product."

- *Look for savings on shipping.* Kristen Kwiatkowski (kriskwi), an eBay PowerSeller, recommends, "Try to get as many items from one seller as possible. Shipping can be expensive, and when you buy from one seller and combine the shipping, you can really save." Lee (efavormart), an eBay PowerSeller, concurs that it's "best to order everything from one vendor. Although it may save $1 or $2 on the bid, shipping from [different] vendors will cost more in the end."

- *Comparison shop.* Angela Bachelor (ajb2103) says, "eBay is a wonderful resource for brides and grooms!! My best advice is to search, search, search! Many times you can find several people who sell the same thing for different prices. Be thorough in your search and bid wisely. Also, since many bride eBayers are first-timers, I would caution them to read the fine print on auctions. Don't make the mistake of bidding on an item that looks like it's priced well, only to find out there is a huge shipping charge for it. As long as brides are careful and buy from reputable sellers, I am sure they will find wonderful success on eBay." Nancy and David Matteis (dnsmartshop), eBay PowerSellers, agree: "My advice is to do a ton of *research*. Some items may be cheaper from other sellers, but then they get you with the shipping charges. My shipping is what it would cost me. I make nothing on shipping or on materials that I use. So I truly believe that you have to research and ask the sellers questions such as return policy, etc."

- *Act on great bargains.* Christopher Rausch (orlandoweddings), an eBay PowerSeller, recommends that "brides take advantage of eBay's pricing when a deal comes around. If they wait, they will run the risk of the seller not having the item available down the road. I have people that have waited and did not get their first choice of items because they were sold out."

- *Ask questions.* Cindy Johnson (jcsm2003), an eBay PowerSeller, says, "The biggest advice that I give brides is to not be afraid to ask questions. Just because you don't see it in an auction or in a store doesn't mean the seller doesn't have exactly what you are looking for. Many times, sellers do not have everything they have available listed, even in their store. I have over 3,000 items, and I only have about 200 items listed. Many times someone will e-mail me asking if I have anything that looks like this or that. If I do, I will e-mail them a picture and a quote. If they want to purchase [the item], I will put up a custom listing in my store for exactly the number they want."

- *Look for quality.* Jackie Carlson (queblessed3x), an eBay PowerSeller, advises brides "to not only search out price but quality. A lot of items being sold are items that you find in a dollar store that people resell or on dollar store Web sites. To me they are not the quality you would want for a wedding, and there's a lot of disappointment when they are received. Look for items that will be true heirlooms that you can pass down through the generations. For example, *everything* we sell is handmade: hankies, pillows, garters, etc. These are items you can't go to a discount store and find. E-mail the seller and ask a lot of questions; check *all* feedback (not just the negative feedback)—we all have bad days and make mistakes because we're human. And most of all, if you have a question, ask it, and don't ever assume. If you make assumptions, you'll wish you'd asked because 'over the wires' it's very hard to know what you're getting, as you can't touch it, feel it, or look closely at it. And lastly, if there's a problem with your purchase, e-mail the seller before heading to feedback—they deserve a chance to right a wrong before you say something bad. Plus you cannot take back your feedback, and some sellers will reciprocate with a bad feedback because of this."

- *Look for good communication.* Maria Cook (humbride), an eBay PowerSeller, claims, "The best advice I have for buyers is that whenever possible, try to have communication with your seller prior to buying. You will feel more comfortable with a transaction if you get to know the seller and the manner in which you are treated and how your questions are answered. Also consider the feedback."

- *Try bidding strategies such as bid sniping.* Shannon and Vance Kane (handykane), eBay PowerSellers, say, "The number one eBay general advice we like to give is to wait 'til the last minute to bid (also known as bid sniping). That's right, write down when your auction is going to end, and when the auction is about 30 seconds from ending, type in the maximum bid you feel comfortable with. The reason we give this advice is because when you bid early on an item that you really want, that draws attention to it, and since most eBayers are girls, they see something in demand, and they *have* to have it. This rarely fails, and is generally the only way I bid unless the item has a good Buy-It-Now price, which is usually easier for me since I'm instant gratification."

- *Read the description carefully.* Lola Tinney (lolasboutique), an eBay PowerSeller, advises brides to "read, read, read. It is so easy to be captivated by the photo. Take time to read the description, about the seller and the seller's feedback. Feedback ratings can be so misleading; the feedback may all be positive, but what did customers really say about the transaction? If the seller has a low feedback rating, ask them questions and see how responsive they are. This will be a good indication of the service you will receive. Speaking of service, will the seller take returns? Generally bridal items are not returnable. Personally, I think this is unfair to the bride, and we are happy to take returns."

- *Look for variety.* Christine Whiting (shadowmom29) recommends that you "look, look, look, and check out the variety of items eBay has to offer. Compare prices, quality, and your likings with the items. Take a couple of weeks at least and check out the offerings and compare them with what you want. Also, if you see something similar to what you like, e-mail the seller and see if they have something to match what you want. You would be surprised, but most do. Actually, a lot of my supplies come from eBay as well. Why? Well, the price and quality are right!"

- *Ask for customization.* Barbara Dimoush (packageperfect), an eBay PowerSeller, says, "Looking for something special and don't see it on eBay? Ask one of your favorite sellers if they can find it for you. The same holds true for special colors; all you have to do is ask. The worst that can happen is that a seller won't be able to accommodate your request. Once you see an item that's perfect for your wedding, you should 'Buy It Now,' bid on it immediately, or determine to watch it and place a last-minute snipe bid. Whichever buying or bidding strategy you choose, be sure to pursue these "ideal items" so that you won't be disappointed when it's no longer available and you had your heart set on it. If that doesn't work with your budget, contact the seller directly and ask how long they plan to have that particular item available."

- *Shop eBay stores.* PowerSeller Karen Mark (daddyskiki) says, "Be sure to check and see if the seller you like has an eBay store, because sometimes the items in the store cost less than a regular auction."

- *Shop eBay sellers' Web sites.* Giselle Bartino (thebartinoco), an eBay PowerSeller, exclaims, "My advice: *research!* I have seen a ton of sellers come and go through the years. It is true that great bargains can be had on eBay, but it is no bargain if you get something you weren't expecting. Granted, mistakes occur, as we are all human, but the key is how the seller/provider deals with those problems. The other great part about research is finding exactly what you like and finding it at the best price. For example, we match any verifiable price plus 5 percent. You may also find that the same seller has a Web site. Prices are usually much lower through a direct Web site because the seller does not incur all of the eBay fees."

- *Verify shipping dates with sellers.* Nick Veradi (veradi) advises you to "check the feedback testimonials of the seller. Also, find out how soon they will ship your order. For art products, make sure you see the fine details in a large graphic before buying; most good sellers have these graphics ready to e-mail to you so you can decide if you really like it or not."

- *Stick to your budget.* Candace Girard (spoolofdesign) says, "Don't lose sight of the fact that you are there to get a deal. Stick to your original maximum bid. Don't get upset if you lose an auction, because sooner or later someone else will come along with the exact same item and maybe you will win that one instead!"

- *Enjoy the convenience and savings.* Jessica Geremia (jessicaspalace), an eBay PowerSeller, states that "it is amazing what eBay has to offer. A bride can simply plan her entire wedding just from eBay, and not have to worry about going broke. You will be able to get the quality at a great deal that you will never find anywhere else! It is all at your fingertips as well. Forget the overspending at the shopping malls, long lines, and nasty sales clerks. Come and visit eBay, where our reputation lies in your hands. Take a peek at your seller's feedback and see how many customers are pleased; you will feel very assured. Not to mention, you can relist almost all of your wedding items on eBay and put the money back into your pocket, then pass the savings on to other brides-to-be. What a dream come true."

Wedding Gown Advice

OK. Now we're ready to hear what the wedding gown experts have to share. Who better to give advice about your dream wedding gown than people who sell gowns for a living?

- *Ask specific questions.* Joyce (buydirectbridals), an eBay PowerSeller, says, "My advice for any bride-to-be who is considering purchasing her dream dress from a seller on eBay is to first e-mail the seller before purchasing the gown. Ask all of the questions you have as far as the designer name. Is the gown a current style? If so, perhaps visit a local bridal salon to try to view the sample gown in person (if you are special ordering). Inquire about the return policy and also if they would consider replacing the special-ordered gown if it should be damaged upon receiving it. Most bridal retailers will offer an exchange gown. Make sure you take proper measurements before purchasing to ensure that the gown will fit. If not, be prepared to have a bridal seamstress near you who will do your 'outside' alterations. A professional bridal retailer on eBay will be able to give you advice on proper measurement taking. And make sure the seller is friendly and helpful."

- *Higher prices don't necessarily mean higher quality.* Xochitl Aramillo (the_dress_co), an eBay PowerSeller, has this advice for the budget-minded bride: "Just because it costs more doesn't mean it's better quality. Many of my competitors sell the exact same dresses I sell for triple the price. I think feedback is very important. It's your eBay reputation on the line, and feedback is the eBay way of telling others that you are trustworthy and that you sell quality items. Ask questions. It's better to ask ahead of time, and most eBay sellers are happy to answer questions, and it also tells you what kind of seller you are dealing with. If they answer questions in a prompt manner and are attentive to your concerns, it's a good sign that they stand behind their products and will contact you if a problem should arise. I would also say that shopping early is best so that they have plenty of time to make alterations and dry clean the gown, as they tend to wrinkle a little during shipping."

- *Check the size chart and your measurements carefully* Wanda Raccagno (bridesgallery), an eBay PowerSeller, says, "My best advice to brides who wish to purchase their bridal gowns on eBay is to check out the seller's feedback to make sure feedback is at least 90+ percent. Then they need to make sure they check over the size chart and compare it against their measurements to make sure [the gown] will fit. If they are between sizes (which most are), they should *always* purchase too big rather than too small. The gown can be taken in several sizes, but can only be let out so much."

    Heiphy (heiphy), an eBay PowerSeller, adds: "How to choose your size correctly? Please remember *not to buy by size alone* because there are so many different size charts even in one country. The best way is to look at the bust, waist, and skirt measurements of the item listed and compare those bust, waist, and skirt measurements to see which size is best for the bride. (For example, if her bust and waist measurements are 38 inches and 30 inches, respectively, choose the dress with bust and waist measurements of 38 inches and 30 inches, respectively, or choose the one with the closest measurements and have it altered later when you receive it.) How to adjust the length of the skirt? Dresses can be suitable for ladies of different heights because brides can adjust the skirt length by wearing a pair of high-heeled shoes or flat-heeled shoes, wearing a full or less full crinoline, or having [the dress] altered by a seamstress. You can take a pair of high-heeled or flat-heeled shoes to adjust your height, too. How to adjust the bust measurement easily? It is easy to adjust the bust measurements. Here are some examples only: (1) Wearing a push-up bra can make the bust measurement bigger easily and achieve a sexier look, too. (2)Wearing a corset underneath the dress can make the overall look much more sexy and beautiful. This can be useful to adjust the bust and waist measurements, too. (3) Adding some bra pads can make the bust measurement fuller and bigger."

- *Consider a custom-made gown.* Jennie Miller (jennieqxw), an eBay PowerSeller, advises, "The best way to save money on a wedding dress is to get a tailor-made gown because the alteration fee can cost much more than what you pay for the dress itself. When ordering a tailor-made gown, it will be very possible that no alterations are needed. In the event alterations are needed, they will be very minor and cost less. But customers need to have measurements taken correctly."
- *Pay attention to the time frame.* Ke Zhao (angelbride520) states, "Pay attention to the time because dressmaking needs enough time to be finished. Make sure to leave enough time for the seamstress to make your custom-made dress. The size is very important to the bride. Although some dresses with firm size are cheaper, sometimes it is better to choose the custom dress."
- *Stick with the gown experts.* Barbara Barrett (valentines93), an eBay PowerSeller, claims, "People who auction gowns as their main eBay business will have the best quality and will provide the best service. I've been in bridal for 11 years and am a wealth of information. We've recently introduced a return policy to help people feel at ease. For $30 you can return anything by contacting us within three days of receiving it and paying the return shipping. It covers our fees and hassle and gives the bride some assurance that we are nice people."

Veil Advice

The right headpiece or veil is a crowning touch to your wedding ensemble on your big day, and you shouldn't have to pay an arm and a leg for it. Here's what one experienced seller had to say about shopping for and choosing the right veil:

- *Try on before you buy.* Norma Pearson (valuveil), an eBay PowerSeller, says that when it comes to buying a veil, "the advice I give to every budget-minded bride would be to visit your bridal shop and find the exact wedding veil (or item) you are looking for, and then come to eBay to see if you can find it at a better price. Bridal shops and boutiques mark their bridal items up a great deal simply because they assume that if you purchase your gown from them, you will also purchase your wedding veil."

Jewelry Advice

To make sure those jewels will be true gems of your wedding experience, here are some tips on wedding jewelry:

- *Educate yourself.* Dorie Miller and Jay Greenberg (djjewelry.com), eBay PowerSellers, say, "Go retail jewelry shopping. Do a lot of research, and learn your correct finger size. The consumer should go to at least three or four jewelry stores to become educated. Ask questions: What is a comfort fit band? What is a half round band? Get the gram weight, if possible, of the ring that you like and then try to match up what you like with a reputable eBay seller. The shopper can save a bundle. We do not have a retail store, so we immediately save on our overhead. There are no salesmen except Jay and myself; that is how we offer such great buys."

- *Look for quality and value.* Jay (mtddiamonds) says, "Remember, cheaper isn't always a better deal. Those that do their homework will be much happier paying only a little more for a quality product. My advice to potential eBay buyers: Especially in diamonds, you have to be educated in what you are buying. Once you understand what you want, then you can search on eBay to find some deals. You should not buy the cheapest item, but know what you are getting. On my main sites http://to-diamonds.com/ and http://diamonds-and-engagement-rings.com/, we have a tutorial to teach people what to look for. There is a lot of information on the Net, so check it out."

Flowers Advice

Ordering floral decorations online shouldn't be intimidating. It should be an enjoyable, and yet affordable experience, one that will enhance your wedding day. Here are some tips from sellers who specialize in creating floral master-pieces for eBay brides.

- *Shop early.* Barbara Grant (affordelegance), an eBay PowerSeller, says, "Buy your silk floral items plenty of time before the wedding (four to six months). If they are high quality, they will last forever and can be one less stress to be relieved of in the final weeks before the wedding."

- *Save time and money with premade arrangements.* Lisa Srey (unique_expressions) states, "When it comes to weddings, this is the most stressful time for a bride. It is your important day, so you want everything to be perfect. eBay is the best place for anything, not just wedding supplies. If you want to make your own bouquet set, you can save even more money. But [most people] are very busy with our normal everyday lives. By buying flowers already made, wedding flower arrangements save a lot of time. Silk is cheaper than fresh flowers, and you can keep the flowers as a keepsake for years to come."

- *Look for experienced florists.* Christina Hartley (designsbykristina), says, "I have worked in the floral business for 12 years now, and I love it. I own and operate my own wedding business, specializing in wedding flowers and home décor. I [advise brides] to always look at the feedback and what the seller offers for returns and customer satisfaction. There are many fly-by-night sellers on eBay, and I find a lot of brides leave things to the last minute, so this could be scary if you found the wrong seller. Second, I would advise brides to look around and see what all the sellers are selling, because there are many different types of styles and flowers."

- *Read the feedback.* When you're looking for good deals at eBay and trying to ensure a smooth transaction, you simply cannot review a seller's feedback too much. Kimberly Frazier (rosesrkim), an eBay PowerSeller, reiterates this important aspect: "My best advice for the budget-minded bride is to read the feedback . . . that tells all. Some shops try to reel you in with $99 specials that promise large packages, and some claim to sell only high-quality flowers and never use 'cheapies' at higher prices. My outlook . . . [is that] each set is different, and if I can keep the cost of a set down to a really good price and use a less expensive flower combined with a really good flower, accent it with beautiful pearls or ribbons, you have a beautiful set at a reasonable price."

- *Ask for customization.* Linda Bailey (teagardenfloral) says, "Communicate with your seller. Ask them if they have 'sample' products sitting around that you could buy cheaply. Ask for the specific items you need and don't pay for extra items you don't need. If your eBay florist won't customize a package to your specific needs, find one who will. Also, make sure you ask a lot of questions about the product. Some florists offer 'premade' bouquets that they buy from factories in China and put up for auction. They can be very inexpensive, so they're not always a bad thing. But if you want custom work and hand-made products, make sure you know what you're buying."

Honeymoon Advice

Your honeymoon should be one of the most romantic and special trips you take together as newlyweds. Here is what you should be looking for while shopping for a fabulous, yet affordable honeymoon vacation.

- *Include the honeymoon in your wedding budget.* Mollie Hill (cruisegoddess), an eBay PowerSeller, says that you should "decide on your honeymoon budget when you set the rest of your wedding budget, so you don't short yourself on one of the last things that seems to get planned by many bridal couples. It is a good idea to stay a shorter time and at a nicer resort for the most enjoyment of your vacation rather than staying longer at a budget hotel. All of our honeymooners really like the first-class and deluxe hotels that we offer with our packages. Several couples decide to stay less days and stay at one of our nicer resorts, if that is what fits their budget. We really try hard to guide the honeymooners to what best fits within their budget during the planning stages. Since we have over 23 years experience in planning honeymoons and travel-based weddings, we are able to offer them the very best value for their travel dollars and honeymoon budget."

eBAY BRIDE SUCCESS STORIES

Now that you've read valuable advice from dozens of eBay wedding sellers, you're probably still wondering, "Will eBay *really* help me save money on my wedding?" You'll be inspired by the following eBay bride success stories, and you'll see how easy it is to become an eBay bride, have fun, and save money on your big day. Let's hear it from the brides and grooms, now.

- Shannon and Vance Kane (handykane), eBay PowerSellers: "We too are an eBay couple. My husband, Vance, and I have been together seven years, married for four, and almost *everything* for our wedding I purchased off eBay. We had such a large, extravagant wedding four years ago, and so many had asked us how we did everything on such a tight budget. They were shocked to find out we had single-handedly created the whole affair. Our invitations were such a huge success; everyone was taken aback by their originality, style, and quality. We know how difficult it was to get married on a tight budget; there is no reason to spend a fortune when the work can all be done for a reasonable price. I also sold my wedding dress on eBay after our wedding for more than I paid for it."
- Lisa Brideau (lilibriluv): "As I decided to take a good six months off after seven exhausting years of university, I got to spend many hours on eBay to prepare my own wedding. Looking for wedding bouquets to buy (and many more items, of course), I realized I could actually do this myself."
- Lisa Srey (unique_expressions): "I got [nearly] everything from eBay for my wedding: my wedding dress, flower girl dress, ring bearer tux, ring bearer pillow, table centerpieces, and our wedding rings. I love eBay."
- Giselle Bartino (thebartinoco), an eBay PowerSeller: "I got started selling through eBay while planning our wedding. We were on a very tight budget, as we were paying for everything ourselves. I was going to rent a gown from a shop and someone mentioned eBay. I had never

heard of it! I bought my gown and realized that there was a market out there for this. At that time people were selling items without pictures! I actually bought my dress just through a description. I paid $90 plus shipping, and the gown came from Alaska. It was a brand new Alfred Angelo dress. I loved it, except that it didn't go with my color scheme because the seller forgot to mention that it was ivory instead of white. I couldn't really complain, since it was a great deal in those days."

- And here's our own success story, Sarah Manongdo (sarspinay) and Dan Joya: "Like many engaged couples out there, we had to pay for our wedding ourselves. We first thought that with our very limited funds, we would have to 'settle for less' and not be able to afford our dream wedding. But after we turned to eBay to find great bridal bargains, we were on a roll—our average savings were about 80 percent off retail prices! Table 3-1 is our little 'worksheet' with some hard numbers—the proof, as they say, is in the pudding."

Are You Ready to Become an eBay Bride?

After reading this inspiring chapter, you're probably anxious to try your hand at being an eBay bride. Not only will you save time and money, but you'll also have the chance to be able to plan ahead for your big day. You can make a similar worksheet of your own when you begin purchasing your wedding items on eBay, in order to better keep track of the phenomenal savings you will accumulate. The next few chapters will address the best tips and tactics for buying wedding goods online, as well as how to use other resources and Web sites that can help you in your wedding planning. Get ready to be an eBay bride, save time and money, and have great fun.

Table 3-1 Sarah and Dan's Savings by Shopping through eBay

Item Name	Cost	Shipping	eBay Seller	Retail Price	Unit Price	Quantity
Wedding dress	$109.00	$25.00	chicbridal	$2,000.00	$134.00	1
Garment bag	$8.99	$4.99	lolasboutique	$30.00	$13.98	1
Wedding shoes	$34.00	$8.45	daddyskiki	$100.00	$42.45	1
Flowers for people	$25.00	$25.00	adidas_bball_chic	$675.00	$1.67	30
Floral candle rings	$35.88	$4.95	adidas_bball_chic	$150.00	$3.40	12
Accessories	$29.99	$15.00	runninghorse1candles	$140.00	$4.09	11
Save the Date cards	$8.00	$3.00	lacedesigns-com	$50.00	$0.22	50
Unity candle + tapers	$24.99	$14.00	kriskwi	$65.00	$13.00	3
Personalized guestbook	$19.99	$5.50	reneehere	$35.00	$25.49	1
R2D2 cake pan	$10.49	$5.25	mcclutts	$25.00	$15.74	1
Wedding veil with ribbon	$15.50	$7.99	veils_by_natali	$100.00	$23.49	1
Tulle satin pew bows	$24.95	$9.95	basketofbows	$60.00	$5.82	6
Brass unity candleholder	$5.00	$4.95	princescat	$35.00	$9.95	1
Soon to be Mrs. hoodie	$29.99	$4.00	spoolofdesign	$65.00	$33.99	1
Pillar candleholders	$5.99	$8.58	doug910	$72.00	$0.61	24
Satin ring bearer pillow	$9.49	$4.50	queblessed3x	$35.00	$13.99	1
Reception place cards	$12.50	$5.99	heather7966	$50.00	$0.18	100
Mauve balloons	$2.50	$4.00	jwac77	$25.00	$0.07	100
Table menus	$10.00	$2.50	shadowmom29	$36.00	$0.83	15

Item				eBay Total	Retail Total			Savings Total
Bridal tiara	$14.53	$7.95	cutebride		$100.00		1	$22.48
Bridesmaid gifts (pashminas)	$72.00	$28.00	joannawei71		$300.00		6	$16.67
Hurricane candleholders	$56.34	$0.00	virgo_baby_27		$180.00		12	$4.70
Altar flower arrangement	$19.99	$8.55	duchess101		$75.00		1	$28.54
Wedding card mailbox	$18.99	$0.00	csmarquis		$100.00		1	$18.99
Precious Moments memory book	$8.50	$4.99	pennys911ks		$30.00		1	$13.49
Precious Moments cake topper	$9.99	$5.95	collectibles4you		$35.00		1	$15.94
Wedding CD favors	$100.00	$18.00	customcreationsforyou		$500.00		100	$1.18
Wedding invitation sets	$119.00	$14.20	jessicaspalace		$250.00		100	$1.33
Floral pew bows/drapes	$133.50	$12.34	ishta2		$500.00		12	$12.15
Rose topiary centerpieces	$75.00	$21.75	peachgifts_com		$600.00		12	$8.06
Totals	$1,050.09	$285.33		$1,335.42	$6,618.00			$5,282.58

79.821396 % Off Retail

4

The Ups and Downs of Buying Wedding Goods Online

It seems like only yesterday that online "e-tailers" opened up shop on the Internet, selling everything from books, CDs, and movies to computers, electronics, and clothing, among other things. Skeptics back then (and some even today) reasoned that the same items could be found at the local store, so why shop online in the first place? Let's take, for example, a book you've been wanting to read. You can very easily hop in your car, drive to the nearest bookstore, and pick up the book there. However, you can also purchase it online. There are several advantages to shopping online, such as sale discounts, free or inexpensive shipping, and/or no sales tax if the Web site does not have a physical location in your state. Use your credit card securely to pay, and you never even have to step outside of your house. Online shopping can save you a lot of time and money.

The same principles apply when you're considering purchasing items on eBay. First, find out if the wedding items you are looking for are available in your local area, and the approximate prices of the items. Then visit eBay to find the same or similar items at a potentially better price. You can almost always find what you're looking for on eBay—you just have to know how to search effectively for what you need (see Chapter 7 for more details). But first, let's discuss some pros and cons that may come to mind when you consider purchasing anything online.

Weighing the Benefits

- *Convenience.* At any hour of the day or night, you can browse eBay and other online Web sites for your wedding items. This is perfect for you, the busy bride, if you hold down a day job (as most of us do) or go to school.

- *Quick results.* Generally, you will receive your items within days of your payment clearing the seller's account. This is not true for custom-made items, of course, so allow extra time if you order anything that will be made according to your own specifications, such as wedding gowns, bridesmaids' dresses, or custom wedding bouquet sets.
- *Orders are trackable.* Shipping services such as the U.S. Postal Service (http://www.usps.gov), FedEx (http://www.fedex.com), and UPS (http://www.ups.com) offer tracking as an option when packages are mailed to you. For your peace of mind, most established retailers will send you e-mails containing the tracking information for your package. Sellers on eBay may also offer tracking as an option (for a modest fee), especially if your items are expensive, rare, breakable, custom-made, or irreplaceable.
- *No sales tax.* If you live and shop within the United States, if you are purchasing items from outside your home state and the Web site does not have a physical location in your state, you don't have to pay sales tax. This can save you anywhere from a few cents to hundreds of dollars, depending on the total price you are paying for your item. Consider purchasing high-end items (such as jewelry or wedding apparel) from an e-tailer or eBayer who is not in your home state—you will most likely save a bundle on sales tax. (Note: this sales-tax savings does not necessarily apply outside of the United States and, if you're in the habit of purchasing top-dollar items beyond preparing your eBay wedding, you may need to pay "use tax." When in doubt, consult a tax advisor.)
- *Delivery to your door.* There's no need to lug your purchases home after you're done shopping. Your items are delivered right to your door.
- *Some items are wholesale-priced or cheaper than retail.* The best part of shopping online is the ability to find the same or a similar item for less than retail prices. The savings do add up. You'll be amazed.
- *Some items are returnable.* If something is not quite what you expected it to be after you receive it in the mail, you may have the option of returning it. Make sure to read the seller's refund/exchange/return policy. If the seller accepts returns, there is usually a period of time during which you can return the merchandise. Read and understand the fine print so that you'll be prepared later on if you have to do a return or an exchange.
- *Bonuses and discounts.* What makes a bargain even sweeter? Free or discounted shipping! If you're able to wait a bit longer for delivery, take advantage of the free shipping that some sellers offer or take them up on their offers of item personalization. If you're shopping for

wedding gifts or gifts for special wedding party members, you can find plenty of gift ideas online that are available for personalization (embroidery and engraving are popular). Make a gift truly unique by personalizing it for the recipient—she or he will remember your thoughtfulness for years to come.

- *No pushy salespeople.* Ever been to a store and been hounded by a wedding salesperson on commission? Sure, we have, too, but not on-line! You can browse to your heart's content and not be bothered by that salesperson who's breathing down your neck, watching your every move and calculating how much you are going to spend in the store. When you shop online, you buy when you're ready, and not before. You can take as long as you like to think about a purchase before making a final decision.
- *Big end-of-season sales and clearances.* Big clearance sales and end-of-season sales are not reserved exclusively for brick-and-mortar stores. You can find great deals online when wedding Web sites and eBay sellers have too much supply compared to the demand. Take advantage of this and grab some online bridal bargains.

The Cons of Online Shopping

Of course, there are some special factors that you'll need to take into consideration when you decide to shop online, for your wedding or whatever else strikes you. Here are some things to take into account when you shop the Internet:

- *You won't be able to see/try on/hold the product before buying it.* Although this is a con, you can try window-shopping in retail stores or malls so that you'll have an idea of what product you want (for example, a Precious Moments wedding album from Hallmark or a Maggie Sottero dress from a bridal salon). Touch it, hold it, measure it, try it on, and make sure it's the item for you. Then find it on eBay for less!
- *You have to wait for the item to be shipped.* If you have to wait for the item to be shipped and arrive at your door, allow for shipping time and purchase it in advance of your wedding date (days to weeks to months). Customizing or personalizing an item also takes extra time, so be sure to take that into consideration. If you are really crunched for time, consider expedited shipping methods.
- *Online fraud is possible.* Avoid online fraud as much as possible by bidding on items from sellers with high feedback ratings (98 to 100 percent) and by using the eBay site and the PayPal Web site properly. Use your credit card to make payments, since credit card companies extend more coverage for purchases than is available for purchases

made without a credit card. Chapter 10 provides some advice in case you encounter problematic sellers.

- *Some items are not returnable.* If the item you purchased is nonreturnable, *make sure* you really want the item before you bid on it. If it's not really to your liking after you receive it, well, it's yours anyway. Don't fret too much about this possibility, though, since you can always give it away as a gift or resell it on eBay and get your money back (or maybe even make a profit).

- *Some items may arrive damaged or defective.* If the seller offers shipping insurance, insure your more expensive or delicate items in case of breakage or damage. (You will get your money back if this happens. You have to file a claim with the U.S. Post Office, FedEx, or whatever shipping company was used.) Contact your seller as soon as possible if your item arrives damaged from shipping or contains a manufacturer's defect.

More details on how to address problems with your purchases and/or your seller are mentioned in Chapter 10, so be sure to read that chapter to learn what to do if things go awry. Otherwise, your online shopping experience on eBay and other official sites should be a fun, convenient way to get things done for your big day.

LEARNING TO SELECT THE BEST ITEMS FOR YOUR WEDDING

It's time to go shopping! Shopping should be fun, right? So why do brides everywhere become so stressed about shopping for their wedding? Perhaps it's the challenge of finding products and services of good quality and still staying within budget. Or maybe it's the stress of coordinating purchases, services, deposits, and balances due with the emotional highs and lows of dealing with loved ones about wedding issues. Although it's enough to take the fun out of shopping, here are a few key things to keep in mind that will help ease your mind when you're selecting wedding items and services to buy.

- *Price.* This is one of the easier characteristics of an item and/or service that you want to purchase to assess. Make sure that the price is within reason and that it fits within your budget. This universal principle can be applied to almost any wedding expense you can think of, including services such as catering, entertainment, and transportation. The only way to know if a price tag is too low, too high, or just about average is to take the time to shop. Compare and contrast, and consider the month of your wedding as well as the location. The best thing about shopping on eBay (we've said it before, but we'll say it again) is that you can expect prices to be as low as 50 percent or more off retail prices. However, price should not be the only thing you judge an item by, as you'll learn next.

- *Quality.* Judging the quality of an item online is a little tricky, but you can do so by reading the feedback the seller has received from buyers of the same or similar items. Pay attention to pictures of the item and its details, and ask questions of the seller if you have any. You should consider both the quality of the item and the customer service you will receive from the seller before you decide to buy. You should also consider the reputation of the brand name (if applicable) of the item you are buying. With reputable manufacturers and designers, you do pay more for quality products, but with eBay, you are able to find both quality and affordability.

- *Authenticity.* If you love the look of a designer wedding gown, but are completely happy with the idea of wearing a duplicate or "designer-inspired" gown on your big day, then you can search specifically for this type of item on eBay. Conversely, if you have to have the real thing and nothing faux (such as diamonds and fine jewelry), you can search eBay for these kinds of items as well, and learn how to filter out what you don't want. (See Chapters 7 and 8 for more details.) Look for items that are new with tags (abbreviated NWT), intact labels, certification documents, and other identifiable characteristics that assure you that you are getting the real thing.

- *Quantity.* Determining the correct quantity is key to ordering wedding items online. You want to order neither too few nor too many. Common examples of wedding items purchased in quantity are invitations, favors, and decorations. Ordering too few will create the hassle and added expense of ordering more, and ordering too many will waste money that would be better allocated to other things. Since most wedding items are sold in lots of 5, 10, 25, 50, 75, 100, and so on or multiples of 12 (12, 24, 48, 96, 120, 244, and so on), estimate how many you need, and order about 10 percent more than that number (the extra 10 percent is to make extra items available in case of errors and/or last-minute changes).

- *Size.* This pertains to any item of wedding apparel and jewelry purchased online. Getting your correct size and measurements for your wedding gown and/or tuxedos is vital to selecting the correct item for you. Ordering the correct size of wedding rings or bands will eliminate the need and added expense of resizing the rings later on. You can very easily obtain your measurements from professional seamstresses or tailors and jewelers, respectively.

- *Convenience.* One of the great things about shopping online is the ability to send payment either electronically or through regular mail, and to expect to receive your merchandise at your address without ever having to set foot in a store. Generally, you do have to pay for this convenience in the form of shipping and handling fees. But if these shipping fees are reasonable (or even discounted or free), the convenience of shopping online will save you time and energy that can be better allocated to other wedding-related tasks.

- *Longevity of use.* Take into account how long you are going to use the item in question. If it is your wedding gown, you will be wearing it for less than a day. If it is your wedding band and/or engagement ring, you will be wearing it (hopefully) for a lifetime. If your budget allows room for only a very few items in the more expensive bracket, think of how long you will be using the item and adjust your budget accordingly. If you want to spend just a little bit more on certain items, such as your wedding gown, reception decorations, and the like, fortunately you also have the option of reselling them after your big day.

- *Resale value.* As previously stated, you will be able to resell any wedding items you no longer need on eBay. The better the quality of your items, the greater the resale value. You can get your money back, and perhaps even make a profit!

When you add it all up, shopping for wedding items is not very different from shopping for just about anything else (such as cars, computers, appliances, and so on). These days, with so many choices available to us in the products we buy or consider buying, being a choosy shopper just makes sense, and choosing to shop and select carefully from the offerings at eBay makes even more sense.

HOW TO SELECT THE BEST SELLERS

It's easy to find the best sellers of wedding items on eBay. First, browse and search for the wedding item you want (for example, a wedding gown). When you look at the seller's information, usually on the top right-hand side of an auction listing, you can see how many positive feedback ratings the seller has, the percentage of positive feedback received, his or her PowerSeller status (if applicable), a link to the seller's "About Me" page (if he or she has one), how long the person has been an eBay registered user, and the country the person resides in (see Figure 4-1).

When it comes to sifting through the sea of sellers, recognize that the "best" sellers on eBay share some common characteristics:

- *High percentage of positive feedback ratings.* Positive feedback ratings could be in the 98 to 100 percent range of feedback ratings received. Look through the negative comments (if any), and try to determine whether the situation was a one-time-only incident and whether the seller consistently gives good service otherwise.

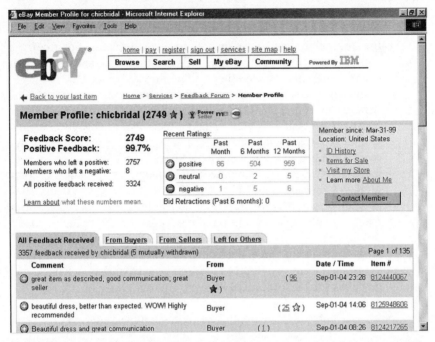

Figure 4-1 Make a point of reviewing the seller's statistics and other information carefully, as you seek to shop from only the best wedding merchants.

- *High number of completed transactions.* The higher the number, the better. You want a seller who has sold wedding items on eBay to other brides in the past.
- *Good and timely customer service.* You can judge this yourself by the promptness of the seller's response to your e-mailed inquiries about an item. You can also judge the seller's past customer service by reading the feedback comments from past bidders.
- *Established on eBay for a number of years.* Generally it is better to shop from an eBay veteran than from a newcomer to eBay, since veterans are more apt to know eBay policies and act accordingly. Newcomers to eBay, if they follow good business practices, eventually become eBay veterans. After making several contacts with a seller regarding the items you want, you can make a more informed decision as to whether you want to bid on or buy an item from a newcomer. Some hardworking newcomers to eBay can earn a high percentage and number of positive feedback ratings in a short period of time. You can take this into consideration when you take note of how long the seller has been on eBay.

- *Detailed auction descriptions and pictures.* It's easy to shop from a seller when the auction description contains all the details necessary for a bride who is shopping for her wedding items. Good pictures are also key when a seller is trying to sell something online, especially if the items are for a once-in-a-lifetime special event. Good sellers will have both detailed descriptions and pictures to help eBay brides shop more easily.
- *Contact information displayed prominently.* It is best if the seller has his or her contact information prominently displayed somewhere in the auction, the "About Me" page, or the e-mailed invoice in case you need to contact the seller for any reason. Good sellers will have this information readily available to their customers, since communication is key to successful completed transactions on eBay.
- *Convenient payment methods accepted.* The best sellers on eBay usually offer convenient methods of payment for the buyer: check, money order, credit card, PayPal, and so on. You are a busy bride, and the more options you have for paying for your wedding items, the better.
- *Fair shipping charges.* Good sellers will charge fair amounts for shipping and will not try to squeeze extra profits from buyers by overcharging them for shipping and handling fees. If you have any questions about a seller's shipping costs, you should e-mail the seller directly.

A select group of eBay sellers qualify to become eBay PowerSellers. What is the PowerSellers program? Here's how eBay itself defines the program:

> PowerSellers are eBay top sellers who have sustained a consistent high volume of monthly sales and a high level of total feedback with 98% positive or better. As such, these sellers rank among the most successful sellers in terms of product sales and customer satisfaction on eBay. We are proud to recognize their contributions to the success of the eBay Community.
>
> **Power Seller** When you see this icon next to the member's user ID, be assured that the member is a qualified PowerSeller who not only maintains a solid sales record but also a 98% positive feedback rating based on transactions with other eBay users. You can feel assured that your transaction will go smoothly and that you are dealing with one who has consistently met the requirements established by eBay.

Furthermore, in order for sellers to become and remain PowerSellers in good standing, they must exhibit the following behaviors as related to their listing and selling activity:

- Uphold the eBay community values, including honesty, timeliness, and mutual respect.
- Maintain a minimum of $1,000 of average gross monthly sales for three months.

- Maintain a minimum feedback of 100 with a 98 percent positive rating.
- Keep the eBay account current—no outstanding balances.
- Be an active seller on the eBay site for a minimum duration of 90 days.
- Maintain a minimum of four average monthly listings for the past three months.

What all this means to you is that if you purchase your wedding items from a PowerSeller, chances are that you will be getting great customer service along with your bridal bargain. PowerSellers are pros at what they do; they help eBay brides like you save a lot of money without sacrificing quality.

Now, to help you begin your own seller selection, please consider these PowerSellers who specialize in wedding items:

Number	eBay PowerSeller	Items Sold
1	cyberexotic	Bridesmaids' dresses
2	fashionwedding	Bridesmaids' dresses
3	www_greatdealbridal_com	Bridesmaids' dresses
4	jcsm2003	Centerpieces
5	bargain-hunter-hua	Custom wedding gowns
6	ds_decals	Engraved bridesmaids'/grooms-men's gifts
7	favors-land	Favors
8	orlandoweddings	Favors, bubbles, petals
9	designsbyheidi	Favors, programs
10	kriskwi	Favors, unity candles
11	ebridemart	Favors, wedding supplies
12	efavormart	Favors, wedding supplies
13	affordelegance	Flowers, bouquet sets
14	rosesrkim	Flowers, bouquet sets
15	packageperfect	Flowers, bouquet sets, favors, pew bows
16	cruisegoddess	Honeymoon vacations
17	cybergetaways	Honeymoon vacations
18	dundeeprinting	Invitations
19	heather7966	Invitations
20	jessicaspalace	Invitations

21	weddings_for_less	Invitations, programs
22	handykane	Invitations, save the date cards, thank-you cards
23	queblessed3x	Personalized items
24	reneehere	Personalized items
25	basketofbows	Pew bows
26	monkeysuits	Tuxedos
27	unitycandles	Unity candles
28	honeymooneve	Veils
29	veils_by_natali	Veils
30	veilsnmore	Veils
31	fashiontiara	Veils, tiaras
32	cutebride	Veils, tiaras, accessories
33	djjewelry.com	Wedding bands
34	facets_wedding_rings	Wedding bands, engagement rings
35	mdcdiamonds.com	Wedding bands, engagement rings
36	signedpiecesinc	Wedding bands, engagement rings, Tiffany & Company
37	mstnggt66	Wedding fortune cookies
38	bridesgallery	Wedding gowns
39	bridewire	Wedding gowns
40	buydirectbridals	Wedding gowns
41	chicbridal	Wedding gowns
42	heiphy	Wedding gowns
43	thebartinoco	Wedding gowns
44	valentines93	Wedding gowns
45	humbride	Wedding gowns, bridesmaids' dresses
46	jennieqxw	Wedding gowns, bridesmaids' dresses
47	the_dress_co	Wedding gowns, formal dresses
48	lolasboutique	Wedding gowns, garment bags
49	bridalveilscustommade	Veils
50	newgowns	Bridesmaids' dresses

The following is a list of other wedding specialists who have not yet reached PowerSeller status (yet, based on the great service and items we've received, we're sure they will do so quite soon):

1	valuveil	Veils
2	beyondwishes	CD-ROM wedding cards, anniversary cards
3	angelbride520	Custom wedding gowns
4	veradi	Custom wedding portraits from photos
5	lacedesigns-com	Favors
6	mema-pops	Favors, chocolate truffles
7	shadowmom29	Favors, custom table menus
8	bigrose_roses	Flowers, fresh roses bulk wholesale
9	cindylynn55	Flowers, bouquet sets
10	duchess101	Flowers, bouquet sets
11	lilibriluv	Flowers, bouquet sets
12	affordable-florals	Flowers, bouquet sets, centerpieces
13	unique_expressions	Flowers, bouquet sets, centerpieces
14	ajb2103	Hair/cake/flower ideas on CD
15	hot-traveldeals	Honeymoon vacations
16	alvarezprinting	Invitations
17	spoolofdesign	Personalized items
18	balloons9695	Pew bows
19	daddyskiki	Shoes
20	mtddiamonds	Wedding bands, engagement rings
21	bridalveilscustommade	Veils
22	csmarquis	Wedding card box holders
23	bridal-gown	Wedding gowns
24	dnsmartshop	Honeymoon items, "Just Married" items

CONTINGENCY PLANS TO KEEP YOUR WEDDING ON TRACK AND ON TIME

When you're planning a wedding, it's not easy to conceive of every scenario in which something doesn't go exactly to plan. Therefore, having a contingency plan to keep your wedding on track and on time is the smart thing to do, especially for a busy bride with a budget.

- Revisit Chapter 2 on how to plan your ceremony, reception, and honeymoon without breaking the bank. Make full use of the suggested calendar of things that must be done in order for your wedding to run smoothly.
- Have a "second-in-command" (such as your mother, your maid of honor, or another close friend) to keep you in check during the wedding planning and to provide unbiased and objective advice whenever you need it.
- Always make note of deadlines or due dates for fittings, deposits, and payments. Write these down in a calendar solely reserved for wedding planning. Inform your fiancé of the existence of this calendar and refer to it often.
- Pay your vendors early if they will let you—this alleviates the stress of forgetting to make the critical final payment right before your wedding day.
- Have everything you need written in your contracts with your vendors, and then keep several copies of the contracts in a safe place.
- Keep vendors' contact phone numbers in one place so that it's easy to access their phone numbers and addresses when you need them. Ask for vendors by name so that you won't be given the run-around if you ever need extra assistance.
- Formulate a "Plan B" for worst-case scenarios (what if the limo arrives late, the flowers are wilted, it rains during your outdoor reception, or the caterer didn't order enough entrees for all your guests?). Discuss possible "Plan B" options with your vendors, and ask a trusted friend or relative (one for each major element of the wedding) to help you map out Plan B if you ever need to do so. For example, you might assign your uncle to provide emergency transportation for the bride if the limousine is late. Or you might ask a close family friend to oversee the reception flowers and replace them with inexpensive but beautiful candles (stored at the reception hall) if need be. Consider ordering a tent or renting an alternative location for your outdoor reception in the event of inclement weather. Ask your catering manager to speak to your maid of honor if anything food-related goes awry during the reception.

- Keep lines of communication open with your eBay sellers. Sometimes a friendly e-mail reminder from you is all that is needed to get your seller to ship you your items promptly or make a correction on your order. Shop and purchase wedding items on eBay early to eliminate the stress of any last-minute hitches.
- Pack for your honeymoon early, and always leave extra time for traveling to and from the airport. Hope for the best but expect the worst in terms of weather, traffic, and flight delays. Bring a good book to read, and wear comfortable clothes when traveling.
- Check the Internet for any quick information you may need (hotel accommodations for guests, traffic information, weather information, bridal registries, and so on). The Internet is one of the fastest ways to obtain information nowadays, and the world is literally at your fingertips.

The point of all this is that shopping at eBay and doing other planning and contingency planning online is the newest and most enabling way to plan a wedding. The Internet is your oyster here, brimming with incredible bargains and opportunities to help you in just about all your wedding needs. Let's continue to the next chapter, where you can find the best wedding-related Web sites for busy eBay brides like you.

5

Other Sources and
Resources to Consider

Our focus so far has been on eBay—and why not, since there are thousands of wedding-related items up for bid or sale on eBay at any given time. However, diversity is key when it comes to bargain shopping, and we've found plenty of other sources that have been helpful in planning a cost-effective yet elegant celebration. Now more than ever, you can use the Internet to find almost anything wedding-related, including wedding advice, items for sale, and wedding services.

In this chapter, we'll steer you to some additional online hotspots that will be of tremendous help to you as you plan your wedding. We'll also offer our insight regarding what makes one wedding Web site different from another seemingly similar one, guiding you to the best sites and thereby saving you having to sort them out for yourself. So sit back, relax, and "mouse" your way to more online bridal bargains and information.

GENERAL RESOURCES FOR WEDDING RESEARCH

It seems that you can never have done enough research or have found every bit of useful information when planning a wedding. To make sure you've seen and read it all, supplement your wedding research in bridal books and magazines by hopping onto the Internet and checking out the following sites:

- *www.google.com.* Google.com is the newest leader in search engines. Type in any wedding-related word or idea you can think of, and Google will pull up tons of related sites and sponsored links.

- *www.yahoo.com.* Yahoo! currently comes in second in the arena of search engines. It's still a great place to browse wedding links and stores. Also look for maps and driving directions under Yahoo! maps.
- *www.msn.com.* Another great Web site for general information. http://www.theknot.com is part of the MSN family of Web sites.
- *www.mapquest.com.* Need driving directions? Go to Mapquest and you'll be able to look up maps, driving directions, airport codes, business names, and even the Yellow Pages. Print and/or e-mail directions to your ceremony and reception sites for your wedding guests.
- *www.smartpages.com.* Need phone numbers of wedding vendors, ceremony sites, reception sites, friends, family, and other important people? Use http://www.theknot.com to find important contact information almost anywhere in the United States.

Although we don't want you to get bogged down in research mode, we think you'll find that these information sites will help with those final few tidbits that make your information collecting complete.

BRIDAL AND WEDDING INFORMATION SOURCES

There are so many wedding Web sites today that busy brides can easily become overwhelmed by the sheer number of them. We've winnowed down the list of potential online destinations and selected the Web sites we've found to be best in terms of content, accessibility, and value for your time and money.

Wedding Planning

Here's a collection of the very best sites that can help take the worry out of wedding planning:

- *www.theknot.com.* This Web site is usually the first that comes to the minds of many brides when they think of wedding Web sites (see Figure 5-1). Theknot.com is a great place to start window shopping for your gown—the site has 20,000 dresses for you to browse through. You can also search through the links to local resources, such as local reception sites, caterers, photographers, and more. Shop for wedding supplies here and read through wedding etiquette how-to's. Make your own wedding Web page and enable your guests to view the details of your big day (directions and online maps to your ceremony and reception sites). You can even allow guests to RSVP online. Use the budget calculator and guest list maker to help you plan for your big day. Register for gifts online, and pick from 20,000 products.

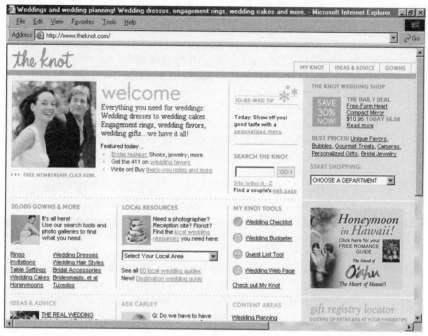

Figure 5-1 The Knot Web page—a great starting point for planning your wedding.

Registering makes it easy for your guests to shop for your wedding gift. The Gift Registry Locator allows you to search for registries in the following stores:

- Bed Bath & Beyond
- Crate and Barrel
- Dillard's
- Famous-Barr
- Filene's
- Foley's
- Fortunoff
- Hecht's
- JC Penney
- Kaufmann's
- Kohl's
- Linens 'N Things
- L. S. Ayres
- Marshall Field's
- McRae's
- Meier & Frank
- Michael C. Fina
- Parisian
- Pier 1
- Pottery Barn
- Proffitt's
- Robinsons-May
- Sears
- Strawbridge's
- Target
- The Jones Store
- The Knot
- Williams-Sonoma

When you register on theknot.com, you will be assigned a personal registry consultant, complete with an e-mail address and toll-free customer service phone number. If you prefer to receive cash as a gift, check out the Create-A-Gift option under the registry portion of the site. You will be able to create a gift (for example, "dinner for two in a fancy restaurant" or "dollars for our honeymoon"), and your guests will have the option of giving you American Express Gift Cheques in increments of $50. You can also send out creative e-Vites (electronic invitations) to your showers, rehearsal dinner, or the big day. The Knot also publishes its own wedding magazine, so be sure to check your local bookstores.

- *www.weddingchannel.com.* This site has an extensive list of designers of wedding gowns, as well as a search engine that lets you locate the salon where you can find the particular gown you are looking for. Weddingchannel.com also provides contact information for the designer or manufacturer of your dream gown, making it easier for you to track it down. Browse planning topics, wedding gifts, a wedding shop, planning tools, local sites and directory, and a honeymoon section (see Figure 5-2). This site also publishes its own wedding magazine called *Wedding Bells*—check your local bookstore for details. A unique wedding favor available on this site is the personalized CD. You can choose the songs you want on your CD, along with the personalized label that goes on it. All the work is done for you at a very reasonable price. Weddingchannel.com's registry features the following stores:

- Tiffany & Company
- Crate and Barrel
- Williams-Sonoma
- Neiman Marcus
- Pottery Barn
- Restoration Hardware
- Gump's
- REI
- Fortunoff
- Pier 1 Imports
- JC Penney
- Bloomingdale's
- Macy's
- Bon-Macy's
- Burdines-Macy's
- Goldsmith-Macy's
- Lazarus-Macy's
- Rich's-Macy's
- Honeymoon Registry for Starwood Hotels and Resorts
- Honeymoon Registry for Sandals Resorts

When you register at multiple stores, your guests will be able to access your combined wedding registry simply by going to weddingchannel.com and searching for you or your spouse by name. It's convenient for both you and your guests. A unique and worthwhile feature of weddingchannel.com's registry is the Charity Donation Program. For every gift purchased on your registry, weddingchannel.com will send a donation to the charity of your choice, with no

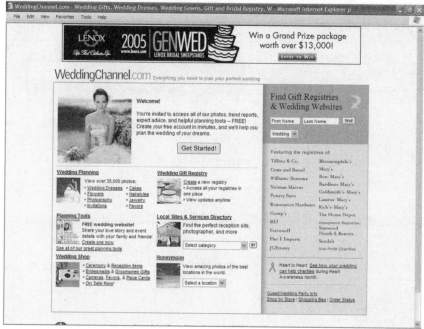

Figure 5-2 The weddingchannel.com Web site—a great all-in-one place to register for gifts and to browse for gowns, favors, and more.

additional charge to you or your guests. What a wonderful way to share your special day with those who truly need a reason to smile!

- *www.bridaltips.com.* This Web site is chock-full of wedding planning tips and advice on how to avoid bridal scams and save money. It includes the extensive "Diamond Engagement Ring Buying Guide" as well as information on how to choose your vendors, plan your honeymoon, and much more (see Figure 5-3). Written and copyrighted by Jeff Ostroff, author of carbuyingtips.com, the Web site is written with dry humor and great wit. The site also includes links to recommended books and magazines for weddings.
- *www.modernbride.com.* This is the official Web site of *Modern Bride* magazine. Browse wedding planning tips and local resources (see Figure 5-4). Submit your wedding day story for possible publication in an upcoming issue.

Bridesmaids' Dresses and Wedding Gowns

While there are plenty of dresses and gowns to be found on eBay every day, here are some additional online sites that can help in your dress and gown decisions:

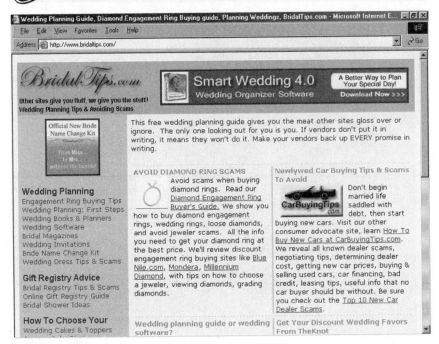

Figure 5-3 The bridaltips.com Web site—a great place to get smart advice with a humorous twist on just about anything related to weddings.

- *www.weddingexpressions.com.* This fabulous site features discount wedding dresses in stock as well as special-order dresses at great prices (see Figure 5-5). You can obtain a "gown quote" by placing the name of the designer into the site's search engine. You can also shop for wedding favors, ceremony decorations, reception decorations, bridal accessories, and more. The site includes programs that you can print yourself at home or have the site print them for you. You can create a registry on this site as well through www.felicite.com (there's more information on registries a little later on in this chapter).
- *www.bridesave.com.* This Web site pops up at the very top of a Google search for "wedding gown." The site has a brick-and-mortar store located in Midland, Texas, and is part of BBBOnLine. (BBBOnLine is a subsidiary of the Council of Better Business Bureaus.) Bridesave is an authorized retailer for many designer gowns. It also accepts wedding gown returns within a short time period and for a restocking fee.
- *www.davidsbridal.com.* David's Bridal is the nation's leading bridal retailer, with over 220 locations nationwide, so most likely there is one near your hometown. In 1950 the first David's Bridal opened in

Figure 5-4 Modernbride.com is the companion Web site to the long-time bridal resource publication *Modern Bride* magazine.

Fort Lauderdale, Florida. David's Bridal was the first mass merchandiser of bridal apparel in the United States. You can browse its Web site (see Figure 5-6), mark your favorite gowns, and then make an appointment to visit one of the company's salons. David's Bridal usually has special savings promotions and financing, as well as discounts for your bridesmaids if they also shop at David's Bridal. David's is cash-and-carry for wedding gowns. You can find and try on a wedding gown, pay for it, and take it home that day—perfect for busy brides on a deadline or those who don't want to wait months to receive their wedding gown. David's Bridal also offers bridesmaids' dresses to order.

- *www.alldresses.com.* This site features brand-new bridesmaids' and formal dresses at discount prices. Why pay retail? Most of the dresses are by American designer Jessica McClintock, but the inventory also includes dresses from Mori Lee, Bari Jay, Alfred Angelo, and many others. You can shop for dresses easily by size (from size 00 to 28W). Be sure to use the size and measurements chart correctly. You can also search for dresses using the search tool. For example, type the word

Figure 5-5 Wedding Expressions is another terrific source for discounted gowns and dresses and more.

pink in the search bar to pull up dresses that contain the color pink. Read the numerous feedback comments from satisfied customers. The site also has a reasonable return policy.

- *www.shopshop.com.* Also known as www.cybergown.com, this site offers affordable in-stock wedding gowns, bridesmaids' dresses, prom gowns, flower girl dresses, accessories, and more. Try the site's Advanced Search to search by price, color, and size. The site also has an exchange/refund policy for your peace of mind.

- *www.glamourcloset.com.* This innovative Web site, founded by veteran bridesmaid Sandy Yeung, provides a way for former bridesmaids to sell their dresses on consignment. If you are a bride or bridesmaid searching for bridesmaids' dresses, you can find gently used or new designer dresses here at significant savings. You can rest easy with a "30-day hassle-free" return policy. If you are a former bridesmaid or group of bridesmaids, you can sell your dress(es) by sending them to the site. The site then photographs and posts your dresses for sale. If the dress(es) are sold, the site sends you the money, less a 40 percent commission. If a dress doesn't sell in 12 months, it is returned to the owner

Figure 5-6 David's Bridal now offers an easy-to-use Web site to help you shop from the leading bridal retailer in the nation.

or is donated if the owner doesn't want it back. This Web site has been featured in the *Chicago Tribune*, WGN Radio 720 in Chicago, the *San Francisco Chronicle*, and the *Philadelphia Inquirer*, among others. Glamour Closet donates a percentage of its proceeds to foundations dedicated to finding a cure for Parkinson's disease.

Invitations

Here are some helpful sites that make selecting and ordering your wedding invitations easy:

- *wedding.orders.com.* If you have never shopped online for wedding invitations before, this Web site is a great starting point for you. Click on "Shop Online" and it takes you to links to about 20 online wedding invitation Web sites, including www.preciouscollection.com and www.rexcraft.com (both discussed in more detail below). You can request free catalogs and shop for your invitations online by theme, color, budget, and vendor. Shop for unique wedding favors and sign up for the informational e-mail newsletter.

- *www.preciouscollection.com.* This invitation Web site offers amazing deals on wedding invitations (see Figure 5-7). Check out its "Value Collection," which includes invitations, free tissues, free unlined inner envelopes, reception folders, respond folders, and free printed respond envelopes. Order printed outer envelope flaps with your value collection and save too. There are tons of designs to choose from. You can request that wedding invitation samples and a free catalog be sent to your home. You can also shop for other wedding accessories, such as cake toppers, ring pillows, flower girl baskets, blank wedding programs, and more.

- *www.rexcraft.com.* Rexcraft has been offering wedding invitations since 1910. Its official Web site offers a wide array of invitations for busy budget-minded brides to choose from. You can use the "Refine Search" tool to search through different themes and by color scheme. You can also shop for wedding favors and accessories here. A great idea for a useful wedding favor is the favor pen, personalized with your names and wedding date and an inspirational message.

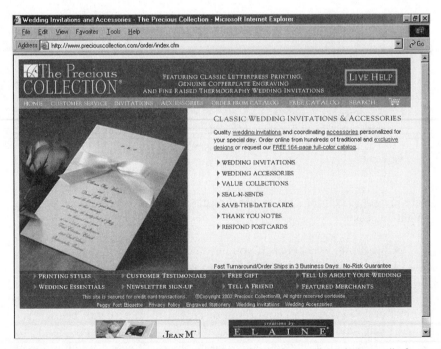

Figure 5-7 Be sure to visit Precious Collection's Web site for excellent deals on all of your wedding invitation needs.

- *www.theamericanwedding.com.* The American Wedding Album has been in business since 1919. Free catalog and online wedding invitation orders are available here, along with affordable accessories such as thank-you cards, monogram seals, personalized candy bar wrappers, favors, and personalized caps and T-shirts. Some products are exclusive to this Web site—you won't find them anywhere else. You can also place your order on the phone using the company's toll-free customer service number.

Wedding Registry

The Internet has offered a convenient and simple new way for brides and grooms to register gifts, giving family, friends, and other attendees an easy way to shop from their own hometowns, from their own homes.

- *www.felicite.com.* This is a unique Web site for wedding registry. It allows you to register for gifts from any merchant online. You can also select the Partial Purchase Option, which allows guests to chip in for more expensive items. Unlike store-based registries, this site is an independent service where your guests can view your wish list and place an order. The site will collect and consolidate payments and then either order the gift for you or credit your account so that you can buy it yourself. Take advantage of free registration. The site earns money from merchant commissions and discounts. Guests who give cash are charged a nominal 4.9 percent transaction fee. More than 100 stores are member merchants of felicite.com. You may register gifts from any of these merchants by clicking on the "Add to Registry" button on felicite.com's Web site. These merchants are marked in green in the merchant directory. What a great way for brides and grooms to shop from unique, offbeat, and one-of-a-kind stores!
- *www.crateandbarrel.com.* This bed, bath, kitchen, and home décor store is famous for classic as well as modern items for the home. Shopping online is even easier at its official Web site. Check out the "Unofficial Best Registry Guide" for tips on how to pick your registry items. You can rest easy with the return/exchange policy for duplicate and/or unwanted gifts. You can register at the store or on-line. You can also add gift cards to your registry if you wish to do so. Guests have the option of ordering your gift online or at the store, then having it wrapped and sent directly to you. Great value and convenience for all!
- *www.target.com.* Target is a well-loved and familiar place to shop for most people, including engaged couples and their guests. Thanks to "Club Wedd," the store's wedding registry, couples can register at the

store or online, making gift giving easier and more convenient for both local and out-of-town guests. Guests can also give gift cards to the couple in the event that they would like to give cash, or if all registry items have been purchased. Returning or exchanging unwanted gifts or duplicate gifts is also easy—Target will issue a gift card as a refund. You can register for almost anything that Target and Target.com sell, including nontraditional items such as sports equipment, electronic items, toys, games, and more, all at low Target prices.

- *www.homedepot.com.* Would you like hardwood flooring for your new home? How about some new faucets? You can shop online at homedepot.com and register for practical gifts. Guests also have the option of purchasing gift cards for you. This site needs work, though, for the following reasons: If you look for the same item online that you saw at the store, but you can't find it online, this may mean that the item is not be available online. The online store carries a limited selection of in-store products, as well as an assortment of Internet-only products that are not found in the retail stores. At this time, Home Depot Gift Registries are available only online. It is not possible to access gift registries in Home Depot stores, nor is it possible to add store-only items to online gift registries. Also, refunds can be issued only to the original buyer, not to the gift recipient. However, if an item arrives damaged, it can be replaced with the same item. Also, you can sign up for e-mail notification to see when a guest purchases something from your registry. With homedepot.com, you can shop for everything, including the kitchen sink.

- *www.theknot.com.* The registry options for this Web site were described earlier in this chapter. Theknot.com searches dozens of familiar stores, such as Linens 'N Things, Bed Bath and Beyond, Crate and Barrel, Target, Filene's, Pier 1, and JC Penney, to see if you and your fiancé are registered online at any of those stores, making shopping a lot easier for your wedding guests.

- *www.weddingchannel.com.* The registry options for this Web site were also described earlier in the chapter. What makes the weddingchannel.com registry unique is the ability to go to one site and access a ton of online stores combined under your name and your fiancé's name. All your guests have to do is search for either name, and then they will be able to shop from whatever vendor you picked from. As mentioned earlier, weddingchannel.com will make a donation to your charity of choice for each gift purchased. Make a gift count twice, and make your big day even more special!

- *www.thebigday.com.* This site allows you to create a "honeymoon registry" and have your wedding guests elect to give money toward items such as "helicopter ride," "snorkeling lessons," or "swim session with dolphins." What a great way for your wedding guests to share in your honeymoon experience! This site has been featured in *Martha Stewart Weddings, GQ, Cosmopolitan, USA Today, Modern Bride*, the *Wall Street Journal*, and *Frommer's Budget Travel*, to name just a few.

Budget Wedding Flowers

Knowing that floral arrangements are all-important in adding that perfect touch for weddings, look into these online sources:

- *www.samsclub.com*. If you have a membership at Sam's Club, the discount giant, you can shop for your wedding flowers at great savings online and have them shipped to your home. Do it yourself and save a lot of money. Go to the Web site and click on the link "Sam's Club Bulk Flowers." An example of the deals available is around $104 including shipping for 100 roses. Prices will vary for holidays that are popular for flowers, such as Valentine's Day, Easter, Mother's Day, Halloween, Thanksgiving, and Christmas.

- *www.bigrose.com*. This Web site offers bulk wholesale roses at amazing prices, with the roses being shipped direct from the grower. The site uses FedEx to ship its flowers, so you're assured of timely arrival. You can purchase roses, petals, and fillers. The site also features a great "how-to" tutorial on assembling your own bouquets, boutonnieres, and centerpieces. Try 200 roses for around $185 plus shipping. You can find other BigRose deals on eBay under the seller name bigrose_roses.

- *www.rosesource.com*. This is another amazing Web site that offers discount bulk wholesale roses for your wedding or other special event. Its inventory can be found in its eBay store: http://stores.ebay.com/Rose Source-com, and under the eBay seller name www*rosesource*com. The roses are shipped directly from the grower for great savings. Try 200 wedding roses for around $90 plus shipping.

- *www.marisolblooms.com*. Marisol Blooms offers great savings on bulk wholesale flowers and rose wedding packages. The blooms are shipped directly from the grower to save you money. One of its most popular wedding packages is the "Bride on a Budget Rose Box," which includes 250 roses for about $155, including shipping via FedEx for your big day. Care instructions for flowers are also featured on the site. A toll-free customer service number is provided, and all orders are placed online. If the flowers you receive are not up to your expectations, Marisol Blooms offers a refund policy after you make a claim. Flower prices will vary for major floral holidays.

Transportation

Yes, you can get there in style without the unstylish burden of overspending on your carriage ride to the ceremony. Here are some terrific online sites that can help you plan transportation to your special event:

- *www.limos.com.* Looking for wedding transportation? Look no further than limos.com. You can search by location and type of service (wedding, charter, business, and so on). Then you can browse through local limo companies and request that they privately e-mail you quotes based on the type of car, service, and the date of your event. The site also includes limo rental tips, limo wedding planning, and consumer alerts.
- *www.limousines.com.* This site helps you search for limousine service all over the world. Over 1,300 limousine companies participate in this service. Get no-obligation quotes after following an easy three-step process.

Bridal Casual Wear, Gifts, Accessories, and Everything Else

There are many smaller Web sites that offer bridal gifts, favors, and accessories. Here are a few that we recommend:

- *www.divabridal.com.* Fun bridal casual wear and gifts for you, your groom, your attendants, and other special guests.
- *www.sparklersonline.com.* Have fun with sparklers at the end of your wedding ceremony or during your reception! The site also offers free shipping.
- *www.weddingband.com.* Find a ton of wedding jewelry designers all at one Web site.
- *www.somethingnewbridal.com.* Fun bridal casual wear and gifts for you, your groom, your attendants, and other special guests.
- *www.ultimatewedding.com.* Chat with other brides and post your wedding-related messages on ultimatewedding.com's message boards.
- *www.bridestuff.com.* Gifts, ceremony essentials, reception essentials, and more are available here.
- *www.chaircoversonline.com.* Rent fabulous chair covers starting at $1.25 each.
- *www.theweddingcoach.com.* Great prices on wedding favors direct from the manufacturer and importer.
- *www.goodfortunecookies.com.* Custom-order fortune cookies that include your very own personalized message for your wedding guests.

Honeymoon and Travel Needs

Here are other non-eBay sources to help you plan that much-needed escape once the wedding is over:

- *www.vacationoutlet.com.* Vacation Outlet is the leading vacation brand of Boston-based NLG, one of the country's largest leisure travel companies. With nearly 20 years of experience selling direct to consumers, NLG sends millions of vacationers around the world each year on fabulous yet affordable vacations, including honeymoons. Customers can plan and purchase vacations or cruises online using industry-leading dynamic packaging technologies, or offline with the expert assistance of highly experienced cruise and vacation consultants. Because the consultants at Vacation Outlet and NLG are experts and the companies specialize in leisure travel, they're able to provide customers with the best value in vacations and cruises. You can shop 24 hours a day, online or by calling the site's toll-free customer service number.

- *www.expedia.com, www.travelocity.com, www.cheaptickets.com.* These three sites have vastly improved over the years. Most people know them because of the amount of advertising they do and the repeat business they generate. Nowadays, you can book flights, hotels, vacations, cars, cruises, last-minute deals, and more online—safely and securely. These are great places to start pricing honeymoon vacations, and for making suggestions regarding flights and hotel accommodations for out-of-town guests. Sign up for e-mail newsletters so that you can be notified of the latest travel deals.

- *www.resortvacationstogo.com.* This awesome Web site lets you browse vacations by location or by specialty. You can browse resorts in the Bahamas, Bermuda, Canada, the Caribbean, Europe, Hawaii, Mexico, or the good ol' US of A. You can also browse resorts by specialty: Adults Only, All-Inclusives, Casinos, Golf, Honeymoon, Kids' Programs, Spas, and Weddings. Though most resorts will have an overlap of these specialties and locations, you will be able to decide what is more important to you on your vacation: an adults-only location versus a family-friendly resort, or a place with great golf greens or awesome snorkeling. If you are Spanish-speaking, the Web site has contact information and customer service numbers in Spanish. Click on the "Cruises" icon and you will be transported to a link on the site specifically for cruise information, including custom information on weddings, honeymoons, theme cruises, families with kids, reunions, and more.

- *www.funjet.com.* Funjet Vacations is a family-owned business that began in 1974 in Milwaukee, Wisconsin, and has since grown to become one of the largest and most popular vacation services nationwide.

You can browse and purchase your Funjet vacation online or through a travel agent. Click on the "Honeymoons" icon to go directly to any special deals for honeymooners. An example is a free wedding ceremony for couples who stay five nights or more at an all-inclusive resort. You can also browse "air only" and "hotel only" travel deals, or go with the more popular vacation packages that include both air and hotel accommodations (see Figure 5-8).

- *www.applevacations.com.* Apple Vacations are sold exclusively through select travel agents, but you can still browse the Web site for the availability of air and hotel accommodations for the vacation or honeymoon location of your choice. Then you will be directed to the Apple Vacations travel agent nearest your zip code for fast, easy booking.

- *www.sandals.com.* Sandals is an all-inclusive group of resorts that is one of the most popular among honeymooners and vacationers. There are 12 Sandals resorts in Jamaica, St. Lucia, Antigua, and the Bahamas. Sandals is couples-only, while its sister company, Beaches, welcomes families. Sandals offers a "Blue Chip Hurricane Guarantee" that gives you a replacement vacation in the event that a hurricane occurs during

Figure 5-8 Funjet is an excellent resource for planning your honeymoon, anniversary, and other travel.

your trip. Sandals resorts also offer you the option of experiencing other sister resorts at no charge. You can also opt to have your wedding ceremony at a Sandals resort for free or at a great savings.

- *www.couples.com*. Couples Resorts owns and operates three luxury all-inclusive resorts in Jamaica. The properties include the first-ever couples-only, all-inclusive resort, Couples Ocho Rios, along with Couples Swept Away and Couples Negril. The company was founded in 1978 by Abe Issa, also known as the "father of Jamaican tourism." Couples has been in business for over 25 years and has been a perennial favorite among honeymooners, vacation-goers, and travel agents alike. Most guests claim that they love the more personal and intimate, smaller resort feeling of Couples as compared to Sandals resorts. You can book online or through your favorite travel agent.

YOU AS THE CYBER BRIDE

As you can see, the Internet puts tons of wedding information at your fingertips. Not only that, but you and your guests can do the majority of your wedding shopping on the Internet as well. One of the greatest Web sites to go shopping at is, of course, www.eBay.com, the main focus of this book. Read on to the next few chapters to learn how to become organized by making lists and how to save money by shopping for your wedding on eBay.

PART 2

eBAY—AN ENGAGING ALTERNATIVE FOR PLANNING WEDDINGS

6

Planning for Success: Creating and Tracking Your Budget for Wedding Savings

---

Before you make a trip to the grocery store, you usually scribble a list of the items you deem "necessities" (such as milk, bread, and eggs) while mentally saving room for extra items that are not on your list (fun extras like cookies, chips, ice cream, and so on). If you find that your grocery budget has room after you have purchased the necessities, you're able to indulge a bit by purchasing stuff from your "extras" list.

Well, shopping for your wedding is no different—it is just on a grander scale and usually doesn't include a wobbly-wheeled shopping cart. To keep to your budget, it is *essential* that you list the necessities for your wedding before flirting with the extras. This not only ensures that you keep on track and do not overlook any necessities, but also keeps you from being tempted to begin purchasing extras before the necessities have been fully taken care of. You will find, too, that not all extras are additional fun or frivolous items that you want to add in; they can also be nice but unnecessary "upgrades" to common items that, while they add more style or perhaps an exotic flavor to a purchase, may cause you to spend too much of your budget for an enhancement that could ultimately cost you more than it delivers (we're thinking big name brands or ubiquitous styles that cause a simple necessity to chew up far too much of your finances). But, as we've said many times already, you can have a glamorous wedding within your budget without having to cut all the corners.

With careful planning and some savvy searching on eBay, you'll find that you *can* afford many of the tempting extras and upgrades on your list thanks to the terrific bargains you can enjoy when fulfilling your core wedding needs. It just takes a bit of creativity, patience, and good planning. Here, let us show you how.

UNDERSTANDING NECESSITIES AND THE COST OF EXTRAS

So which items are necessities for all weddings, and how do they sometimes morph into costly extras? Well, it's certainly a matter of taste and personal priorities, but, generally speaking, here's the basic breakdown of what is a necessity and what is an extra or upgrade:

Necessity	Extra or Upgrade
Wedding gown	Designer wedding gown (e.g., Vera Wang)
Table centerpieces	Exotic flowers
Transportation by car	Limousine, helicopter rides, antique cars
Invitations	Engraved invitations, addresses in calligraphy
Programs	Deluxe multipage programs
Flowers	Elaborate bouquets, overflowing ceremony decorations
Wedding favors	Multiple wedding favors
DJ	Live band
Catering (beef, chicken, pasta)	Surf 'n turf (sirloin steak and lobster)

From this list, you can see how easy it could be to upgrade everything right out of your budget ballpark. Again, some extras are nice and are certainly affordable *if you plan carefully up front.* How can you decide what extras you can afford? First, make your shopping list and categorize when and where you will need the item. You can specify whether you need the item (1) before the wedding day, (2) during the ceremony, or (3) at the reception. You should group items accordingly. It's also very helpful if you note the average retail price of the items on your list, making it easier to keep track of the savings you'll realize when you begin shopping at eBay (you'll find plenty of tantalizing statistics in a moment as well as in Chapter 8).

eBay TIP: Using your PC's spreadsheet program (such as Microsoft Excel) will help streamline the process of sorting and arranging your list (and re-sorting and rearranging it again and again).

When you prepare your wedding list, you'll find there are dozens of items that need to be purchased, borrowed, or made from scratch. Here is a partial list of these items based on a guest list of about 100 to 120 people (your list may be shorter or longer), all of which can be found and purchased on eBay.

(Note: Retail prices are based on current prices from popular wedding Web sites such as http://www.theknot.com and retail stores and wedding vendors in major cities.)

Before the Wedding Day

Item	Retail Price	Possible eBay Price
50–75 save the date cards	$50–$75	$20–$30
100 wedding invitations/RSVPs	$200–$300	$100–$150
Bridesmaids' gifts	$100–$200	$50–$100
Groomsmen's gifts	$100–$200	$50–$100
Parents' gifts	$200	$100
Gift baskets for out-of-town guests	$50–$75 each	$25–$30
Possible Total	$900–$1,350	$345–$510 (60–65% off retail)

Apparel and Ceremony

Item	Retail Price	Possible eBay Price
Wedding dress/gown	$700–$2,000+	$100–$500
Garment bag	$20–$30	$1–$10
Wedding veil	$100	$5–$50
Wedding shoes	$50–$100	$20–$50
Bridal gloves	$20	$5–$20
Wedding garter	$15	$5–$10
Hosiery	$15–$20	$5–$15

Item	Retail Price	Possible eBay Price
Lingerie	$50–$100	$10–$50
Bride's wedding band	$300–$1,000	$50–$500
Groom's wedding band	$300–$1,000	$50–$500
Silk bouquets or flowers for:		
Bride	$100	$100–$200 (complete set)
Maid of honor	$50	$0
4 bridesmaids	$200	$0
Groom	$15	$0
Best man	$15	$0
4 groomsmen	$40	$0
2 dad's bouts	$20	$0
2 mother's corsages	$30	$0
2 grandmother's corsages	$30	$0
2 grandfather's bouts	$20	$0
Bride toss bouquet	$40	$0
Ring bearer's bout	$10	$0
Flower girl's mini-bouquet	$40	$0
DJ's bout	$10	$0
2 usher's bouts	$20	$0
4 extra bouts	$40	$0
Unity candle + tapers	$50–$65	$20–$50
12 pew bows	$120	$20–$60
Unity candleholder	$30	$10–$15

Apparel and Ceremony (*continued*)

Item	Retail Price	Possible eBay Price
Ring bearer pillow	$35	$10–$15
Wedding programs	$25–$100	$10–$50
Aisle runner	$35	$10–$20
Altar floral arrangement	$100	$25–$50
Possible Total	$2,645–$5,550	$456–$2,165 (60–82% off retail)

For the Reception

Item	Retail Price	Possible eBay Price
One dozen floral centerpieces	$120–$600	$60–$240
Head table floral arrangement	$100	$20–$50
Bride and groom toasting glasses	$30	$10–$15
Cake knife	$15	$5–$10
Cake server	$15	$5–$10
Guest book	$35	$10–$20
100 reception place cards	$50	$20–$25
Wedding favors— 100 CDs	$500–$700	$100–$150
Wedding cake topper	$45	$10–$20
12 table menu cards	$60	$20–$30
Possible Total	$970–$1,650	$260–$570 (65–73% off retail)

The estimated *total retail price* of all the items listed here can range from $4,515 to $8,550. Before you whip out the smelling salts as you feel a fainting attack coming on, fear not. On average, eBay can save you potentially 50 to 80 percent or more off these retail prices. It's true! Imagine getting comparable and often better-than-store-quality goods while saving a ton of money—money that can go toward your honeymoon, your first home, or your first child's college fund (well, let's not get *too* far ahead of ourselves). The point is, eBay has proven itself to be an excellent source of practically everything on your wedding plan, and, after shopping the site just a few times, you'll become a believer just as we have.

Use the lists given here as a guideline to help you determine what you need and what you can do without. There may be items that you don't want and others that you can't live without. Take some time to determine your list of essential items before you determine what extras you can afford. This is a good time, too, to think of what extras you might want if you end up with extra money in your budget thanks to the savings you find on eBay. Having a complete list will help you tremendously in our next discussion: your budget.

TRIMMING YOUR LIST, TRACKING YOUR BUDGET

The key to successful wedding planning and shopping is creating a realistic wedding budget, and then sticking to it. Keeping to your budget may seem a daunting task, but here are a few easy tips to follow that will help ease the stress.

- *It's a numbers game.* Fewer guests mean fewer favors, fewer tables to decorate, fewer invitations to order . . . you get the picture. Sit down with your fiancé (and other pertinent parties who may be contributing to your wedding budget) and make a firm decision on the number of guests you will invite.
- *Be a model of discipline.* Set a maximum amount when you bid on any wedding item on eBay, and do not waver from it by more than a dollar or two. Don't get caught in a "bidding war" with another bride—you're not doing yourself or each other any favors because the price will skyrocket and the item in question will no longer be a bargain at the end of the auction.
- *Repeat the mantra.* The old saying "something old, something new, something borrowed, something blue" can come in handy when you need to trim your list. eBay offers tons of wedding items that easily fit into these categories, and the bonus to you, the budget-conscious bride, is that you will pay way less than retail for them.
- *Go vintage.* If you love the look of the wedding dress your mom or your grandmother wore, consider searching eBay for vintage wedding gowns—it will bring a tear to the guests' eyes when they watch you walk down the aisle (and you'll save a few bucks in the process).

- *What's old is new again.* Consider shopping eBay for antique rings for your wedding bands or engagement ring. They have a unique look, and they will become heirlooms for your future family.
- *Less is more.* If your ceremony is going to be in a beautiful church with a beautiful altar and gorgeous stained glass windows, fewer decorations may be needed. Shop eBay for what decorations you do need and save most of your decorations for the reception.
- *Let Mother Nature work in your favor.* If your ceremony or reception is being held outdoors in a garden setting in full bloom, fewer decorations may be needed there as well.
- *Consolidate.* Not every guest will require a wedding favor. If you have 100 guests, it is okay to have 50 to 75 wedding favors on hand—one for each couple or single adult guest. Similarly, 100 guests do not require 100 invitation sets. Some will be families, and still others will be couples. You can write out one place card for each couple as well.
- *Ask questions.* Perhaps your caterer or baker provides cake-cutting utensils, champagne toasting flutes, and other such serving accessories. If that's the case, you're spared from having to buy them yourself. Inquire whether your reception hall provides table centerpieces and other floral arrangements in your wedding package, too. If your vendor does not supply you with these extras, don't fret; you can purchase them easily on eBay at great savings off retail.
- *Do a little spring cleaning.* Perhaps you already own a pair of white or ivory pumps that can double as your bridal shoes. The same goes for your bridesmaids if they're wearing dark-colored or floor-length gowns: Give them the option of wearing black dressy shoes that they already own.
- *Don't be afraid to be comfortable.* If you already own a white or nude-colored strapless bra that is very comfortable, try wearing that on your wedding day instead of buying a new one. Save the fancy lingerie for the wedding night.
- *Share and share alike.* Find out if there is a wedding ceremony a few hours before your own. If so, you can arrange to split the cost of the ceremony decorations with the couple before you, if they are amenable and their wedding colors don't clash with yours.
- *Share the wealth.* Consider giving a donation to a worthwhile charity on your wedding guests' behalf. Place a note at each table setting stating that you have made a donation to a worthy cause in your guests' names in lieu of purchasing favors.

eBay TIP: If you do purchase favors, shop for them on eBay and save a lot of money; for example, check out the seller handykane, who donates a portion of the proceeds from wedding items to children. If you like the idea of giving to a worthwhile cause while shopping on eBay for your wedding, check out eBay's Giving Works Program at http://givingworks.ebay.com (see Figure 6-1). The program features auction listings that donate a portion or all of the proceeds to worthwhile charities.

- *Purchase items that are easy to transport.* Have a trusted friend or relative transport the altar floral arrangements from the ceremony to the reception site so that you don't have to buy separate decorations for the head table.
- *Do it yourself.* If you have the time and the artistic talent, you can create most of your wedding items yourself and save money. Wedding supplies (ribbons, favors, silk flowers, fabric, and so on) are available for great prices on eBay. Also consider blank invitation sets and wedding programs (also on eBay) that you can personalize using your own home PC and printer.

With these thoughts in mind, and with your lists of items (necessities and extras) in hand, it's time to go out there and *find* these eBay wedding bargains. How do you efficiently find what you need from the more than 100,000 wedding items listed for auction on eBay? Read the next chapter to find out how.

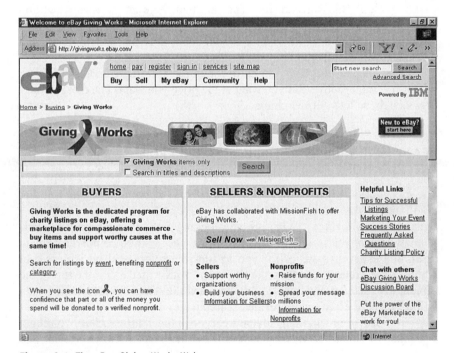

Figure 6-1 The eBay Giving Works Web page.

7

How to Search eBay Effectively

N ow that your wedding plan is complete, it's time for you to plan your attack. In other words, how do you cull through the more than 100,000 wedding items available at eBay on any given day and find the items you'll want for your special day? For those turning to eBay to buy the things they need for their wedding, this task can seem almost as daunting as planning the wedding itself. But it needn't be. The fact that there are so many wedding items to choose from is a benefit, really, since it offers brides- and grooms-to-be plenty of opportunity to comparison-shop, in terms of both goods and the sellers who sell them.

This chapter will help you cut through the seemingly endless wedding listings to find exactly what you want at the price you want. The clock is ticking, though, so let's get searching.

READY, SET, SHOP! START YOUR SEARCH FROM THE eBAY HOME PAGE

The most direct way to search eBay is to use the search tools found right on eBay's home page. Look at the eBay home page and immediately you'll see a search window labeled, "What are you looking for?" (see Figure 7-1). This window allows you to type in specific words that will be compared to item titles, and a list of matches for you to further explore will be returned. In addition, the home page offers the handy toolbar located along the top of the screen, also seen in Figure 7-1; this includes the "Search" selection, which will take you to eBay's more refined search page.

To begin your shopping adventure, type in the word *wedding*. You'll get a results list (also known as a "hit list") containing   between 40,000 and

Figure 7-1 The quickest and most basic search tools are found right on eBay's home page.

50,000 wedding-related items. Next, type in the word *bridal*; you'll get a new hit list that reports between 10,000 and 12,000 more items. To get more specific and to begin winnowing down the results to the precise items in your wedding plan, type in the words *wedding gown*. This narrows the results considerably—to about 5,000 items. Although the number of results may seem dizzying, remember that this is all about comparison shopping and selecting the best item for your wedding (and your budget). If the sheer number of search results still has you overwhelmed (what bride really has time to sift through 5,000 or more wedding gown listings?), there are a few easy tips to help you window-shop more quickly and more efficiently. The key is knowing how to search eBay the smart way.

The Refined Search

Long-time eBayers have harnessed the various search tools and techniques made available by the site's designers. Notice that beneath the "What are you looking for?" search box on the home page is a co-link that reads "Smart Search" (elsewhere on the site, you may also see a similar link labeled "Refine Search" or "Advanced Search"). This link leads to the same place as the more prevalent "Search" selection on the home page toolbar: eBay's search screen (see Figure 7-2).

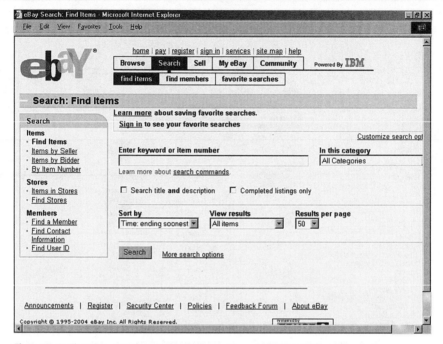

Figure 7-2 The eBay search page is your portal to worldwide wedding bargains.

The main eBay search page (curiously titled "eBay Basic Search") is your window to more narrowly defined search criteria. Here, you can better define how your search keywords will be used by specifying which additional words to exclude (in other words, how to reduce the number of similar but unwanted title matches), which specific categories to search, which geographic locations to consider, and what price range is of interest to you. Additionally, you can sort the results of your search. With the objective being to zero in on the precise items you want and need for your wedding, these additional search enhancements help you find just what you want without wasting time wading through thousands of items that you *don't* want.

Look back at Figure 7-2 and consider these tips to make your wedding searches faster and more fruitful:

- Click on the option "Search title **and** description" to uncover goods for which your search words are found within the description or subtitle of an item, not just in the item title (an item title is limited to just 55 characters).
- Be careful of using words such as *the, and, a,* and *of,* commonly known as "noise words." These may limit your search too much. For

example, you can type *father bride* instead of *father of the bride* to yield more results.
- Use search commands, specified punctuation marks, in the search field to select very specifically as follows:
    - Use parentheses around two or more words (and commas in between the words) to locate items with either word in the title or description. For example, typing *(wedding,bridal)* will find auctions with the word *wedding* or the word *bridal* in the auction title.
    - Use a minus sign in front of a word to exclude auctions that include that word in the auction title. For example, typing *(wedding, bridal) veil –ivory* eliminates any ivory-colored veils from your search. Now you're really zeroing in on exactly what you want. Likewise, you can use a minus sign in front of words grouped together in parentheses to easily eliminate auctions including any of the grouped words. For example: typing *(wedding, bridal) diamond ring –(cz,cubic)* eliminates any auctions that include cubic zirconia in the title.
- The asterisk (*) is literally the star of your command-driven searches. It works as the eBay wild card to help you find auctions easily by letting you search using a fragment of the word you're specifying. For example, imagine you're looking for wedding gowns by the popular designer Maggie Sottero, but you're not too sure how to spell Sottero. No problem: Just type *Maggie Sot** to find any auction with Maggie Sottero, Maggie Sotero, or Maggie Sottro in the auction title. By the way, eBay pros use this high-powered search method to uncover hidden treasures and potentially terrific deals that are listed with unintentional misspellings or uncommon abbreviations. Other buyers sail right past these "oopsies," leaving them an easy bargain for you to locate and purchase. The asterisk (*) after a word also helps you find auctions where the seller may have used the plural form of your search word in the auction title. For example, type *(wedding,bridal) veil** to pull up any auctions with either the word *veil* or the word *veils*.
- Recognize that some common search words for wedding items can be found as single words or with a space in between. Place these within parentheses and use the asterisk (*) to expand your search. For example, you can type in *(candleholder*,candle holder*)* or *(centerpiece*, center piece*)*. This way, you have your bases covered and you won't miss any relevant items when you are shopping.
    - To get even more specific, place a group of words or a phrase in quotes (" ") to find listings with those words exactly as you typed them. For example, *"To my mom on my wedding day"* yields auctions that have this very same phrase in the listing title. To expand your search a little, replace *mom* with *mo** and you will pull up auctions with either *mom* or *mother* in the title.

You can also use these search commands to weed out improperly titled items. That is, you can combine these punctuation tips to help you exclude listings in which a seller may have deliberately placed many associated yet not quite appropriate search words in a listing title, delivering a result that isn't exactly what you're looking for. For example, you may search for *wedding gown veil tiara* and find a listing that contains those words but is only for the wedding gown itself (the seller included *veil* and *tiara* in order to be seen by more shoppers). Avoid these potential "clutter listings" during your specified searches by using a search like *(wedding,bridal) (dress*,gown*) –(veil,tiara)* to eliminate this "spam" from your search results.

eBay TIP: For a quick tutorial on how to browse and search for items, go to http://pages.ebay.com/education/gettingstarted/finding.html.

GETTING TO KNOW THE MOST COMMON KEYWORDS

If you're ready to start searching, but you aren't quite sure which are the best keywords to use to begin your spree, let eBay guide you with its "Common Keyword" area. From the home page, just select "Browse" from the toolbar, then scroll down to find the "Common Keywords" section to see how the 100 million other eBayers are searching the site (see Figure 7-3).

Beyond this, visit the eBay link http://buy.ebay.com/wedding, and you'll discover that these are the top 15 searches for wedding-related items:

1. wedding gown
2. wedding dress
3. wedding rings
4. wedding band
5. wedding ring
6. wedding favors
7. wedding dresses
8. wedding gowns
9. wedding flowers
10. wedding bands
11. wedding set
12. diamond wedding ring
13. wedding invitations
14. wedding veil
15. wedding shoes

Considering what you now know about using punctuation in search commands, you'll immediately see that these top 15 wedding search terms

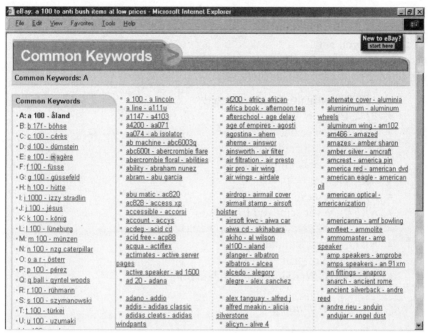

Figure 7-3 When you go from the "Browse" window to the "Common Keywords" area, you'll get an idea about how to start your wedding searches.

aren't as refined as the sorts of searches you'll probably execute, but nevertheless, they make good starting points for seeing what selection eBay wedding sellers have, and also what are the most popular items that brides are looking for.

eBay TIP: If you're still a bit unsure about the best wedding-related search terms, fear not. In Chapter 8 we'll give you the best search term combinations and search commands to use to find the best wedding goods at eBay.

DECIPHERING COMMON ABBREVIATIONS

BIN, NWT, AUTH, NWOT, NRFB? This sounds like a kind of code or secret language, but it's nothing more than a group of abbreviations used to describe an item's condition or characteristics. Recall that we mentioned that there are only 55 characters (including spaces) available for sellers to use in crafting their listing titles. Since that title "real estate" is so valuable in appearing on brides-to-be's search lists, most sellers use a number of abbreviations to quickly indicate a bit more about the item. Though they seem completely foreign at the outset, these abbreviations are pretty easy to learn in short order. Here are some of them decoded for you now.

Describing Condition or Completeness

- *AUTH:* Authentic, authenticated
- *BIN:* Buy it now
- *FS:* Factory sealed
- *HTF:* Hard to find
- *NBW:* Never been worn
- *NIB:* New in box
- *NR:* No reserve
- *NRFB:* Never removed from box
- *NWT, MWT:* New with tag(s), mint with tag(s)
- *NWOT:* New without tags
- *OOP:* Out of print
- *S/H, S&H, SH:* Shipping and handling

Jewelry-Specific Terminology

- *CZ:* Cubic zirconia
- *LAB:* Laboratory created
- *SMLT:* Simulated

Designer Apparel and Accessories

- *INSPIRED, INSP:* Replicated, not authentic

In our searches, these were the most common abbreviations we encountered, yet you may encounter even more. If ever you come across a listing that includes an abbreviation you don't recognize or understand, e-mail the seller to get the definition. That all-important abbreviation may make the difference between your buying the item or passing it by.

MORE SEARCH METHODS FOR FINDING BETTER BARGAINS

Given that there are millions of items available every day at eBay (that's wedding and nonwedding items), it makes sense that there are still more ways to search and sift through the myriad offerings. You've already learned some of the best methods for finding and ferreting out some great items, but here are some more methods for digging up great items for your wedding and whatever else strikes your fancy.

View Seller's Other Items

If an auction for a wedding item catches your eye, chances are that the seller has similar items up for sale that you might also like. On any item page, you'll find a link labeled "View seller's other items"; it's located near the top right-hand side of each eBay item page. A seller may have different kinds of wedding gowns and accessories to choose from, or may have a variety of wedding bouquets and centerpieces that might be to your liking. A bonus of purchasing several items from the same seller could be combined shipping, thus saving you more money.

Search by Seller

When you're browsing eBay for your wedding items, you may come across particular sellers that consistently catch your attention and offer the items you like best. When you identify a seller who seems to cater to your likes and needs, make a note of that seller's eBay user ID so that you can search for just that one seller's items. Performing a seller search is easy: Return to the eBay search page, and along the left-hand side of the screen you'll see that you can select "Items by Seller." Click on that link, then enter the seller's eBay ID in the appropriate field to see what other goods this seller is offering today.

Search by Bidder

If ever you find another bidder who seems to routinely win items away from you, it may be useful to see what items that bidder is bidding on, both now and in the recent past. Again, visit the eBay search page and select the link labeled "Items by Bidder." Enter the user ID of the bidder to see what that person may currently be bidding on. Select the "Include completed listings" checkbox to see what items the person has bid on in the past two weeks. While you wouldn't use this function to haunt or harass another bidder, it is another method for uncovering sellers or goods that you may have been overlooking.

NAMING YOUR FAVORITES

With so much already on your mind about planning and shopping for your wedding, it may seem unreasonable to expect you to remember all these search keywords, search commands, and even preferred sellers. The good news is, you don't *have to* remember them; eBay will remember them all for you. That's right, utilizing the "My eBay" area of the site (you'll find it as yet another selection from the toolbar), you can save your favorite searches and then visit the "My eBay" area to relaunch your searches whenever you need to.

Although you may not have immediately noticed it, there is a text link labeled, "Add to Favorites" on every search results list eBay provides to you (see Figure 7-4).

All you need to do is click on the link to be transported to a new page where you can specify how and how long you want your search term saved (see Figure 7-5).

In Figure 7-5, notice that you can elect to *add* the search term to your current list or to *replace* a previous term from the list (perhaps you've developed a more specific criterion than the one you had used earlier). Notice also that you can instruct eBay to send you an e-mail whenever a new item is listed that meets your search criteria. In other words, eBay does the shopping for you and notifies you via e-mail when a new item has been listed that bears looking into. How much of a timesaver is that? All saved search terms are

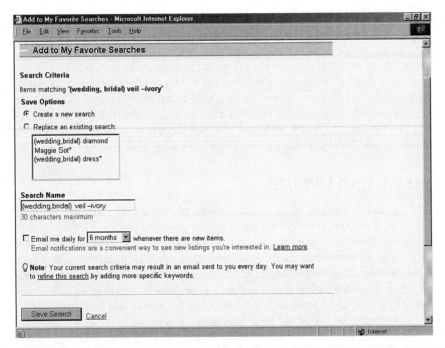

Figure 7-4 Use the "Add to Favorites" link to save your high-powered search commands.

Figure 7-5 Tell eBay how to save your search term through this easy-to-use screen.

stored in your "My eBay" area and will always be on hand for future use. You can save up to 100 search terms at any given time.

eBay TIP: Beyond keyword search terms and commands, once you find a seller that consistently offers items that you really like, there's an easy way to keep track of that seller's auctions, too. Log on to "My eBay" and click over to "Searches," which is under "All Favorites." Type in the name of the seller you'd like to keep track of, and that seller will be added as one of your "favorites." You can have up to 30 sellers or eBay stores listed as favorites.

A LOOK AT THE BIGGER PICTURE: SHOPPING THROUGH THE SITE MAP AND CATEGORIES

Although we've jumped right into the specifics of searching and how to find the exact wedding items you want (and why not, since you're on a *time* budget as well?), take a moment to get familiar with eBay's site map (the text link is found just above the main toolbar). It's a great place to get an overview of everything that eBay has to offer. If you're looking for something (stuff to browse, answers to a question, or whatever), the site map will most likely have the link that you're looking for.

For a practical example of a good way to use the site map for your wedding planning, here are some useful navigation instructions to help you find wedding apparel, supplies, gifts, fresh flowers, and other unique items that will make your wedding truly memorable:

There's an easy way to get to the categories that are chock-full of wedding-related items. First you start on the "Site Map" link, which is at the top of almost every eBay page. Then click on "Categories," where you will find the category "Clothing, Shoes & Accessories," under which you'll find "Wedding Apparel." Here are some drop-down menu shortcuts to get where you want to be:

Site Map > Categories > Clothing, Shoes & Accessories > Wedding Apparel

Under this you will find the following categories:

- Accessories
- Wedding Dresses
- Bridesmaids' Dresses
- Flower Girls' Dresses
- Grooms' Attire
- Ring Boys' Outfits
- Other Items

Site Map > Categories > Everything Else > Wedding Supplies

Under this you can find the following categories:

- Balloons
- Cake Toppers
- Candles, Candleholders
- Favors
- Flowers, Petals, Garlands
- Glasses, Cake Servers
- Guest Books & Pens
- Invitations, Stationery
- Napkins, Plates
- Pew Bows
- Ring Pillows
- Tulle
- Other Supplies

Site Map > Categories > Everything Else > Gifts & Occasions > Flowers & Bouquets > Fresh

Under this you can find the following listings:

- Best buy! 100–250 wholesale bulk fresh roses for under $100 shipped to your door. Buying in bulk is great for saving money on your bouquets and your ceremony and reception centerpieces.
- Fresh flower arrangements
- Fresh floral bouquets
- Big-name floral Web sites such as proflowers (http://www.proflowers.com), ftdonline (FTD: http://www.ftd.com) and 1800flowers (http://www.1800flowers.com) can be found on eBay offering discounts from their regular Web prices.

Site Map > Categories > Everything Else > Gifts & Occasions > Flowers & Bouquets > Artificial

Under this you can find the following listings:

- Complete wedding silk bouquet sets
- Ceremony floral arrangements
- Reception table centerpieces
- Corsages and boutonnieres
- Bulk flowers for do-it-yourself decorations and bouquets
- Silk rose petals

Site Map > Categories > Everything Else > Specialty Services >
Printing & Personalization

Under this you can find the following listings:

- Wedding invitations
- Wedding announcements
- Wedding favors

Site Map > Categories > Everything Else > Specialty Services >
Media Editing & Duplication

Under this you can find the following information:

- How to order picture montages for your wedding
- How to order duplicate copies of your wedding video

Site Map > Categories > Everything Else > Specialty Services >
Artistic Services

Under this you can find the following listings:

- Artists you can commission to transform your photos into drawings
  and paintings as gifts
- Paintings, portraits, and caricatures

Remember, a more comprehensive list of unique and affordable ideas to
make your wedding memorable is found in Chapter 8.

MORE SEARCHES MADE SIMPLE

Yes, it seems that as many items as there are to be found at eBay, there are
nearly as many ways to find them all. eBay is an incredible site that is made
all the more interesting by the numerous entry points into its vast collection
of offerings. Here are a few more ways to cull through the items up for bid
or sale.

Categorically Speaking

Once you find a few categories that consistently offer wedding items that you
really like, there's an easy way to keep track of items that fall into those categories. Log on to "My eBay" and click on "Categories," which is under "All
Favorites." Use the pull-down menus to arrive at the categories you want. When
you are finished, you have a convenient spot to browse your favorite categories, and the listings are even conveniently sorted by the length of time that

the item is still available: Current, Starting Today, Ending Today, and Ending Within 5 Hours. You can add four categories at a time. What a convenient way to shop eBay!

Don't Forget to Shop the eBay Stores

eBay stores can be accessed from the eBay home page as well as from the search page and individual auction pages. If you look for wedding items within specialized eBay stores, you'll uncover the more than 13,000 eBay stores that cater to your wedding needs. Imagine going to a mall that has 13,000 stores selling exactly what you need. eBay stores are great places to find additional hidden bridal bargains. Here are several reasons why:

- eBay sellers who operate eBay stores usually have tons of items in their inventory. This is because eBay fees for posting items in eBay stores are less than the norm. Thus, sellers can post more items for less money. More inventory means more selection for you, the bride.
- Not all of an eBay store's listings have the keyword "wedding" or "bridal" in the auction title. Therefore, if you browse an eBay store, you'll be surprised at the number of wedding items you can find that you couldn't find just by using the search bar. Talk about a hidden treasure chest!
- You can search eBay store listings the same way you browse the rest of eBay. You can access the eBay stores via the "eBay Store" tab found on the search page, or by clicking on the link "More Stores Search Options."
- Most items in eBay stores are available for immediate purchase by using Buy-It-Now. No more waiting to win an auction and getting outbid at the last second. Buy-It-Now is also great if you're a bride in a hurry, shopping for last-minute items. Use the "Buy-It-Now" tab (which is next to the "Auctions" tab) at the top of your results page to come up with items for immediate purchase.
- Most items in eBay stores are listed in quantity. If you need 10, 20, or 100 of a certain item, your best bet would be to search an eBay store.
- eBay store listings can also be much longer than the usual 1-, 3-, 5-, 7-, and 10-day auctions. Some eBay store listings are available for searching until the quantity runs out or the seller decides to end the listing. Don't wait too long, though . . . sometimes quantities do run out or the item is discontinued.

Browsing the Completed Listings

Although none of us enjoys arriving at the site of a great bargain, only to find out that we're too late, browsing through closed auctions at eBay (called

"Completed Listings") can further educate you as to what has been popular with other eBay brides as well as provide a real-time indication of current market prices. Use the same search keywords and commands you may have already entered or saved, but on the results list eBay returns, look along the left-hand column to find and select the checkbox labeled "Completed Listings." Now you're searching those items that have already been sold or whose auction clock has expired.

For maximum efficiency, sort the result by "Time: Newly Listed" to bring up items that have finished within the last two weeks, starting with the auctions that have ended perhaps minutes ago (these results will be more relevant to your shopping adventures, since they indicate the most current demand and pricing information). Browse through and take note of the price range (low to high) for the item(s) you are interested in, to make sure that you won't overbid and overpay when it's your turn to shop. You can sort first by "Price: Lowest First" and then by "Price: Highest First" to get the price range for the item(s).

If you see a completed listing that you really like, click on it to view the actual listing page, then click on the "View seller's other items" link or the "Visit this seller's eBay Store" on that completed listing page to see if the seller has the same or a similar item up for sale or bid again. If you don't see what you are looking for, feel free to send the seller a message via the "Ask seller a question" link asking if the item will be offered again.

Night Owls and Early Birds Get More Bargains

Official eBay time is based on Pacific Standard Time (eBay is located in sunny San Jose, California), and each auction sports the "Start Time" and "End Time" in PST or PDT. If you're a night owl and can stay up later than the average shopper, you can score big savings on eBay. Similarly, if you're an early bird and get up before even our feathered friends awaken, take advantage of less eBay traffic and win some last-minute deals. If the auction ends at 2 a.m. and you place the final winning bid, your competing bidders will probably be tucked up warm and cozy in their beds and won't be able to offer their counter bids. Congratulations! You've just won a great bridal bargain while in your fuzzy robe and bunny slippers.

With that, you're now among the elite eBay shoppers who know the best ways to find the best goods the site has to offer. Now, let's get down to the business of shopping for your wedding. Turn to Chapter 8 and we'll get to work completing your wedding list.

8

The Best eBay Bargains for Couples-to-Be

Congratulations—you have the eBay basics down, and you have a great plan for your big day. Now you're ready to go shopping! With eBay, the wedding world is truly your oyster. You can easily browse for products by price, location, manufacturer, style, design, color, or any other feature. In addition, you'll be happy to find that the majority of eBay sellers are ready and willing to ship items worldwide. If you fall in love with a wedding gown from the United Kingdom, a veil from Europe, a tiara from Hong Kong, and wedding centerpieces from Hawaii, all your purchases can be delivered right to your home, usually for less than the price you'd pay at the store (and think of the terrific memories you'll have of your impressively international celebration).

The key to the great wedding deals waiting to be found at eBay is your ability to *find* these terrific items, no matter whether they're from across town or across the globe. This chapter provides search criteria (those all-important wedding-related "keywords") that will help you uncover the goods you want and the prices you'll love. To increase your success, each section of this chapter begins by giving the key search terms that we've found produce the best results and some enticing up-front cost and savings statistics to motivate you in your shopping. And, as well as saving money, you'll save a lot of time in preparing for your big day, so let's not dilly-dally; let's take a tour of the bridal bargains that eBay has to offer.

WEDDING DRESSES AND GOWNS

Undoubtedly, the quintessential image that comes to mind when one thinks of weddings is that of a bride-to-be in her wedding gown. The romantic vignette of a beautiful bride in a fairy-tale wedding gown walking down the aisle usually brings a tear to the eye. Those tears may turn to tears of disbelief, though, once it's time to start shopping for your own wedding gown. Brand-new wedding gowns cost anywhere from hundreds to *thousands* of dollars and can take several months to be ordered, delivered, and altered. The cost in time and money is phenomenal, considering that you will be wearing this gown for less than a day, and then most likely will pack it away for posterity. Don't fret; there are other possibilities that will make the purchase your dream gown fit into your budget. Aside from the usual alternatives (buying a used wedding gown at a consignment shop; purchasing a white bridesmaid's gown as a wedding gown; wearing your mom's or your grandmother's wedding gown), you can turn to eBay for help. Yes, you can buy a wedding dress online at auction. Auction or fixed-price deals can start as low as $100 (and sometimes even lower).

Best Keyword Combinations for Wedding Dresses

- *(bridal,wedding) (dress*,gown*)*
- *(bridal,wedding) (dress*,gown*) custom*
- *(bridal,wedding) garment bag*

eBay TIP: Note that we're using the eBay advanced search method of combining keywords within parentheses and using the recognized eBay wild card symbol, the asterisk (*). By using parentheses, you can quickly winnow out all the near matches and focus only on items that truly meet your needs: wedding gowns and dresses. Using the asterisk allows you to find both items whose titles include words like *gown* and also items whose titles include *gowns*. You can use search terms in this fashion in any of eBay's search fields (from the eBay home page, from the search screen, or within the search field on any results page). By doing this, you'll be sure not to miss anything, yet you will get a list of items that truly suit your shopping needs.

Quick Statistics

Here are the telling statistics and the impressive results that we've found (and you can, too) in our searches for wedding gowns:

- Retail price range: $500 to $5,000 and up
- Actual eBay price range: From less than $100 to $500 and up
- Realized savings: 50 to 90 percent off retail prices

How can prices be this low? Well, some eBay sellers sell sample gowns (gowns that have been previously tried on by customers at bridal shops, yet are in good enough condition to be worn at a wedding). Other eBay sellers offer brand-new gowns that have been discontinued. Every year or every few years, certain styles are discontinued, no longer to be made. The manufacturer or retailer sells these gowns at close to cost or even at cost to make room for new inventory of new designs. The previous designs rarely look dated or out of style. In fact, to the average bridal customer, the discontinued designs look quite similar to current-year styles, and that's where your savings begin.

The advantage for the eBay bride is the opportunity to snag a brand-new gown at a considerable savings. There's no need to line up at 5 a.m. at some bridal chain's semiannual "$99 Wedding Gown Sale," fight the rabid crowd, and try to grab something off the rack that is close to your size—and there may not be much of a selection there at the store that is close to your size. Instead, you can do it all from the comfort of your own home.

But to be truly successful, you first need to do some homework. Browse through bridal magazines to see what kind of dress you would like. Visit bridal salons and department stores and try on the kinds of dresses you're considering. Take a trusted friend along to give you her honest opinion lest you get carried away by bridal salespeople ooh-ing and aah-ing at the dress you're trying on in hopes of motivating you to buy. Narrow down the kind of dress you'd like (strapless, ball gown, sheath, and so on) and the color you prefer (gowns come in all shades of white, ivory, and ecru, and some even have splashes of color). Cut out pictures of the gowns you especially like and keep them handy. Note the time of day your ceremony will take place, and how formal or informal your wedding gown has to be. Your bridal gown will set the tone for the rest of your bridal party (bridesmaids), so the sooner you get your own shopping accomplished, the sooner your bridesmaids can start shopping for their own dresses.

There are many different silhouettes, necklines, and sleeve styles to consider when choosing your gown. You also have to consider what styles are allowed in your church if you are going to have a religious ceremony (some churches frown on the popular strapless and spaghetti-strap wedding gowns, and therefore you must have a shawl or wrap at least during the ceremony).

Consider these different gown silhouettes:

- *A-line.* This is just what it sounds like: The bodice hugs the body and then flares out toward the base like an "A."
- *Ball gown.* This silhouette has a fitted waist with a full, flared floor-length skirt, perfect for the "fairy-tale princess" look.
- *Dropped-waist.* This style features a waist seam that falls below the natural waistline.
- *Empire waist.* This style incorporates a slim skirt falling from just below the bust.
- *Fishtail or mermaid.* This silhouette is fitted but flares out from the knee down.

- *Princess line.* This style is characterized by a seamless waist, a fitted top, and a slightly flared hem.
- *Two-piece.* This is a dress that is made with a top that is separate from the skirt.
- *Sheath or column.* This style is form-fitting from top to bottom.

Next, consider the style of neckline you like best:

- Cowl
- Halter
- Jewel
- Portrait
- Queen Anne
- Sabrina
- Scooped
- Sweetheart
- Square
- V-neck

Then consider the sleeve styles:

- Cap
- Juliet
- Tulip
- Poet or kimono
- Shoestring or spaghetti straps
- Sleeveless
- Strapless

eBay TIP: When you are buying your bridal gown, keep in mind that bridal gowns are sized smaller than street clothes. A size 8 woman can very well require a size 14 wedding gown. Therefore, it's very important that you do not shop on the basis of the *size* noted on the gown's label, but instead shop on the basis of the actual *measurements.* Have a professional seamstress take your measurements: bust, waist, hip, and hollow-to-hem. Sure, it's tempting to try to do this yourself, but remember that taking these measurements correctly the first time will save you a bundle of money through finding a dress that fits properly and doesn't require costly alterations. Some bridal stores provide measurement services for free. You can also visit your local seamstress (or a skilled and trusted friend who is handy at dressmaking and tailoring). The bottom line is, avoid guesswork and get reliable measurements to ensure that your ultimate purchase fits you beautifully.

Armed with your correct measurements, you're now ready to browse eBay for your wedding gown. Use the search terms we've already noted to browse through the selection available on eBay. Use the sorting feature to arrange the auctions according to price or by ending date (you can even specify only Buy-It-Now listings if you are ready to purchase and don't want to wait for an auction to end or for some other bride to outbid you), or specify locations for items if you're particular about where you want to purchase your dress.

When eBay returns the list of items that match your query (the "hit list"), carefully read each auction's description of the dress's condition (brand-new, new, used once, and so on) and the measurements. Once you identify the dress size closest to your measurements (always go one size up if you find you are between sizes—it's easier to alter a dress to make it smaller than to make it bigger), go ahead and place the size you need in the search criteria. For example, *(wedding,bridal) (gown*,dress*) 14*. By doing this, you're truly zeroing in on the perfect gown.

eBay TIP: A little-known eBay tool is the "Wedding Dresses Finder," a search tool similar to the search engines on popular Web sites such as www.theknot.com. To find this tool, start at eBay's site map (from the convenient link located at the top of every eBay page), then click on the "Clothing, Shoes and Accessories" category, and then on "Wedding Dresses" under "Wedding Apparel." You'll find the "Wedding Dresses Finder" on the left-hand side (see Figure 8-1). It enables you to search for wedding dresses and gowns by your desired sleeve length, size, color, condition, and keywords. Keywords can be the name of the gown designer or manufacturer (e.g., Vera Wang, David's, Maggie Sottero), a style you like (e.g., corset, empire), or a fabric you prefer (satin, lace).

By this time, you may be wondering who are these sellers offering these gowns on eBay? The majority we've shopped sell brand-new dresses. Most of them own or operate brick-and-mortar bridal stores and have begun marketing on eBay to help expand their customer reach (a great idea, by the way). Many of these are offering discount deals because they're trying to clear their warehouses of overstocked (yet still brand-new) gowns. Some sellers own their own dress stores and can manufacture a custom-made gown just for you, again finding eBay to be an excellent way to reach far more customers than those in a local geographical area. And many of the sellers are actually brides who have already gotten married and want to sell their wedding gown on eBay (remember the adage, "Something old, something new, something borrowed, something blue"?).

If you are bidding on a wedding gown that has been tried on by other people at a bridal salon (i.e., a "sample" gown) or worn by a bride to her own

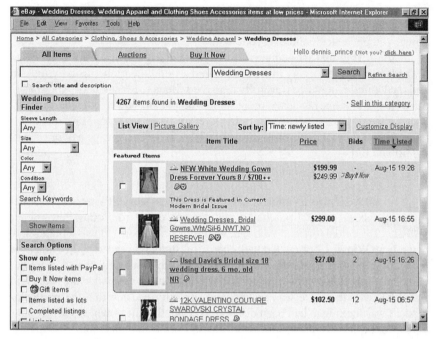

Figure 8-1 "Wedding Dresses Finder" is another excellent eBay search tool to help brides-to-be.

wedding, be sure to read the description carefully. Here are some questions to keep in mind (and to ask the seller if the auction description does not give you the answers):

1. Has the gown been altered from its original size?
2. How long was the gown used on the wedding day? (Typically it is worn for less than 12 hours.)
3. Was the gown dry-cleaned after being used?
4. How and where was the gown stored?
5. Is the bride offering any of her matching bridal accessories for sale as well?
6. Are there any parts of the gown that need to be restored (i.e., missing sequins, buttons, and so on)?
7. What is the overall condition of the gown?

Tips for buying a used gown are very similar to those for purchasing a new one—shop by measurements, not by tag size. And always ask the seller questions before you commit to purchasing. You may find that a bride who paid thousands of dollars for her Vera Wang wedding gown at a bridal salon is willing to part with it for less than half of what she paid. She sells her wedding gown, you get a steal, and everyone wins.

You'll find that while many of eBay's wedding gown sellers are located in the United States, many more are located around the globe, usually in Asia and the United Kingdom. Carefully read the seller's feedback and "About Me" page (if there is one) to learn more about the person you're considering purchasing from. Carefully read the seller's return policies (if any) and make initial e-mail contact if you have any doubts whatsoever. Always ask questions *before* you bid.

eBay TIP: Here's another eBay bride success story: It's my own personal success story. I purchased my wedding dress from eBay PowerSeller chicbridal (official Web site: www.chicbridal.com). It was a brand-new gown from Winnie Couture that had a beautiful strapless beaded bodice and nine layers of tulle skirt scattered with rhinestones. The gown was posted at a phenomenally low Buy-It-Now price of $109. What a steal! I e-mailed the seller and asked her why the price was so low, and she informed me that the particular model I was looking at had been discontinued, but that the gown was brand-new, had never been tried on, was in stock, was still in the manufacturer's packaging, and was ready to be shipped from the warehouse. I was hooked, and after determining the correct size with my measurements, I bid on and won the dress. Later, my seamstress informed me that she had just finished altering a dress very similar to mine, and that the bride had paid close to $2,000 for the dress alone! Wow!

eBay TIP: While we're talking about wedding gowns, eBay seller bartinoco also has an official off-eBay Web site at http://www.bridal-gown.net/. Among other great wedding items, this seller offers wedding gown preservation kits for $65 to $70 (retail price $150 to $200). While you're planning your wedding is a perfect time to think ahead about preserving your wedding gown and memories should you decide not to part with it (see Figure 8-2).

eBay TIP: Don't forget to purchase a garment bag (vinyl or breathable ones are best) to store your wedding dress in, to keep it clean and looking new. Search eBay and you'll find plenty of sellers offering garment bags at prices much lower than retail.

You may also fall in love with a particular designer's gowns. Go ahead and place the designer's name in the search box to narrow down your search. Usually

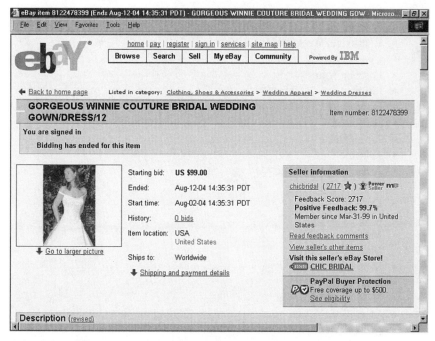

Figure 8-2 In addition to finding this fabulous new wedding gown on eBay under $100 you can also inquire about gown preservation at the same time.

placing only part of the designer's name (for example, Maggie or Maggie Sot* instead of Maggie Sottero) in the search box will yield more results, since sometimes the sellers either don't have enough space to give the entire name or happen to misspell the name. The following is a partial list of popular wedding gown designers and manufacturers you may choose to search:

- Alex Hanson
- Alfred Angelo
- Alvina Valenta
- Amsale
- Bonny
- Bridal Originals
- Casablanca
- Christina Wu
- Christos
- David's
- Demetrios/Ilissa
- Diamond

- Eden
- Emme
- Exclusives by ACE
- Eve of Milady
- Forever Yours
- Ian Stuart
- Impression
- Jacquelin
- Janell Berte
- Jasmine
- Jessica McClintock
- Jim Hjelm
- Lazaro
- Maggie Sottero
- Marisa
- Mary's
- Mon Cheri
- Monique
- Monique L'Huillier
- Moonlight
- Mori Lee
- Paloma Blanca
- Private Label by G
- Pronovias/St.Patrick
- Reem Acra
- Scaasi/Forsyth
- Scott McClintock
- St. Pucchi
- Sweetheart
- Tomasina
- Venus
- Vera Wang
- Watters and Watters (or Watters Bride)
- Winnie Couture

Since you're purchasing your gown online, it's up to you to arrange for any necessary alterations to be made. Bridal salons are notorious for refusing to alter gowns that were not purchased from their store (what happened to that "friendly service"?). You'll typically fare better if you approach your local seamstress or tailor (at her or his own shop or at your regular department store) or a talented relative who can do this for you (perhaps as a wedding gift). Make sure you allow ample time (several weeks to months, depending on how busy your seamstress is) for alterations to be completed. Alterations can cost as little as $25 for a simple hem, or up to $200 for a multilayer dress made of different kinds of fabrics. Keep this in mind and mentally factor it into the cost of the gown you are considering purchasing on eBay.

A Perfect Alternative to Alterations

If you want minimal alterations, try searching for a custom-made wedding gown. Many eBay sellers are ready to use your *own* measurements to make the gown of your choice. That's right; the dress is *custom-made* just for you. It's like getting the bridal salon treatment without paying the hefty salon price. Going this route can save you a bundle, since you'll most likely need very few alterations, given that the dress was made with your measurements from the outset. eBay seller jennieqxw, who offers tailor-made wedding gowns, comments: "The best way to save money on a wedding dress is to get a tailor-made gown because the alteration fees can cost much more than what you pay for the dress itself. When you order a tailor-made gown, it will be very possible that no alterations are needed. In the event that alterations are needed, they will be very minor and cost less. But customers need to have measurements taken correctly."

Your choice of wedding gown is limited only by your imagination (and your willingness to cull the auction listings), but thanks to eBay, the possibilities abound.

WEDDING VEILS, TIARAS, AND OTHER HEADPIECES

Amazing as it may seem, bridal veils can retail for around $100 or more. That seems like a lot of money for a few yards of white, frothy material, and the excuse that some salespeople may give is, "Well, the veil is *only* $100, and the gown is $1,000. You're getting a steal!" Don't fall for this argument. Most brides swallow the lump in their throat and cough up the dough because they erroneously think that they have no other option. Quite the opposite! There are tons of beautiful, affordable veils listed on eBay every day, and the best news is that some start as low as $5.99.

Best Keyword Combinations for Veils

- *(bridal,wedding) veil**
- *(bridal,wedding) (tiara*,headpiece*,head piece*)*
- *(bridal,wedding) hair*

Quick Statistics

- Retail price range: $100 and up
- Actual eBay price range: From less than $6 to $50
- Realized savings: 50 to 95 percent off retail prices

Veils are categorized by color, number of tiers, and length. Colors are generally white, ivory, and diamond white. Veils can have one, two, three, or even up to five tiers. Lengths include shoulder length, elbow length, fingertip length, and the cathedral veil (the longest length). Veils can be plain, pencil-cut, or ribbon-edged. They can be decorated with rhinestones, Swarovski crystals, or pearls. They can be attached to tiaras or headpieces or sold separately. A Spanish type of veil called the mantilla is a classy veil that is draped close to the head. Choose the veil that will best complement your wedding gown, hairstyle, and face shape.

While the salon prices may lead you to think that the tiaras are made of precious metals and stones, most are only costume jewelry quality. Why, then, do they cost so much at the store? When you pay retail, you are paying for overhead: the store's rent, the salaries of the salespeople, and the electricity that powers the lighting of the fitting rooms. Is there a better alternative? That's right; you can find the same tiaras and headpieces on eBay starting for less than $10 (see Figure 8-3).

Begin by considering what kind of hairstyle you would like to wear on your wedding day. If you want ideas for your wedding-day updo, check out the offering of CD-ROMs on eBay that feature hairstyle ideas specifically for brides (it's true!). One such seller, known simply as ajb2103, offers an inexpensive

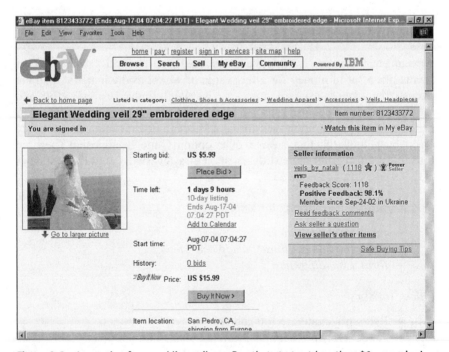

Figure 8-3. An auction for a wedding veil on eBay that starts at less than $6—amazing!

CD ($5) with over one thousand wedding hair ideas. Go this route and you'll eliminate the necessity and expense of purchasing dozens of expensive bridal magazines just to search for wedding hairstyles. Your bridal hairstyle and headgear can look like a million dollars, but only you will know that it didn't cost anywhere near that.

WEDDING SHOES

Realistically, if you are wearing a floor-length wedding gown, the only time your guests will even notice your shoes is during the infamous garter ritual at the reception (when your new husband slyly inches up your skirt without using his hands to get at your garter, accompanied by hoots and whistles from rowdy guests). Nevertheless, the shoes are a necessity, but paying retail prices is definitely out of style in our book.

Best Keyword Combinations for Shoes

- *(bridal,wedding) (shoe*,sneaker*,slipper*,formal)*
- *(bridal,wedding) (pump*,flat*,ballet)*
- *(bridal,wedding) dyeable*

Quick Statistics

- Retail price range: $50 to $100 and up
- Actual eBay price range: From less than $20 to $50
- Realized savings: 50 to 80 percent off retail prices

You can purchase your wedding shoes (usually white or ivory to match your gown) at the store, but to make them memorable and one-of-a-kind, go on eBay to find them. Make sure you include your shoe size in the keyword search combinations to narrow it down for you. One of the most popular styles is wedding sneakers similar to those seen in the movie *Father of the Bride* (see Figure 8-4). I purchased mine for just $34.95 (wedding sneakers at the stores and on Yahoo! retail for about $100). For comfort, you can also browse for ballet slippers to wear on your wedding day. They're soft and comfortable, and they have won rave reviews from brides. You can also purchase dyeable shoes for your wedding party, and if you're buying them from the same seller who's offering your own wedding shoes, you can probably save on shipping costs, too.

Aside from landing some terrific bargains, when shopping for wedding shoes, remember that comfort is key, since you'll be parading about in them (or just standing, walking, and sprinting to the limo while dodging rice and birdseed from exuberant guests) for an entire day. And don't forget posing for formal photography, greeting the guests in the receiving line, and dancing at the reception. Therefore, make sure you break your bridal shoes in long before

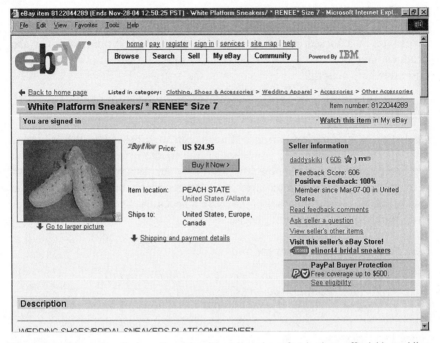

Figure 8-4 Take your walk down the aisle with style and comfort in these affordable wedding sneakers from eBay.

your wedding day, to make them more comfortable. Wear them for a few hours at a time at home while you're running around doing laundry, doing the dishes, vacuuming the living room, or evading your mother or future mother-in-law who may be visiting and trying to wheedle an extra guest or two into the invitation list. Most of all, have fun choosing your bridal footwear. When else can you get away with wearing sneakers trimmed with lace, elegant ballet slippers, or white satin shoes embroidered with your initials? Just remember to put your best foot forward and shop for your wedding footwear at eBay first.

BRIDAL ACCESSORIES

So you've finished shopping for your wedding gown, and you've saved yourself quite a bundle. Give yourself a pat on the back and some congratulations, but wait! You're not quite done. According to the salespeople in the bridal salons you've window-shopped in, the dress is not quite the only thing you need to complete your wedding-day attire. There's still the lingerie to shop for, and the bridal accessories that go with your dress. eBay to the rescue.

Best Keyword Combinations for Accessories

- *(bridal,wedding) (shawl,wrap,shrug)*
- *(bridal,wedding) glove**
- *(bridal,wedding) garter**
- *(bridal,wedding) jewelry*
- *(bridal,wedding) (lingerie,bra,crinoline,slip,corset)*
- *(bridal,wedding) (hose,hosiery)*
- *(bridal,wedding) (purse,bag)*

Quick Statistics

- Retail price range for each item: From $25 to $75 and up
- Actual eBay price range: Usually starts at less than $10
- Realized savings: 50 percent or more off retail prices

You might want to consider buying a shawl or wrap for your dress, as well as gloves to complete the look. A matching bridal purse or bag might be a neat addition to your ensemble. A crinoline would help give your wedding gown a fuller look, and a corset or girdle might help you attain a beautiful slimmer shape for your big day. Don't forget the garter for the infamous garter-toss ritual at the ceremony.

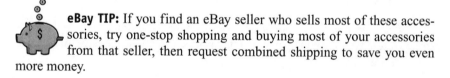

eBay TIP: If you find an eBay seller who sells most of these accessories, try one-stop shopping and buying most of your accessories from that seller, then request combined shipping to save you even more money.

- *Shawl or wrap.* This is ideal for a glamorous addition to a strapless or sleeveless wedding gown. It also allows the bride to bare a little more skin at the reception but be more covered up for the ceremony.
- *Gloves.* Lengths include wrist length, elbow length, and opera length. Fabrics range from lace to shiny satin and matte satin. Gloves may be plain or adorned with pearls or rhinestones (see Figure 8-5).
- *Garter.* This can be made of combinations of lace and satin. It may be white or a myriad of other colors.
- *Jewelry.* This includes earrings, necklaces, bracelets, and tiaras.
- *Lingerie.* This is traditionally white or ivory.
- *Crinoline or slip.* This is worn to give the skirts a fuller look.
- *Hosiery.* Thigh-highs or pantyhose are the norm.
- *Bag or purse* This holds your "wedding-day necessities": lipstick, compact, handkerchief, lucky penny, whatever you like.

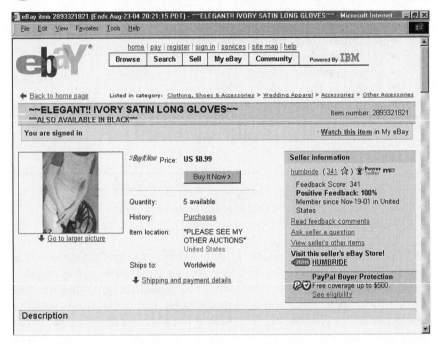

Figure 8-5 Gloves like these retail for up to $40; get them on eBay for a fraction of the cost.

Traditionally, these items are found in bridal salons and department stores, where you will end up paying retail prices. But you won't have to, because you can shop eBay!

WEDDING BOUQUETS, BOUTONNIERES, AND FLOWERS

Wedding flowers essentially set the tone of romance for your wedding. According to estimates from florists, wedding packages range from $600 for a minimalist package to thousands of dollars for elaborate bouquets and arrangements for the church and reception hall. If you don't have the space in your budget for expensive floral arrangements, eBay can once again come to the rescue by providing amazing deals on your wedding floral needs. Your guests will marvel at the professional look of your floral arrangements, while you saved both time and money by purchasing them on eBay.

Best Keyword Combinations for Flowers

- *(bridal,wedding) (flower*,bouquet*,set*)*
- *(bridal,wedding) (corsage*,boutonniere*,bout*)*

Quick Statistics

- Retail price range: $600 to $5,000 and up
- Actual eBay price range: From less than $100 to $250 and up
- Realized savings: 50 to 80 percent off retail prices

There are two types of flowers that you can use for your wedding: fresh flowers and silk ones. It is very easy to find fresh flowers offered at wholesale prices. First, you go to the "Site Map" link, which is at the top of every eBay page. Scan the page and locate "Categories," where you will find a section called "Everything Else." Under this heading, you will find "Gifts & Occasions," and under that you will find "Flowers & Bouquets," where you can sort through "Fresh" or "Artificial." To review, here is the quick way to get your floral shopping done on eBay:

Site Map > Categories > Everything Else > Gifts & Occasions > Flowers & Bouquets > Fresh

You can easily find auctions for 100 to 250 wholesale bulk fresh roses for under $100 shipped to your door. What a steal! That's less than you'd pay for *one* bridal bouquet or *one* floral arrangement of one or two dozen roses ordered from your local florist! Buying in bulk is great for saving money on your bouquets and your ceremony and reception centerpieces. Try the seller www*rosesource*com (more info about this seller is at its official Web site, http://www.rosesource.com) or the seller bigrose_roses (shop this seller's eBay listings to save 50 percent off the regular prices at the official Web site, http://www.bigrose.com).

The majority of the wedding flowers offered on eBay are silk. Now, before you scoff at the idea of silk flowers, you need to realize that the silk floral industry has improved to the point where a guest may be hard-pressed to distinguish silk from the real thing. Silk floral arrangements and bouquets can also serve as mementos that your bridal party and guests can treasure long after the ceremony is over. The flowers can also double as home décor for your guests.

If you want to include fresh flowers, you can mix them with silk and have the important bouquet (i.e., the bride's) contain live flowers, while the others (tossing bouquet, bridesmaid bouquet, flower girl basket) contain silk. You can get good deals from other sellers averaging about $150 to $200 for *complete* wedding sets, making eBay essentially your one-stop shop for wedding flowers. A complete set might include the bride's bouquet, the bridesmaids' bouquets, the groomsmen's boutonnieres, corsages for important guests, and even the flower girl's basket (see Figure 8-6).

Excellent sellers of wedding flowers include affordelegance, rosesrkim, and unique_expressions. Their silk flowers look amazingly gorgeous and very real and are a great value. Silk flowers also minimize the hassle of making sure that the flowers are delivered on time and remain fresh. Silk flowers can

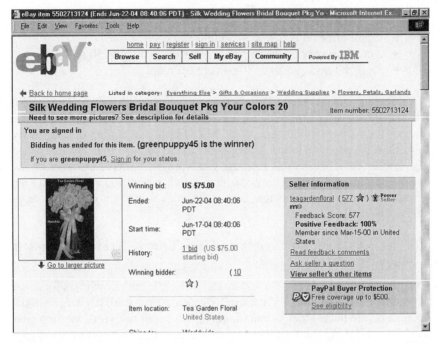

Figure 8-6 Check out complete wedding bouquet sets on eBay that start at less than $100.

also be stored well (in a cool, dry place), and therefore you can feel free to shop for your wedding flowers as early as one year ahead of the big day. Also, in the event that you need more flowers, all you have to do is contact your seller of choice and place another order. Many even offer price breaks or other such incentives for repeat business.

If you have a favorite blossom that you would like to incorporate into your wedding flowers, most eBay sellers are more than happy to customize your order. To make your flowers even more special, pick ones that have special meanings to them. Here are the meanings attached to certain flowers:

Amaryllis: splendid beauty
Apple blossoms: temptation
Aster: amulet of love
Bluebell: constancy
Buttercup: riches
Camellia: perfect loveliness, gratitude
Carnation: pure, deep love
Daffodil: regard
Daisy: purity and innocence

Forget-me-not: don't forget
Freesias: innocence, friendship, and trust
Gardenia: joy
Honeysuckle: genuine affection
Hyacinth: sporty and playful
Ivy: fidelity
Jasmine: amiability
Jonquil: affection returned
Lily: purity
Lily of the valley: happiness
Myrtle: love
Orange blossom: purity, loveliness
Orchid: rare love and beauty
Pink rose: happiness
Red rose: I love you
Red tulip: love declared
Rose: love
Sunflowers: adoration
Sweet peas: continued pleasure
Tulip: perfect lover
Violet: modesty, faithfulness
White camellia: perfect loveliness
White daisy: innocence
White lilac: first emotions of love
White lily: purity and innocence
White rose: purity and innocence
Yellow rose: friendship

eBay TIP: You can also choose from and possibly request different types of bouquets from your eBay seller, or search for these arrangements via the pictures of the flowers in eBay auctions:

- *Posy, round bouquet, or nosegay:* A tight cluster of flowers bound or hand-tied to form a round overall shape; easy to hold and/or throw.
- *Cascade, shower, or waterfall bouquet:* A top-heavy arrangement that tapers into a trail; more dramatic than the posy or nosegay.
- *Teardrop bouquet:* Similar to a posy, but with a tapering trail.
- *Arm spray:* A bouquet designed to be held in the crook of the elbow; it can be made of longer-stemmed blooms.
- *Freestyle bouquets:* Bouquets that are abstract in shape and can be modern.
- *Single-stem bouquets:* These are most dramatic with a simple dress, e.g., a single, long-stemmed calla lily stem for your bridesmaids.

Thanks to eBay, you can have beautiful, affordable wedding flowers that reflect your personal taste and personality and still have money left to plan a great honeymoon!

CEREMONY DECORATIONS

Why spend a fortune on ceremony decorations? You don't have to. The ceremony lasts for one hour or so and will be photographed and videotaped. You don't have to break the bank to make the church or ceremony site look amazing. The most beautiful sights inside your ceremony venue are actually you, your fiancé, and your loved ones dressed to the nines watching you exchange wedding vows. The decorations merely enhance the romance of the moment. Therefore, consider the eBay alternative to great decorations at terrific prices.

Best Keyword Combinations for Ceremony Decorations

- (bridal,wedding) pew bow*
- (bridal,wedding) aisle runner
- (bridal,wedding) unity candle*
- unity (candleholder*,candle holder*)
- (wedding,bridal) (ceremony,altar,alter) flower*
- (wedding,bridal) altar (flower*,arrangement*)
- (wedding,bridal) (ringbearer*,ring bearer*,pillow*)

Quick Statistics

- Retail price range: $200 to $5,000 and up
- Actual eBay price range: From less than $10 to $100 and up
- Realized savings: 50 to 80 percent off retail prices

Remember to check with your ceremony site and/or officiant and inquire about what kinds of decorations are allowed in your church, synagogue, or hall, and how much time is available to you for setup and removal of decorations pre- and postceremony. If you're having your ceremony outdoors, the beauty of Mother Nature may eliminate the need to purchase numerous decorations. To save even more money, you can ask trusted friends and relatives to transport some of your ceremony decorations to the reception site in order to get double use out of your beautiful arrangements and other such decor.

Common ceremony decorations include pew bows (up to $10 each at retail), aisle runners (up to $30+ at retail), the unity candle ($50 to $60 at retail) and candleholders ($20 to $100 at retail), and floral arrangements for the altar and/or entryway ($50 to 100+ each at retail). As you can see, ceremony decorations can easily cost hundreds of dollars, but not if you use eBay!

Search eBay and you'll find plenty of sellers specializing in creating magnificent pew bows, such as the seller basketofbows. Seller packageperfect also sells pew bows, available either in full sets or a la carte (meaning that you can buy whatever quantity you need). To keep your guests abreast of the ceremony proceedings, consider browsing eBay for personalized wedding programs, many of which you'll also find on eBay for prices far less than retail. The seller weddings_for_less offers beautiful wedding programs that have especially impressed us. The seller efavormart offers a nice selection of aisle runners and other decorations at really low prices, as well as arts and crafts supplies if you want to create your own masterpieces. The seller angelafre sells amazing rose-shaped ring pillows for your ring-bearer to carry. The rose-shaped pillows can also serve as wonderful bridal party gifts. The seller affordelegance has gorgeous altar arrangements that can be transferred to your head table at the reception. The seller kriskwi offers hand-carved unity candles and tapers. Its unity candles even feature a replaceable tealight so that you can keep your unity candle new for years and years to come. Your unity candle becomes a memento of your ceremony. Another awesome seller of unity candles is unitycandles. Its candles are hand-carved, gorgeous, and wonderfully priced well below retail! Its official Web site is http://www.weddingunitycandles.com (see Figure 8-7). These are just a few examples of how you can decorate your ceremony site beautifully and affordably through eBay.

RECEPTION DECORATIONS

Most likely, your reception site provides catering and linens, but minimal decorations. Therefore, you may have to purchase additional decorations yourself, all the while attempting to stay within your budget. Ask your reception site coordinator what decorations are allowed at the site. Florists give estimates of about $20 to $100 or more per arrangement per table, and once you do the math, you'll see that the tally goes up pretty high pretty fast. You can control the cost and still have fabulous reception decorations simply by browsing and shopping on eBay.

Best Keyword Combinations for Reception Decorations

- *(bridal,wedding) candlering*,candle ring**
- *(bridal,wedding) pillar (candle*)*
- *wholesale (candleholder*)*
- *wholesale (candle*)*
- *(wedding,bridal) reception (decoration*)*
- *(wedding,bridal) (topiary,topiar*)*
- *(wedding,bridal) (centerpiece*,center piece*)*

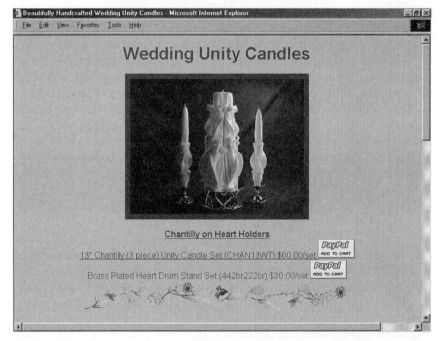

Figure 8-7 Visit sellers' official Web sites (such as this one by seller unitycandles) to learn more about the sellers and their businesses.

- *(wedding,bridal) card (box,holder)*
- *(wedding,bridal) cake (top,topper)*
- *(wedding,bridal) balloon**
- *(wedding,bridal) swag**

Quick Statistics

- Retail price range: $20 to $100 and up per reception table; $50 to $100 for head table floral arrangement
- Actual eBay price range: From less than $10 to $35 and up per table; $35 to $50 for head table
- Realized savings: 50 to 90 percent off retail prices

You can start by searching eBay using the search words shown. Make full use of the thumbnail gallery pictures of the items in the auctions to see what first catches your eye. Remember, when searching eBay, you can sort by price or narrow your search to Buy-It-Now items if you want to make your purchase immediately rather than bid against another bride. If you like a certain item from a seller, don't forget to browse that seller's other auctions or eBay store (if he or she has one), as you might find other items that you can purchase at the same time (remember, you can usually save money on shipping costs when you combine items in a single purchase).

When shopping for decorations, make a rough estimate of how many table arrangements you will need, calculated from the approximate number of guests who will attend and therefore the number of tables, place cards, menu cards, and so on. For example, if you plan on having about 120 guests, and your reception coordinator informs you that each table seats 10 guests, you can shop for one dozen or so table centerpieces when searching and buying on eBay.

The most popular reception table centerpieces are topiaries, candle rings with candles or hurricane lamps, floral arrangements, potted flowers, potted plants, fishbowls with floating candles, helium balloon arrangements, wicker baskets, fruit bowls, or a simple grouping of candles (see Figure 8-8). Topiaries and flower arrangements may be made of real flowers or silk ones (silk is less expensive, is more easily portable, and can be

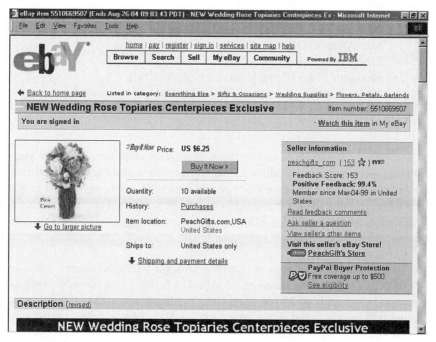

Figure 8-8 Decorate your reception tables with beautiful yet affordable centerpieces from eBay, such as this one.

130   How to Buy Everything for Your Wedding on eBay

given away at the end of the reception as long-lasting home décor gifts to guests).

Place cards allow guests to find their table quickly and easily, and table menu cards (usually one on each table) are an elegant way to announce to your guests the order of the delicious courses to come. Helium-filled balloons can decorate each table or highlight the bridal table; a balloon-filled archway can be a beautiful addition to the entryway to the reception hall or a fun backdrop for photographs. Floral swags can decorate the cake table and/or the head table. The wedding cake (which will be on prominent display at your reception) may be topped with live or silk flowers, or with a traditional (bride and groom statuettes) or nontraditional cake topper. At the gift table, you can place a birdcage wreathed in flowers or a mailbox-shaped wedding card box with a card slot that can safely collect wedding cards from guests.

As you ponder your purchases for your reception decorations, think of a theme that would make your reception unique and convey your and your new spouse's interests and hobbies. Some examples of popular wedding themes are

- Romantic Hollywood movies
- Medieval theme
- Precious Moments theme
- Kim Anderson theme
- Ethnic theme (e.g., Asian, Western)
- Romantic cities (Paris, Venice, Rome, Madrid)
- Holiday theme (Valentine's Day, Christmas, New Year's Day)
- Beach theme
- Cinderella (fairy-tale) theme

A theme can unify your reception decorations and even simplify your shopping process. Simply add a search word to your eBay search to narrow down your choices. For example, type in *Cinderella (wedding,bridal)* in the search bar to immediately bring up hundreds of items that can be used for a Cinderella-themed wedding. Whatever you decide to include in table decorations, add the appropriate keywords to the keyword combinations we've already noted.

When purchasing items in quantity, look for auctions that sell items in lots. Most wedding decorations come in lots of 6, 10, 12, or more for decorations and increments of 25 for items such as place cards and wedding favors (favors will be addressed in the next section). You can place the number you need in the search bar to narrow down the auctions that have the exact number of decorations you need. For example, you can type in *10 (wedding,bridal) centerpiece**.

Read the auction description carefully for shipping charges to avoid overpaying for an item. Ten floral centerpieces may not be the best bargain around if the final winning bid price was $30 but the shipping was $50. Factor this in when shopping for items in lots.

eBay TIP: Just a timely reminder: As mentioned in Chapter 3, add the total bid amount (or Buy-It-Now price) to the total shipping charges, and divide the total cost by the number of items you are receiving. This is the *per-unit cost*. If the amount is less than what you would pay retail at the store, you have a bargain, without a trip to the store and the effort of lugging your purchases home. If the amount is the same as or higher than store prices, you may want to consider browsing other sellers of the same or similar items. Wedding decorations purchased on eBay are shipped to your door, with little or no assembly required. It's very easy to find quality, value, and convenience when shopping on eBay.

Most wedding sellers on eBay sell items that cross different categories (decorations, favors, invitations), so be sure to browse their selections. The seller jcsm2003 offers wonderful candle and flower centerpieces in affordable sets of 10 to save you money. Sellers affordelegance, unique_expressions, and peachgifts_com also offer candle rings, swags, and gorgeous silk flower centerpieces. The seller hamptonwholesale offers candles at wholesale prices, which are perfect for wedding decorations. This seller has an official Web site at http://www.hamptonstore.com/. The seller csmarquis offers beautiful custommade wedding card boxes that can be handed down to future brides in the family (if not resold on eBay). The seller shadowmom29, whose official off-eBay Web site is http://www.labelsbuydesign.com/, offers customized table menus for an elegant touch for each reception table.

Your reception should be a joyous gathering of your family and friends, and the first social event at which you and your spouse will be stepping out as husband and wife. With eBay, you can make your reception as fantastical or as simple as you choose while avoiding the financial stress that often accompanies dressing up the party.

WEDDING FAVORS

Wedding favors are fun mementos that guests get to take home with them after the wedding. With eBay, the sky's the limit for wedding favors—they can be as unusual and as much fun as you would like; it just depends on how much you want to spend per favor, and whether your guests will really like a particular favor and bring it home. Popular wedding favors include mini-picture frames that double as place card holders, magnets, candy wrapped in personalized candy wrappers, bookmarks, candles, bubbles, matchbooks, birdseed, and just about anything else you can conjure up.

Best Keyword Combinations for Favors

- *(bridal,wedding) favor**
- *(bridal,wedding) magnet**
- *(bridal,wedding) bookmark**
- *(bridal,wedding) CD**
- *(bridal,wedding) (candle*,favor*)*
- *(bridal,wedding) frame**
- *(bridal,wedding) camera**
- *(bridal,wedding) bubble**
- *(bridal,wedding) (matchbook*, match book*)*

Quick Statistics

- Retail price range: $3 to $10 and up per guest
- Actual eBay price range: From less than $1 to $3 per guest
- Realized savings: 50 to 80 percent off retail prices

The average cost of a wedding favor is a few cents to a few dollars apiece. Most favors feature the bride and groom's names along with the wedding date to commemorate the occasion. Some couples have edible wedding favors, keepsake wedding favors, or both. A CD wedding favor with some of your favorite songs as a couple can be a touching gift to your guests, one that they may actually use more than once. With so many legitimate music download sites online today, you can easily compile the songs and master the CDs yourself, then purchase personalized CD wedding labels on eBay. If you'd rather leave the work to someone else, find a reputable eBay seller to put together the entire CD for you and master the appropriate number of copies for your guest list. A bookmark favor personalized with a poem or a picture of you and your new spouse will be a beautiful reminder of your big day. Wedding-day bubbles are a fun way for your guests to shower you with good wishes as you dance your first dance together.

To save money, take into account that not every guest will need a wedding favor, especially if your wedding favors cost more than a dollar each. Couples usually take only one, and children don't normally get to take home your magnets, matchbooks, candles, or picture frames. But be sure to order enough so that most of the adult guests can take one home. Have fun child-friendly favors for your younger guests. As with wedding decorations and anything else you purchase for your wedding in lots or in bulk, keep the per-unit cost in mind (the total winning bid price or Buy-It-Now price plus the total shipping charges, divided by the number of items you are receiving). If the per-unit cost is lower than retail, you have yourself a bridal bargain. If not, keep browsing and you'll be sure to find a better deal from another eBay seller.

The seller designsbyheidi specializes in favors with themes from Precious Moments, Kim Anderson, and other popular wedding themes (see Figure 8-9). The seller favors-land offers affordable silver-plated favors such as frames (around $1 or so each) and ice-cream scoops (around $1.99 each) that will wow your guests. Its official off-eBay Web site is http://disposable-cameras-wedding.com/. The seller orlandoweddings offers great favor ideas like bubbles, rose petals, and more. Its official off-eBay Web site is http://www.orlando-weddings.com/.

The seller ebridemart offers excellent disposable camera favors for $2.99, with awesome AGFA film for beautiful prints. Put one on each table, with instructions for guests to take whatever candid shots they would like to take and then leave the cameras on the tables at the end of the night. Collect the cameras, develop the film yourselves, and get *hundreds* of wedding candids for less money than any photographer would charge. Use popular film-developing Web sites such as http://www.snapfish.com and http://www.shutterfly.com; they offer online albums that can be shared with your guests, as well as discount

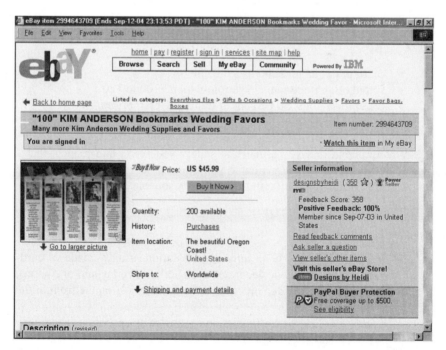

Figure 8-9 Wow your guests with wedding favors from eBay that start at less than a dollar each!

film developing and the ability to offer your guests the chance to purchase copies of the pictures.

The seller mema-pops offers delicious chocolate truffles as wedding favors. Go gourmet without paying a lot! Its off-eBay Web site is http://www.truffle-trolley.com. If you're artistically inclined and would like to make your wedding favors yourself, you can purchase art supplies (ribbons, lace, boxes, tulle, and so on) from the seller efavormart, then host a "favor party" with your bridal attendants or relatives and have a fun time making your favors a personal labor of love. With eBay, your wedding favors are limited only by your imagination.

WEDDING INVITATIONS

The wedding invitation is your guests' first impression of your big day. There are thousands of designs, textures, sizes, and colors from which to choose, and all of them are waiting for you at terrific prices on eBay.

Best Keyword Combinations for Invitations

- *(bridal,wedding) invitation**
- *(bridal,wedding) invitation* (Precious Moments, Kim Anderson)*
- *(bridal,wedding) invitation set**
- *"save the date"*

Quick Statistics

- Retail price range: $200 to $300 and up
- Actual eBay price range: From less than $100 to $200
- Realized savings: 50 percent or more off retail prices

While images of wedding invitations in an eBay listing are nice, we highly recommend that you e-mail the sellers you select and request that a sample of their invitation be mailed to you. Most sellers we've talked to were happy to fulfill our request (some charge a reasonable fee to offset postage costs, and that's fine).

Types of Invitations

- *Single panel.* This is an unfolded invitation, usually made of cardboard stock. It may be decorated with vellum overlay and/or ribbons.
- *Folder.* This is a folded invitation. The print is only on the front of the folder.
- *Z-fold type.* This type of invitation resembles an accordion. There may be print on all three sides of the invitation, for maximum space.

Types of Response Cards

- *RSVP card with envelope.* Requires a first-class stamp
- *RSVP postcard.* Requires postage for postcards (usually less expensive than first-class mail).

Types of Envelopes

- *Lined.* These may feature your wedding theme colors on the inside of the invitation envelope for a fancier, more elegant look.
- *Unlined.* Just the basics

Types of Printing

- *Engraving.* The most expensive method of raised printing. Engraved printing raises your lettering above the surface of the invitation while leaving slight indentations on the reverse side of the paper. Engraved stationery is produced by filling the crevices of an etched copper plate with ink, feeding the paper into the press, and then stamping the paper—the result is three-dimensional lettering.
- *Thermography.* Similar to engraving in look and feel, but costs much less.
- *Flat printing.* Can be done on laserjet or inkjet printers. This is the least expensive way to go.

Extras

- *Calligraphy.* This involves commissioning a calligrapher to address your envelopes. It can be a very pricey option.
- *Return address printed on envelope flap.* This is considered more formal than handwriting your return address again and again. Clear address labels printed using your home computer can be an inexpensive alternative.
- *Return address printed on RSVP envelope.* This option guarantees that all your guests have to do is mail the RSVP back to you.

The best invitation deals average about $1 to $2 *per invitee*, which includes the following: invitation, envelope, response card with envelope or response postcard, raised printing (if offered), reception card (if available), and return address preprinted on the RSVP. This is an amazing deal, since catalogues and retailers routinely charge more than $1 for each item in the invitation set. You do the math, then hurry to eBay to save yourself money from the get-go (see Figure 8-10).

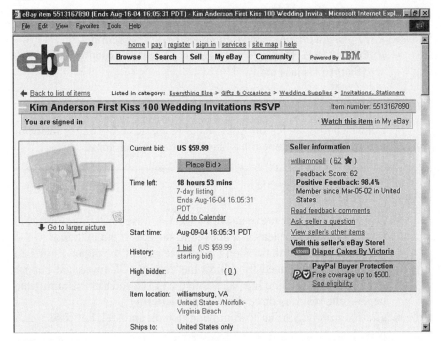

Figure 8-10 Beautiful, elegant, and affordable wedding invitations can be found on eBay. It's advisable to narrow your search by placing the quantity you desire (for example, "100") in your search keywords.

eBay TIP: Most brides are not aware that there are alternatives to expensive wedding invitations from catalogues and printers. Many eBay sellers are professional invitation printers who have their own small businesses, and some may be designers who work from home rather than at a larger printing firm or a bridal salon.

You can make an educated decision about your invitations after receiving samples by comparing quality, prices, and the level of customization the seller can offer. Does the seller offer thermography, engraving, or flat printing? Can the invitation include reception information at no extra charge? Will proofs be sent for your approval via e-mail or regular mail before the printing of your total order begins? What is the turn-around time for completion? Once again, consider the per-unit cost of each invitation set.

Sellers such as heather7966, alvarezprinting, dundeeprinting, and handykane offer a wide variety of wedding invitation sets at affordable prices. The seller weddings_for_less has official Web sites at http://www.weddingnook.cceasy.com/ and http://weddingnook.regency.ac. The seller handykane offers unique Cinderella-themed and photo invitations and thank-you cards that are simply breathtaking . (We especially appreciated that this seller donates a portion of the proceeds to charities that help children's causes.) Its off-eBay Web site is http://www.handykane.com.

To save money on postage, consider the size of your wedding invitations. The size should be specified in the auction description (for example, four inches by six inches, five inches by seven inches, and so on). Generally, the smaller the invitation, the cheaper the postage will be. Postcard response cards also require less postage than traditional RSVP cards with envelopes. Keep in mind that oddly shaped invitations (like square ones) can cost you extra at the post office. Take a completed invitation set to the post office and have it weighed; this will help you estimate how much money you should set aside for postage for sending the invitations out. Then calculate how much money you should set aside for return postage (usually one first-class stamp for each RSVP).

eBay TIP: Another alternative for RSVPs is to create a wedding Web site (for example, at www.theknot.com) that enables guests to RSVP online. Include your wedding Web site address in your invitations on a small paper insert and give your guests the convenience of responding online.

Ask sellers plenty of questions. Look at their past feedback from buyers to see if they gave good customer service. Allow plenty of time to shop for and pick out your invitations so that you won't be rushing to mail them out—ordering them at least four to six months before your wedding is ideal. Sellers with free 800-number customer service phone numbers, prominent e-mail contact information, and brick-and-mortar locations are good, since invitations are some of the most personalized purchases you will make for your big day.

eBay TIP: Look for auctions of invitations where the seller specifically states that he or she will e-mail or mail you a proof for your approval *before* printing begins. There's nothing worse than receiving 100 invitations with the bride or groom's name misspelled, or the wrong time and date printed. Hey, it happens.

Also consider purchasing blank invitation sets on eBay and printing them out yourself on your home computer. Order 10 to 20 percent more than you think you'll need, to allow for errors in addressing the envelopes and to have extra invitations on hand for last-minute additions to your guest list. Have fun choosing your wedding invitations. Make sure to save one or two to be framed later on as a treasured keepsake. With eBay, your invitations can be as simple or as fancy as you would like, and you do not have to worry about trimming the guest list to be able to afford beautiful invitations. Remember, it's never too soon to start browsing and asking for samples. Most sellers also sell matching reception place cards, save-the-date cards, and thank-you notes, again making eBay a one-stop shopping resource for most of your wedding stationery needs.

BRIDAL PARTY AND PARENTS' GIFTS

Naturally, in return for their help, support, and active involvement, it's traditional to present suitable gifts to your bridesmaids, groomsmen, and parents. Choosing the perfect gift can sometimes be a bit of a challenge, especially if your wedding budget is tight. Not to worry; there's a whole slew of affordable and/or luxurious gifts on eBay that you can browse and buy and that will let everyone know how much her or his participation means to you.

Best Keyword Combinations for Gifts

- (bridesmaid*,groomsman,groomsmen) gift*
- "to my (mom,dad,parent*,brother,sister) on my wedding day"
- (bridal,wedding) parent*
- (bridal,wedding) (engraved,engraving)
- (bridal,wedding) party gift*

Quick Statistics

- Retail price range: $20 to $50 each
- Actual eBay price range: From less than $10 to $20 and up
- Realized savings: 50 percent or more off retail prices

You'll be pleased to find that many sellers who offer such items also offer customization through engraving or embroidering of names and monograms for little or no additional cost, unlike retail stores, which charge you for the item and then charge you *again* for the personalization services (see Figure 8-11). It's usually a good idea to buy multiple items from one eBay seller for uniformity and savings on shipping costs. Remember that the gifts don't necessarily have to be beer mugs or keychains (not that there's anything wrong with those). If you want to offer something a bit more unusual, you'll be happy to find that eBay sellers are ready to help you be as creative as you like. And your bridal party will feel really special when they receive items that were hand-picked or personalized just for them.

Traditionally, the bride and groom purchase identical gifts for the members of their wedding party, but these days, most people feel freer to have some fun

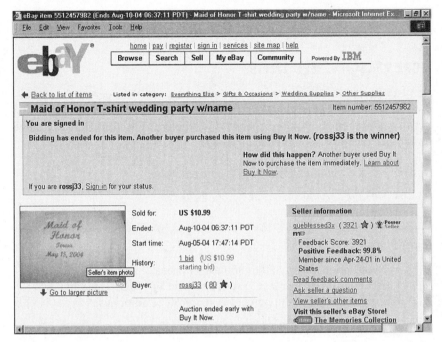

Figure 8-11 Make your attendants feel special with personalized wedding party gifts from eBay.

with shopping for bridal party gifts. Great ideas for the bridesmaids include spa gift certificates, scarves, perfume, wallets, a small piece of jewelry, jewelry boxes, cute handbags, tickets for the two of you to a musical or dinner theater, or a framed picture of the two of you together. Browse eBay for bridal tote bags that you can personalize with your bridesmaids' names and fill with goodies specific to each bridesmaid. Great ideas for the groomsmen include flasks, beer mugs (there, we said it), wallets, money clips, pocket watches, sports memorabilia from their favorite team, gift subscriptions to their favorite magazine, or tickets to a sporting or music event that they like. Browse eBay for these gifts and many more.

You can also pick out a "To My Mother on My Wedding Day" poem, plaque, or picture frame with a picture of you and your mother together; you can choose this type of gift for virtually any special family member who took part in your wedding. Give your father a handkerchief embroidered with his initials, so that he can shed tears of joy and nostalgia as he gives you away at the ceremony. Give both sets of parents a framed picture of you and your new spouse taken during your wedding day. Surprise your parents with a thank-you gift of a pair of tickets to a symphony, play, musical, or dinner theater. Thank-you gifts need not break the bank to be amazingly touching and heart-warming. We like the items offered by the seller ds_decals, who sells beautiful and afford-able bridesmaids' and groomsmen's gifts with free engraving services.

MORE PERSONALIZED ITEMS

Remember, nothing says it's *your* big day quite as much as personalized wed-ding items. Placing your names and your wedding date or your monogram on items makes them even more special after the wedding day. Here are some more great personalized items to consider.

Best Keyword Combinations for Personalized Items

- *(bridal,wedding) (custom*,personalize*)*
- *(soon be, hoodie)*

Quick Statistics

- Retail price range: $50 to $60 each (varies)
- Actual eBay price range: From less than $10 to $30 and up (varies)
- Realized savings: 50 percent or more off retail prices

Get personalized items from the seller queblessed3x (hankies, ring bearer pillows, blankets, T-shirts) as gifts for your wedding party and special relatives or friends. They'll remember your thoughtfulness for years to come. Purchase a personalized wedding guest book from the seller reneehere for less than you'd pay for a regular, nonpersonalized guest book at the store. Order yourself a per-sonalized wedding "treat" if you wish, and surprise your fiancé by purchasing one of the most popular current wedding items: the "Soon to be Mrs" hoodie (a sweatshirt with a hood made famous by pop star Jessica "Soon to Be Mrs. Lachey" Simpson). The seller spoolofdesign offers this popular hoodie, person-alized with your future last name in colorful embroidery thread of your own choosing (the official Web site is www.spoolofdesign.com). It's a great conver-sation starter, as friends and even strangers will come up to you to wish you well and congratulate you on your engagement and your upcoming wedding. Along with the "Soon to Be Mrs." clothing items (see Figure 8-12), you can purchase "Mrs. (Your Last Name Here), Established (Your Wedding Date Here)" T-shirts, to be worn after the wedding to proudly proclaim your new status as a newly-wed. It's your special event, just for you and your spouse-to-be, so have fun.

WEDDING BANDS AND RINGS

The jewelry pieces you choose for your wedding are special—they symbolize your union and the vows of fidelity you exchange with each other, and they will be worn by you and your spouse for a long, long time. They must be of

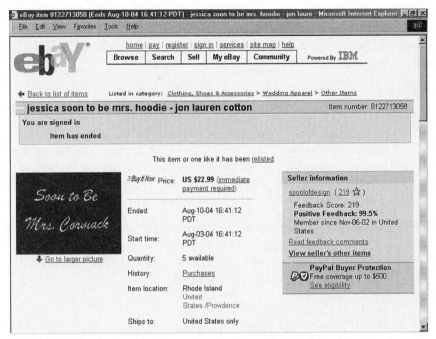

Figure 8-12 Proudly proclaim your bride-to-be status with this personalized sweatshirt "hoodie" from eBay.

great quality and beauty, and it is a bonus if you are able to find them at an affordable price. eBay can help you do that.

Best Keyword Combinations for Rings

- *(bridal,wedding) band**
- *(wedding,engagement,solitaire) ring**
- *(EGL,GIA,IGI) cert*—this keyword combination allows you to search for certified diamonds*
- *(bridal,wedding) diamond ring –(cz,cubic,lab,created,fn,smlt)*

Note that the last search term eliminates any items that are cubic zirconia, lab-created, or simulated. You want only *authentic* jewelry for your wedding.

Quick Statistics

- Retail price range: Varies
- Actual eBay price range: Varies
- Realized savings: 30 to 50 percent or more off retail prices

Do your homework first; read up on how to buy a diamond (we recommend the book *How to Buy a Diamond,* by Fred Cuellar) and how to buy fine jewelry (gold, platinum, and so on). A great Web site about how to buy diamonds is at http://www.bridaltips.com/diamond.htm.

A Quick Review of the Four C's of Buying Precious Gems:

- *Cut.* Cut is commonly confused with shape (round or brilliant, princess or square, emerald, pear, marquis, heart-shaped, trilliant, or oval). However, according to Tiffany & Company's educational brochure on diamonds, cut "refers to the faceting proportions on the surface of a diamond. More than any other factor, the precise positioning of these facets determines the brilliance of the stone."
- *Color.* Diamonds range from colorless (the most highly prized) to almost colorless, to brownish, to highly colored (also highly prized). The GIA (Gemological Institute of America) scale goes from D to Z.
- *Clarity.* The amount of imperfections or flaws within the stone. The scale ranges from flawless to included.
  - FL: flawless
  - IFL: internally flawless
  - VVS1 and VVS2: very very slightly included
  - VS1 and VS2: very slightly included
  - SI1 and SI2: slightly included
  - I1, I2, and I3: included
- *Carat.* A measure of the diamond's weight, not the size as most people think. One carat equals 100 points, which in turn equals 200 milligrams (approximately 0.007 ounce).

Become an educated consumer by taking the time to explore the jewelry stores in your city's diamond district and malls to see for yourself what the wedding bands and engagement rings you like are selling for in retail settings. Keep the four Cs of diamond shopping in mind, then go look for similar styles and quality on eBay.

eBay TIP: A word of caution in buying *any* high-end item such as jewelry: Check the seller's feedback, "About Me" page, and all item page fine print *before you bid*. Seek out sellers who have feedback ratings in the 98 to 100 percent range, then carefully review the actual comments posted by previous customers.

The sellers djjewelry.com, mdcdiamonds.com, signedpiecesinc, mtddiamonds, and facets_wedding_rings are all excellent sellers who provide great quality and value. You can shop mdcdiamonds.com's excellent ring selection by diamond shape. The seller djjewelry.com educates its customers by describing differences in methods of manufacturing wedding bands, and even offers free engraving with its beautiful and affordable wedding sets. The seller mtddiamonds manufactures its own brand-new diamond jewelry and is able to provide you with excellent personalized customer service. Its official off-eBay Web site is http://diamonds-and-engagement-rings.com/. The seller signedpiecesinc sells designer pieces from Tiffany & Company as well as other well-known designers. The seller facets_wedding_rings (a division of signedpiecesinc) manufactures its own line of wedding bands and engagement rings. Its statements on its "About Me" page are quite impressive:

> Facets is a brand of jewelry created in platinum and 18K gold, using only collection quality diamonds—diamonds that are F-G color and VVS-VS clarity. Every piece of Facets jewelry comes with a Facets certificate. Facets diamonds of 0.40ct or more are GIA certified, D-H in color and IF-VS2 in clarity. These diamonds are only ideal and premium cut with depth ranging from 59% to 62.7% and table ranging from 53%-61%. Minimum standards for polish and symmetry are "Good/Good". Each Facets diamond ring comes with a GIA certificate and a Facets certificate.

If you did your homework, you would realize that facets_wedding_rings has diamond cut/color/clarity standards similar to those of Tiffany & Company, the esteemed jewelry company that diamond expert Fred Cuellar describes as "practically beyond reproach. They represent quality with a capital 'Q.'" We heartily agree.

There is a little-known program on eBay called the "Authenticator Pre-Certified Jewelry Program (APJ)." You can read about this program by going directly to http://pages.ebay.com/apj/index.html. Here is what the program is all about:

> The Authenticator Pre-Certified Jewelry Program is a relationship between eBay and Saleslink, an eBay approved third-party logistics company. This relationship enables buyers to purchase fine jewelry on eBay with greater confidence and peace of mind. By combining the assurance of independent certification and laser inscription of all APJ items by either the Gemological Institute of America (GIA) or the International Gemological Institute (IGI) with the auditing and in some cases direct shipping by Saleslink, the APJ program assures buyers are getting the quality jewelry that they are paying for.
> - APJ items are graded by either of the two leading gemological laboratories (GIA or IGI).
> - Buyers receive a GIA or IGI grading certificate, which can assist in a quicker, more accurate appraisal of your item.
> - The laser inscribed serial number provides verification of authenticity and assists law enforcement investigative processes in the event of theft or loss.

As you can see, by searching for jewelry items under the APJ program, you can be doubly assured that you will be getting what you paid for (see Figure 8-13). The APJ program has very strict and stringent qualifications for sellers—they have to have high feedback scores in addition to a high percentage of positive feedback (more on seller qualifications on http://pages.ebay.com/apj/qualifications.html). To search for jewelry that qualifies for the APJ program, go to

Site Map > Categories > Jewelry & Watches > Authenticator Pre-Certified

You can also search for certified diamonds on eBay with the keyword combination *(EGL,IGI,GIA) cert**. Certified diamonds include a certificate of appraisal from the International Gemological Institute (IGI), the Gemological Institute of America (GIA), or the European Gemological Laboratory (EGL). Certification allows the buyer to have peace of mind about the stone and/or jewelry he or she is purchasing. It also allows for a quicker, more accurate appraisal of the item's value for insurance and investigative purposes. You can shop eBay for great deals on amazing diamonds.

Figure 8-13 Find amazing deals on jewelry that qualifies under the APJ program.

It takes a bit of bravery to purchase jewelry online, but if you take the time to do research on a seller's reputation, store policies, return/exchange policies, and items for sale, you can save big when purchasing your wedding jewelry.

eBay TIP: Visit a jeweler or jewelry sales professional to measure your ring size before you begin your shopping. This service is usually offered free of charge at your local jewelry store. Ring size is critical when ordering rings online. Having the correct ring size eliminates the need (and extra cost) to resize a ring. And it's always easier to size *down* than to size *up*. If you need a size 6 and there's only a size 5 or 7 up for auction, you're safer with a size 7.

Most of the wedding jewelry on eBay is brand-new items. However, there are some items that have been previously worn (i.e., vintage jewelry, antiques, or estate jewelry) and pieces that are being sold by sellers who no longer have the occasion to wear them (perhaps because of financial and/or personal circumstances). You can get a bargain on eBay if you know where to look and what questions to ask. If the piece you are eyeing was previously owned, ask for documentation that certifies the item (such as an insurance appraisal, a laboratory certificate, or the like). Ask the seller how long the item has been in his or her possession, and how the owner has been caring for and storing the item.

If you have any doubts or further questions concerning jewelry items (new or used), e-mail the seller your questions. Most sellers want your business and are extremely helpful if you have any questions. Obtain an independent appraisal of your purchase as soon as you receive it. Always pay for a high-end purchase with a credit card, on PayPal or by other means, so that if there is any dispute over the transaction, you have a means of obtaining a refund or compensation. If all goes well, congratulate yourself on finding beautiful and affordable pieces of jewelry that you and your spouse will wear for a lifetime.

BRIDESMAIDS' DRESSES AND GROOMSMEN'S TUXEDOS

Yes, you can buy bridesmaids' dresses and even grooms' and groomsmen's tuxedos online (see Figure 8-14). Prices can start as low as $100 or even lower. There's no need to gather the girls together for a group shopping trip to the local bridal salon and have everyone pay retail prices, or to pack the boys into a pickup truck and trudge to the local tux shop for an unwelcome fitting. You can do it all from the comfort of your own home, and have the finished garments shipped direct to your door. (This is especially convenient for the out-of-town attendants.)

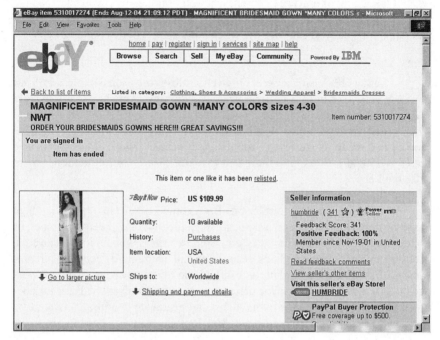

Figure 8-14 Affordable bridesmaids' dresses for your entire wedding party can be found on eBay.

Best Keyword Combinations for Bridesmaids' Dresses and Groomsmen's Tuxedos

- *bridemaid* (dress*,gown*)*
- *(prom,homecoming) (gown*,dress*)*
- *(groom,groomsmen,wedding) tuxedo**

Quick Statistics

- Retail price range: From $100 to $200 and up
- Actual eBay price range: Usually starts at less than $100
- Realized savings: 50 percent or more off retail prices

Before you begin shopping for the dresses, your bridesmaids have some homework to do. They should browse through magazines to see what kind of dresses you and they would like. They might choose to visit bridal salons and department stores to try on different kinds of dresses. Prom gowns and other formal event gowns can also be a good alternative for a bridesmaids' dress, by the way.

eBay TIP: Just as with the bridal gown, be sure a professional seamstress or tailor takes each bridesmaid's measurements: bust, waist, hip, and hollow-to-hem. Remember, some stores will take the measurements free of charge.

If you want your bridesmaids to all have the same style and color gown, consider ordering all the dresses from one eBay seller. The easy way to find out if an eBay seller is able to deliver matching dresses for everyone in your bridal party is to check out the seller's current and past auctions—usually the description will say that multiple orders are welcome and that a variety of sizes are available. Generally there is no extra charge for multiple orders. Most sellers even give a discount on shipping for group orders (usually to a single address). Always shop and order early (four to six months before the wedding) to prevent any mishaps or miscalculations. Allow extra time for any alterations if needed. Sellers humbride, fashionwedding, www_greatdealbridal_com, newgowns, cyberexotic, and jennieqxw offer amazing selections of bridesmaids' dresses.

And, yes, the guys can also find good deals on eBay. They, too, should have a professional tailor take their measurements before shopping. The seller monkeysuits (natch) offers tuxedos for sale for the price of a regular rental. Its official off-eBay Web site is http://www.formalwearoutlet.com/. Although it is not traditionally the role of the bride or groom to pay for the bridal party's outfits, you will still earn their gratitude if you help them save money on their apparel. And eBay is one of the best places to show them how.

TAKE A BREATHER

Congratulations! You are well on your way to having an elegant, affordable wedding the eBay way. After reading through this chapter, you may have realized that eBay is far more than what you previously thought it could be—it is not just a "swap meet" or "garage sale" for collectible enthusiasts. Now you can see that eBay can actually be your one-stop shopping source for your wedding items! But we're not done yet. Go on to the next chapter to find exciting wedding shower and honeymoon gift ideas, as well as honeymoon travel bargains and anniversary ideas, all available on eBay.

9

Sweetening the Honeymoon

Ah, yes, the honeymoon. You waltzed through the ceremony and reception with grace, style, and an unwavering bargain-conscious demeanor. Now comes the alone time for your and your love. Every bride and groom lucky enough to be able to afford a honeymoon no doubt have stars in their eyes and can't wait to sail off on the most romantic trip of their lives, one that they hope they will remember forever. Some, unfortunately, lurch to a sudden stop when they are confronted by the retail costs of a fantasy getaway and all that goes into it. Don't worry, though, because just as we saved you a bundle on the wedding itself by using eBay, we can also sweeten your honeymoon (and subsequent anniversaries) by saving at eBay. And if you're looking for great deals on shower and going-away gifts for another lucky couple, eBay's got those goods at great prices, too.

SHOWER AND HONEYMOON GIFT IDEAS

Before we get to saving money on your honeymoon, let's look quickly at shower and honeymoon gifts. Are you fresh out of ideas about what to give your soon-to-be new spouse? Or maybe you are stumped about what to give another bride and groom as a truly unique wedding gift? eBay offers a myriad of fun, unique, and affordable items in this category. Some examples are "Just Married" items, such as T-shirts and slippers, visors, lingerie, and stuff that the honeymooners can pack into their suitcase. Other examples are personalized items with the newlyweds' names on them, such as towels, pillowcases, picture frames, and so on. Use your imagination by using eBay.

Best Keyword Combinations

To find the perfect gift for a couple or for your new spouse, try using any of the following keyword searches on eBay:

- *(bridal, wedding) shower gift**
- *("just married", wedding) (bride, groom)*
- *(honeymoon, wedding) gift**
- *(bride, groom) gift**
- *("just married", wedding) –dvd –vhs*
- *(bridal, wedding) (honeymoon, lingerie)*
- *(bridal, wedding) portrait*

Quick Statistics for Gifts for the Newlyweds

- Retail price range: $20 to $100 and up
- Actual eBay price range: Starts at less than $10 to $50
- Realized savings: 50 percent or more off retail prices

Imagine the scene: You're at a bridal party, and the bride is about to open the gift you bought her on eBay. In your mind, you can already hear the "oohs" and "aahs" as she opens a present from you that is truly unique—one that no one else has thought of yet. Or imagine the fun that you and your new spouse will have on your honeymoon, sporting "Just Married" hats, shirts, and even flip-flops and collecting best wishes and congratulations from people during your honeymoon travels (as well as airline or hotel upgrades!).

The seller dnsmartshop offers the ever-popular "Just Married" sandals and honeymoon items for the new couple (see Figure 9-1). The seller queblessed3x offers personalized "bride" and "groom" T-shirts with the couple's names and their wedding date on them. The seller designsbyheidi sells Precious Moments–themed "Just Married" items such as shirts, mugs, tote bags, and pillowcases, all personalized.

Would you like a memento of your wedding day that will beautify your new home? How about a painting made from one of your favorite poses at your wedding? The seller veradi (whose official Web site is http://www.studioveradi.com) offers custom-made Impressionist-style 8- by 10-inch paintings on lacquered canvas made from your own wedding photo starting at $15 or less. You spend minimal bucks and get maximum "oomph" for your dollar—the guests at your housewarming party who see your painting will think you spent hundreds.

For a truly unique way to congratulate a bride and groom, or to send anniversary greetings to each other, the seller beyondwishes offers creative, one-of-a-kind CD-ROM greeting cards for weddings, as well as anniversary cards and birthday cards. For more information, its official off-eBay Web site is http://www.beyondwishes.com.

You can also shop for wedding lingerie on eBay, without being embarrassed by pushy salespeople at the local department store. You can enjoy the convenience of having your presents shipped directly to the bride, especially if you are an out-of-town guest (your eBay seller will usually be amenable to this, but check first just to be sure).

Figure 9-1 You can find unique honeymoon gifts for the engaged couple on eBay, such as these matching bride and groom hats.

HONEYMOON TRAVEL NECESSITIES

It's your honeymoon, hopefully one of the most special and memorable trips the two of you will take together. eBay has everything that you need to make your honeymoon affordable. In fact, eBay comes in handy for saving money on everything for your honeymoon, from items you need to take with you to the actual travel arrangements themselves.

Make sure you have a great set of luggage to take all your necessities with you. What, you forgot about luggage? Go on over to eBay, then, for more great deals.

Best Keyword Combinations

To find the best luggage deals, use the following keyword searches:

- *(luggage,backpack,duffel)*
- *luggage set**
- *(Samsonite,Tumi,Kenneth Cole)*

eBay TIP: Bonus search strategy: From the eBay home page, click on "Travel" in the "Categories" side panel, then select "Luggage" from the subsequent page.

Quick Statistics

- Retail price range: $100 to $5,000
- Actual eBay price range: Starts at less than $10 to $200 and up
- Realized savings: 50 percent or more off retail prices

You can choose luggage sets, backpacks, duffle bags, garment bags, suit-cases, or carry-on bags. eBay has an excellent selection at reasonable prices, and most are below retail. You can easily find great brands such as Samsonite, American Eagle, American Tourister, Pierre Cardin, and Tumi, among others (see Figure 9-2). Look for popular features such as retractable handles, wheel-bearings, and the ability to nest one piece of luggage inside another for easy storage when you come back home.

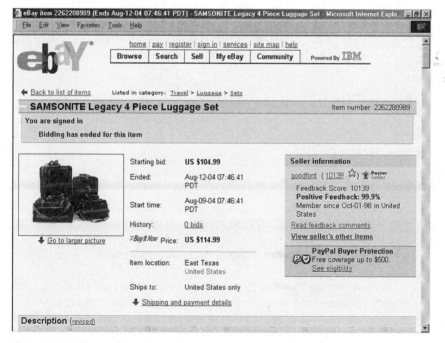

Figure 9-2 Pack your bags! Find a great deal on a complete luggage set such as this one using eBay.

You can also shop for the following honeymoon essentials on eBay:

- Cameras (digital and/or regular film cameras)
- Film
- Swimsuits
- Hats
- Fun Hawaiian-style shirts
- Tote bags
- Sunglasses
- Binoculars
- Snorkel gear
- Towels
- Swim shoes
- Tank tops
- Shorts

HONEYMOON TRAVEL BARGAINS

Best Keyword Combinations

- *(honeymoon,vacation,trip,resort) (INSERT LOCATION HERE)*
- *"all inclusive"*
- *7 (night*,nt*) (honeymoon,vacation,trip,resort)*—you can place the number of nights you desire in your keyword search

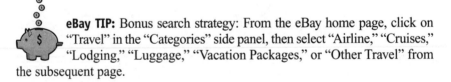

eBay TIP: Bonus search strategy: From the eBay home page, click on "Travel" in the "Categories" side panel, then select "Airline," "Cruises," "Lodging," "Luggage," "Vacation Packages," or "Other Travel" from the subsequent page.

Quick Statistics for Honeymoon Vacations
(Average 7 Nights)

- Retail price range: $3,000 to $5,000 and up (varies)
- Actual eBay price range: Less than $500 to $3,000 and up (varies)
- Realized savings: 50 percent or more off retail prices

Yes, you can find a great honeymoon vacation deal on eBay! You can make eBay your one-stop shop for travel vacation packages and luggage. The easiest way to access these auctions is to click on "Travel" on the "Categories" side panel on the eBay home page. You will then find separate travel categories you can choose from: airline tickets, cruises, lodging, luggage, vacation packages, and other travel. If you are honeymooning, you may be most interested

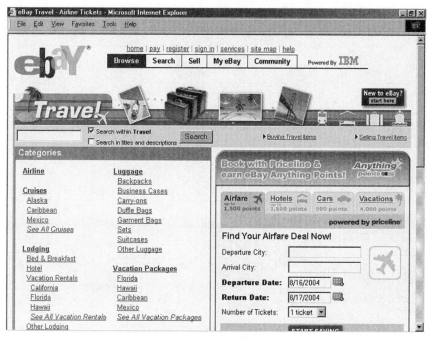

Figure 9-3 The eBay travel page—your starting point for honeymoon searches.

in the categories "Vacation Packages" and "Cruises" (see Figure 9-3). You can pick from lots of auction-style listings as well as affordable Buy-It-Now listings.

eBay TIP: Use the "Vacation Packages Finder" to narrow down your search for the perfect vacation. You can sort by destination, primary activity, travel date, whether airfare is included or not, length of trip, and keywords (see Figure 9-4).

Now you can browse through your options, looking for what you most desire. You can specify the *location* of your honeymoon, the *number of nights*, whether it is *with* or *without airfare*, whether it is *all-inclusive* or *à la carte* (paying separately for each activity or meal), and so on. Bid only on auctions hosted by trustworthy eBay sellers (you can identify them by checking both their feedback and their concurrent listings). eBay does a preliminary screen of these travel package sellers via SquareTrade before permitting them to list in the "Travel" category (see http://pages.ebay.com/community/news/travel_verification.html), but it is still up to you to do your homework before bidding and buying. Look for customer service phone numbers (if offered) and do not hesitate to contact

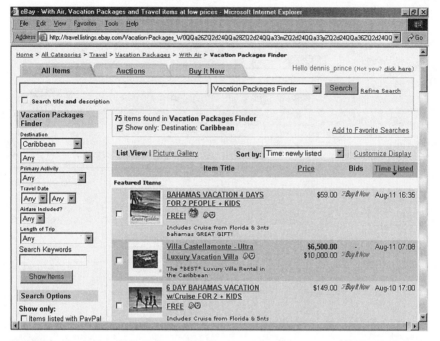

Figure 9-4 Use the "Vacation Packages Finder" tool, an easy shortcut to finding the honeymoon of your dreams.

the seller directly (by e-mail or phone) if you have any questions whatsoever about the auction. If the seller has an official Web site, check that out, too.

> **eBay TIP:** One of the most common features of these vacation deals is the need for the customer to have *flexible travel dates*. Read the fine print carefully to see if there are any blackout dates, any extra fees and taxes, and refund and cancellation policies. Always pay with your credit card (via PayPal or some other official means) so that if any problems arise, your credit card company can assist you in resolving the disputes.

The following is a list of the most popular honeymoon destinations that can be found on eBay:

Caribbean

1. Aruba
2. Cayman Islands

3. Little Dix Bay, British Virgin Islands
4. Montego Bay, Jamaica
5. Nassau, Bahamas
6. Negril, Jamaica
7. Ocho Rios, Jamaica
8. Paradise Island, Bahamas

Mexico

1. Baja California region
2. Cancun, Quintana Roo
3. Guadalajara, Jalisco
4. Isla de Cozumel, Quintana Roo
5. Puerto Vallarta, Jalisco

South Pacific

1. The Marquesas
2. Tahiti

Europe

1. Greece
2. Spain
3. England
4. France
5. Rome
6. Italy
7. Germany
8. Austria
9. Switzerland
10. Sweden
11. Finland
12. Norway
13. Monaco

United States

1. Alaska
2. Hawaii
3. Grand Canyon National Park, Arizona
4. Niagara Falls, New York
5. The California Pacific Coast Highway
6. Hilton Head, South Carolina

7. Pocono Mountains, Pennsylvania
8. Disneyland, Anaheim, California
9. Walt Disney World, Orlando, Florida
10. Massachusetts beach resorts: Cape Cod, Martha's Vineyard, and Nantucket
11. U.S. Virgin Islands

Other Continents

1. South America
2. Australia
3. Asia (China, Thailand, Singapore, etc.)

Sellers cybergetaways, cheap_airfare, cruisegoddess, and hot-traveldeals offer amazing vacation deals—you save up to 50 percent or more compared to full-price vacations (see Figure 9-5). Many travel sellers on eBay, such as vacationgetaways (www.lalalink.com), have their own official Web sites, which you should check out—those Web sites usually offer more information about the seller and perhaps have other great online deals.

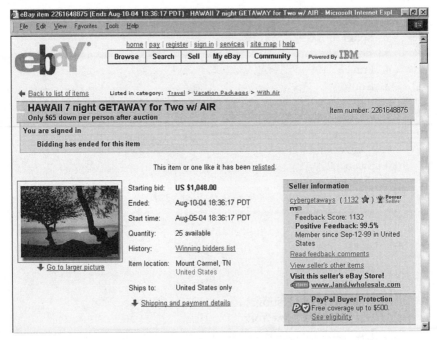

Figure 9-5 Find the honeymoon of your dreams at rock-bottom prices on eBay Travel.

eBay TIP: Check for feedback from other bidders on past transactions who have already gone on their vacations—you can get a better feel as to how great a travel bargain you will get, as well as how good the seller's customer service was. A good example is the seller cruisegoddess—satisfied customers have left feedback *after* taking their vacation. If you really enjoy the honeymoon vacation you find on eBay, consider sending a family member or good friend on a similar vacation as a "thank you." If the service from a particular eBay travel seller is really excellent, consider taking a similar vacation for your anniversary.

THINKING AHEAD: ANNIVERSARY IDEAS

Congratulations! You've already begun considering how to celebrate your first wedding anniversary (or fifth, or tenth, or fiftieth . . .). Looking back with fondness at the year(s) of married life you've spent together, isn't it time to treat yourselves to something wonderful for your anniversary? Or maybe you are shopping for someone else's anniversary. Why not shop eBay for convenience, value, and one-of-a-kind gifts? (See Figure 9-6 for an example of the sort of personalized anniversary gifts you can find at eBay.)

Best Keyword Combinations

- *"wedding anniversary"*
- *anniversary gift**

Quick Statistics

- Retail price range: $50 to $500 and up (varies)
- Actual eBay price range: Less than $25 to $250 and up (varies)
- Realized savings: 50 percent or more off retail prices

Many of the gift ideas mentioned in this chapter and in the previous chapter may apply, of course, so here's a quick review:

- Anniversary jewelry (diamond rings, necklaces, earrings)
- Event tickets (musicals, dinner theaters, concerts)
- Personalized apparel
- Vacation getaways (second honeymoon, and so on).
- Restaurant gift certificates (try the seller restaurant.com)
- Monogrammed handkerchiefs, towels

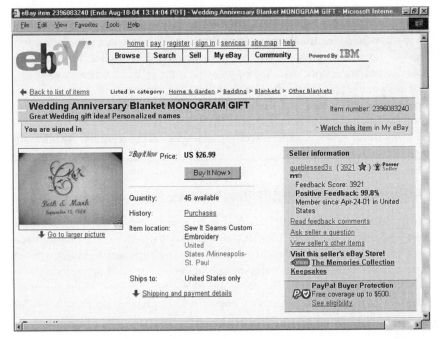

Figure 9-6 An example of monogrammed anniversary gifts at 50 percent or more off retail.

- Engraved picture frames with your favorite photo
- Gift baskets
- Portrait painting from photos (try the seller veradi)
- Hand-drawn sketches or caricatures from photos

eBay TIP: To search for artists who can transform your photos into works of art, go to eBay's site map to search for the category "Everything Else," then click on "Specialty Services," "Artistic Services," "Painting & Drawing." You'll be glad you did.

Remember that list of traditional anniversary gifts based on what year you are celebrating? You can give these traditional anniversary gifts a fun, eBay "twist" by searching for gifts made of the appropriate material. Here is the list:

Anniversary Year	Traditional Gift	Fun eBay Gift Ideas
First	Paper	Gift certificates
Second	Cotton	Personalized apparel (robes, shirts)
Third	Leather	Leather wallets, jackets
Fourth	Linen	Linen clothing
Fifth	Wood	Weekend in a log cabin
Sixth	Iron	Golf clubs
Seventh	Wool	Wool sweaters
Eighth	Bronze	A tan from a sunny vacation
Ninth	Pottery	Unique vases for home décor
Tenth	Tin, aluminum	Cookware
Eleventh	Steel	Grilling equipment
Twelfth	Silk	Silk lingerie or apparel
Thirteenth	Lace	Lace lingerie
Fourteenth	Ivory	Tickets to a piano concert
Fifteenth	Crystal	Swarovski crystal
Twentieth	China	Anniversary plates
Twenty-fifth	Silver	Silver jewelry
Thirtieth	Pearl	Pearl jewelry
Thirty-fifth	Coral, jade	Scuba/snorkeling lessons
Fortieth	Ruby	Ruby rings, pendants
Forty-fifth	Sapphire	Sapphire rings, pendants
Fiftieth	Gold	Gold jewelry
Fifty-fifth	Emerald	Emerald jewelry
Sixtieth	Diamond	Diamond jewelry

Of course, when you're planning a party or get-together to celebrate your anniversary, make sure to shop on eBay for party decorations and favors. Have a great wedding anniversary eBay-style that's reminiscent of your fabulous eBay wedding!

10

Troubleshooting Problems
with eBay Sellers

It's absolutely true that 99.99 percent of all eBay transactions are completed successfully, but try to convince a buyer who has just endured a nightmare deal of this glowing statistic. Yes, once in a while a deal on eBay does go along a rocky path; sometimes the problems can be resolved, and other times the deal remains bogged down in the realm of disappointment and disenchantment. Don't worry, but do be prepared. This chapter offers proven methods that will keep you ready to redirect a deal that's going astray, while also helping you ultimately steer clear of sellers who may not be as committed to doing good business as they should be.

WHEN GOOD DEALS GO BAD

So you've bid on and won a great bridal bargain on eBay; terrific. You've paid the seller promptly, and now you are eagerly awaiting the arrival of your great wedding items; that's the fun of eBay. And so you wait and wait, and then wait some more. You think to yourself, "Wow, it sure is taking a long time for those items to arrive." You continue to wait, and soon fear that your items may *not* arrive after all begins to creep in—that the seller who took your money has taken it on the lam. No, this *isn't* the fun of eBay, and it's not the way it generally works.

If you think there's a problem on the seller's end, don't panic and don't jump to harsh conclusions too quickly; there may be a reasonable explanation. It's possible, after all, that your merchandise was lost in the mail or has been otherwise unexpectedly rerouted. It's also possible that the seller is quite behind on completing business at his or her end (never a good excuse, but a reality nonetheless), or that the seller has forgotten to ship your goods. Leaving aside the possibility of a truly nefarious deed for the moment, here are some action plans you can use to attempt to complete the transaction to your satisfaction.

Step 1: Open the Lines of Communication

Return to the listing page of the item you purchased (you can search by completed items, search the search page by specifying your ID in the "Items by Bidder" area, or go to "My eBay" and locate the item you've won). Once you've navigated to the listing page, click on the "Ask seller a question" link within the "Seller Information" block. In the next screen that's provided, send your seller an e-mail note asking for the status of your item: Was payment successfully received, when was the item shipped, when can you expect it to arrive, and what carrier tracking information is available to monitor the package's journey to you?

By doing this, you're reminding the seller of her or his commitment to complete the transaction, and you may find that you've just jogged the seller's memory or alerted the seller to a wayward shipment that he or she, too, believed should have already arrived. Again, this could be a carrier's problem, or it could be an unintentional oversight on the seller's part. Don't jump down the seller's throat; be courteous but firm and ask the seller for reassurance that your item is on its way.

Most often, sellers will respond promptly and will be eager to work with you to clear up the situation. If your seller responds and e-mails you with appropriate shipment information, wait a few more days to see whether your merchandise arrives. Perhaps there was a delay on the seller's part, or perhaps there was a hold-up at the post office.

If your merchandise arrives without any additional problems, and all is well, leave your seller positive feedback and send a short e-mail to let him or her know that you received the package. Ask the seller nicely to leave you positive feedback as well, to mark a successful completed transaction between the two of you.

Step 2: Obtain the Seller's Contact Information

If the seller does not respond to your e-mail inquiry and you're concerned that this may be a case of deliberate avoidance, you can request the seller's contact information, that is, his or her phone number and address. (Remember that you provided this information when you registered? The purpose of that was to enable eBay members to contact each other if situations like this arise. It's certainly nothing to request on a whim, because others can request your contact information as well. Consider it a silver bullet of sorts and use it sparingly.) When preparing to request a seller's contact information, make sure you have the item number for which you're inquiring (you'll need it to prove that you have a completed transaction with the seller), then navigate to the eBay search

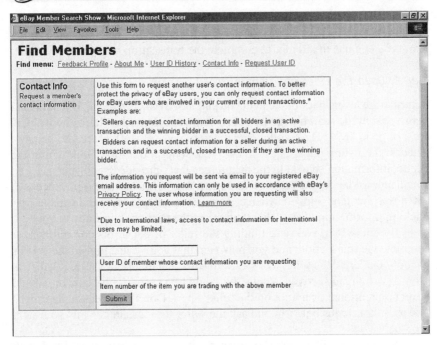

Figure 10-1 If the situation truly warrants it, use the eBay "Find Members" area to request contact information.

page and select the "Find Members" button from the toolbar submenu. Scroll down and submit your request for the contact information (see Figure 10-1).

In the "Find Members" screen shown in Figure 10-1, type in the seller's user ID and provide the item number of the listing from which you purchased. eBay will respond by sending an e-mail to *both* you and the seller: You'll receive the seller's phone number and address in accordance with your request, and the seller will receive *your* phone number and address. This dual notification keeps everything fair and on the up and up, leading members to be truly certain before requesting such sensitive information.

Now, give the seller a phone call and see if you can work out the situation on a person-to-person basis.

If the seller's phone number has been disconnected or is misleading, and you suspect that you may not be able to reach the seller by phone, you can contact eBay and report the situation. eBay's "SafeHarbor" area was designed to assist users with potential problems such as this. Navigate from the site map to "Safe Harbor (Rules & Safety)," then navigate further to the "A–Z Index," and finally to "Investigations" (see Figure 10-2).

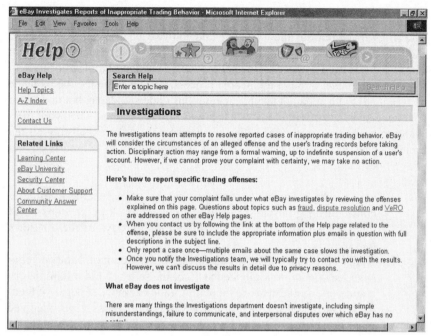

Figure 10-2 The eBay SafeHarbor will assist you in your investigations of sellers who seem reluctant to ship the items you've purchased.

Scroll down to "Contact Information/Identity Offenses," where you will find a link called "False or Missing Contact Information." Find the "Report" link to issue your complaint about the seller's false or missing contact information. Be very specific and include information such as the item number, the date you sent payment, and whether the seller responded to your attempts to make contact. eBay will then take the appropriate steps to contact the seller. If the seller fails to respond to eBay's official inquiries in a timely manner, eBay may suspend the seller's eBay privileges indefinitely, or until the seller complies with eBay's rules and regulations.

If, at this point, your seller finally contacts you and promises to send the merchandise, take the high road: Allow the seller to complete the transaction without further complaints from you. Even if everything comes out all right in the end, you may elect not to purchase from that seller in the future. If, however, you still do not receive your items in a reasonable amount of time, if the seller claims to have sent the item but is unable to provide you with tracking information, or if the seller fails to contact you at all, you may elect to utilize the "Official Last-Resort Options" detailed in Step 3.

Step 3: Official Last-Resort Options

OK, you've been faithful and forgiving, and you've tried everything reasonable and within your power to complete a wayward deal: You've requested shipment details, you've tried contacting the seller, you've engaged SafeHarbor to help prod the seller, and, through this whole process, you've exhibited the patience of a saint, all to no apparent avail. Frustration is understandable, but don't lose your head; there are official last-resort options that you can use when your merchandise never arrives and the seller never responds. After exhausting all the avenues detailed in Steps 1 and 2, here is what you can do to, you hope, get your money back.

1. Go to eBay's Fraud Protection area (http://pages.ebay.com/help/ confidence/isgw-fraud-protection.html) and follow the steps listed there. Make sure that you do this within 30 days of the auction's end.

2. Notify eBay that you have possibly been the victim of fraud and consider leaving appropriate feedback for the seller. Avoid inflammatory comments, and instead be factual. A good example of negative feedback that is not a personal attack would be, "Items never received after payment sent. No contact from seller." Be prepared, though, for the seller to leave negative feedback for you in return.

3. Try dispute resolution services such as SquareTrade (www.square-trade.com). Dispute resolution allows buyers and sellers to interact to resolve conflicts with the help of a neutral third party. The majority of the buying and selling disputes on eBay are resolved with Square-Trade's help. As mediation incurs a fee, be sure the cost of the goods purchased will warrant enlisting outside help. Mediation works only if both parties agree to resolve the issue.

4. Contact your payment provider, such as PayPal or your credit card company. Most credit card companies offer 100 percent protection for online purchases (remember the discussion in Chapter 1 regarding your card issuer's warranties as you registered with eBay and an online payment site).

eBay TIP: Go to http://www.paypal.com/cgi-bin/webscr?cmd=p/gen/ protections-buyer-outside for more information on how to possibly get reimbursed using the PayPal Buyer Protection Program. PayPal can investigate the possibility of deducting the amount of your claim directly from the seller's PayPal account. Note, however, that PayPal's Buyer Protection Program is effective only for transactions amounting to $25 or more.

5. To utilize eBay's Standard Purchase Protection Program, visit http://pages.ebay.com/help/confidence/programs-fraud.html to begin the process. First you must file a "fraud alert" to let officials at eBay know what is going on. According to eBay customer service,

> eBay's Fraud Alert encourages communication between a buyer and seller by prompting a seller to get in touch with a buyer to resolve an incomplete transaction. eBay encourages buyers to file Fraud Alerts as necessary because these reports are internally tracked and weighed when considering a seller for possible disciplinary action. Please note that the time frame for filing a Fraud Alert is between 30 and 60 days after the listing ends. To file a Fraud Alert with eBay, please see the following eBay Help page: http://pages.ebay.com/help/confidence/isgw-fraud-protection.html and follow the instructions provided.

6. Next, file a protection claim (make sure you file with your credit card company first, before filing with eBay). eBay can reimburse you up to $200 (less a $25 fee) for your loss.

7. To cover all your bases, consider filing a report with the Internet Fraud Complaint Center, a division of the Federal Bureau of Investigation. The IFCC can be reached at http://www.ifccfbi.gov:

> The Internet Fraud Complaint Center (IFCC) is a partnership between the Federal Bureau of Investigation (FBI) and the National White Collar Crime Center (NW3C). IFCC's mission is to address fraud committed over the Internet. For victims of Internet fraud, IFCC provides a convenient and easy-to-use reporting mechanism that alerts authorities of a suspected criminal or civil violation. For law enforcement and regulatory agencies at all levels, IFCC offers a central repository for complaints related to Internet fraud, works to quantify fraud patterns, and provides timely statistical data of current fraud trends.

8. Consider contacting a law enforcement agency in your hometown or in the seller's hometown.

eBay TIP: Here's another bride success story: It may seem as if it involved a lot of filing and official paperwork, but in the end this may be worth the time and energy you put into it. An eBay buyer bid for and won 100 wedding CD favors from a seller who has since been suspended. She had paid $100 + $18 shipping for her purchase promptly. Weeks turned into months, and after a single e-mailed promise from the seller that "the CDs are on their way," she was $118 poorer with no wedding favors. She first contacted other winning bidders from this seller's past auctions and found out that she was not alone—this seller had done a vanishing act on others as well. She was angry, but she channeled her anger into energy instead, filing reports with eBay, PayPal, SquareTrade, and the IFCC.

eBay was able to reimburse her claim amount (not including the money she spent on shipping), minus a $25 processing fee. Through a stroke of luck, she found the fraudulent seller back on eBay (after being suspended), illegally using an alternative user name. She contacted the seller to demand either a refund or her merchandise. She reported the seller to eBay again, and eBay suspended the seller again. The seller finally agreed to deliver the merchandise. She was so grateful that the issue was resolved, via eBay's excellent customer service, that she voluntarily returned the $75 she received from eBay.

MATTERS OF MISREPRESENTED MERCHANDISE

Sometimes a problem with a transaction doesn't occur until you actually *receive* the goods. What if you receive your merchandise and it's the wrong color, size, or quantity? Or, what if it arrives broken or damaged? Here are some easy steps to resolve the situation:

- Review the sales policies listed by your seller on the auction page. Determine whether he or she offers exchange or refund options if the merchandise is below your expectations.
- Contact the seller immediately and apprise him or her of the situation. If the seller offers a refund or exchange policy, begin the process right away.
- For items damaged in transit, the post office or shipping company will reimburse you only if you purchased insurance on the item. Take your merchandise and all original packaging to your nearest post office to start the paperwork on your claims. Unfortunately, if you elected not to purchase insurance on the item, and it arrives damaged, the seller is not liable for compensating you. That's why it's a good idea to purchase insurance on expensive and/or breakable items. Go to http://www.usps.gov or http://www.fedex.com to look up prices for insurance (they are very reasonable).

As in the case of missing merchandise, try to work with the seller to rectify such a situation; it could be an embarrassing surprise to the seller. If the seller seems apathetic to your needs or has gone outright AWOL on the transaction, you can employ the same resolution steps previously noted. And, in the end, if you're unable to exchange or return a wedding item that doesn't fill the bill, consider offering it on eBay and recouping some or all of your money (or maybe even turning a profit). You know the old adage about what to do when life gives you lemons.

CHALKING IT ALL UP TO GOOD LESSONS LEARNED

Although it's highly unlikely that you'll ever be besieged with bad eBay deals, if a deal does go sour, look for the silver lining. As the best protection is prevention, here are some steps you can take to avoid getting tangled up in unwieldy transactions:

1. Always review a seller's feedback and carefully read what past bidders have had to say about that seller. Sort the feedback to review comments from other buyers only.
2. Be wary of sellers with "private" feedback (feedback that's hidden from public view)—they most likely have something to hide. Steer clear of these sellers—there are plenty of other sellers on eBay who are good businesspeople and are eager to satisfy you.
3. Give strong consideration to the benefits and protections that you'll gain when you pay via an official method such as PayPal or with your credit card.
4. Read auction descriptions carefully. Look for the fine print. Look for ambiguities or inconsistencies. Don't make hasty decisions to purchase expensive items, especially those that are accompanied by a "no returns" sales policy. Since there are so many great wedding items up for bid and sale every day, you have the luxury of mulling over your potential purchases and shopping around.
5. If your item is personalized, expensive, or rare, consider purchasing tracking information and insurance on your item. It's a small price to pay for peace of mind when the item is in transit and until it arrives on your doorstep.
6. Communication is key. It is one of the most important elements of online shopping on eBay. Make sure the e-mail address and contact information that you have recorded at eBay are current at all times—this is how sellers and eBay will contact you. Check your e-mailbox carefully for correspondence from eBay and from your sellers—you don't want the seller's invoice to land in your junk folder before you've had a chance to read it.
7. Just as brick-and-mortar stores and retail Web sites have 30-day limits on purchases, so do the Web sites that can help you (eBay, PayPal, SquareTrade). Don't wait more than 30 days after the auction to take action if something's gone awry.
8. Rest easy knowing that 99.99 percent of the transactions on eBay end successfully, and that if and when the less-than-1-percent specter visits you, there are options and actions you can take to sort things out to your satisfaction.

9. If a bad deal ever befalls you, don't let it leave you jaded about eBay. Just chalk it up to experience, learn from the experience, and continue with your eBay shopping.

After all that shopping, planning, and hectic activity before, during, and after your wedding day, it's time to go on your honeymoon. Relax and bask in the sun, and congratulate yourselves on having had a glamorous, affordable wedding, eBay-style. When you return home, what happens after the honeymoon? Read the next few chapters to find out how you can resell your eBay wedding items on eBay, recoup some of your wedding expenses, and perhaps even turn a profit! If you end up liking the experience of selling on eBay, consider becoming an eBay wedding seller yourself. Read advice from established eBay wedding sellers on how they themselves did it, and how you can, too. It's fun, it's easy, and you'll be helping other eBay brides have their own glamorous yet affordable eBay wedding. By reading the next few chapters, you'll learn how to pass the bouquet (and everything else) to the next couple.

PART 3

AFTER THE HONEYMOON—
GOING INTO BUSINESS
FOR YOURSELF

11

Passing the Bouquet (and Everything Else) to the Next Couple

Congratulations! You're a newly wedded couple, and you are about to embark on a journey together that you hope will last the rest of your life. As all the excitement and activity winds down and you look back on your eBay wedding and honeymoon memories with fondness, you are also looking forward to settling down and settling into your new life together. Often you'll find that this means you have some things left over from the celebration that, well, you no longer want or need. The great thing about having an eBay wedding is the fact that you can recoup some of your wedding expenses and perhaps even turn a postwedding profit by selling on eBay those items that you have no use for. Here are some easy steps on how to pass the bouquet (and everything else) to the next couple, eBay style.

TAKING INVENTORY

As the dust settles following the festivities, take stock of the wedding items you have that you believe served their purpose well, and, if some of those items truly don't have any sentimental value to you, ask yourself if they would be of interest to other budget-minded brides and grooms. That's right, this is where you can thin out the wedding goods you no longer need and possibly recoup some of the investment (frugal though it was) that you laid out. Items that will sell are, of course, those that are in good-as-new condition. And since you most likely used your wedding items only once and only for a few hours, they are the ideal items to post on eBay. Some examples include (but are not limited to) your

- Wedding gown, veil, tiara, gloves, shawl, shoes, garment bag, and other bridal accessories
- Bridesmaids' gowns, gloves, shawls, shoes, and bridesmaids' accessories
- Florals: silk bridal and bridesmaids' bouquets, boutonnieres, corsages, flower girl basket, ring pillow
- Ceremony decorations: silk floral arrangements, pew bows, aisle runner, unity candleholders, and so on
- Reception decorations: silk floral table centerpieces, candleholders, extra favors, extra place card holders, wedding card box, wedding banners, wedding lights, cake topper, and so on
- Wedding supplies: extra ribbons, bows, tulle, thank-you cards, unused balloons, and so on

Basically, anything that you are willing to part with can be listed on eBay. Remember, keep the stuff that you'd like to have as keepsakes (for example, your toasting goblets, the cake topper, or your personalized unity candle). Sort through your wedding stuff, and make it a joint effort with your new spouse to see how much money you can recoup while still having fun. You can even reuse the original packaging and boxes that you received while you were shopping for your eBay wedding. Save money and save trees at the same time.

GETTING READY: SETTING UP YOUR SELLER'S ACCOUNT

Of course, before you can venture into selling on eBay, you'll need to revisit the registration process, where you first signed up as a buyer. The fastest way to create a seller's account is to click on the "Sign In" text link at the top of eBay's home page. When you enter your user ID and password, eBay will recognize that you're not yet registered to sell and will provide a link to complete this process. eBay will then guide you through the process to create your seller's account, as shown in Figures 11-1, 11-2, and 11-3.

To become an active seller on the site, you'll need to provide valid credit card and checking account information for eBay to keep on file. This is another sensitive area that has been a topic of controversy in years past: Users are uncomfortable with having to surrender sensitive financial information to a Web site. However, to avoid fraud and prevent general tomfoolery, eBay instituted the verification of credit card and bank account information to ensure that users are of legal age to use the site, are identifiable via their chosen financial institutions, and are serious about selling on the site. All of the information you'll enter in this form is protected by the SSL (Secure Sockets Layer) protocol, a secure method whereby sensitive information is transmitted in an encrypted format and is unreadable unless a specific decrypting key is

Figure 11-1 Begin creating your seller's account by providing credit card information.

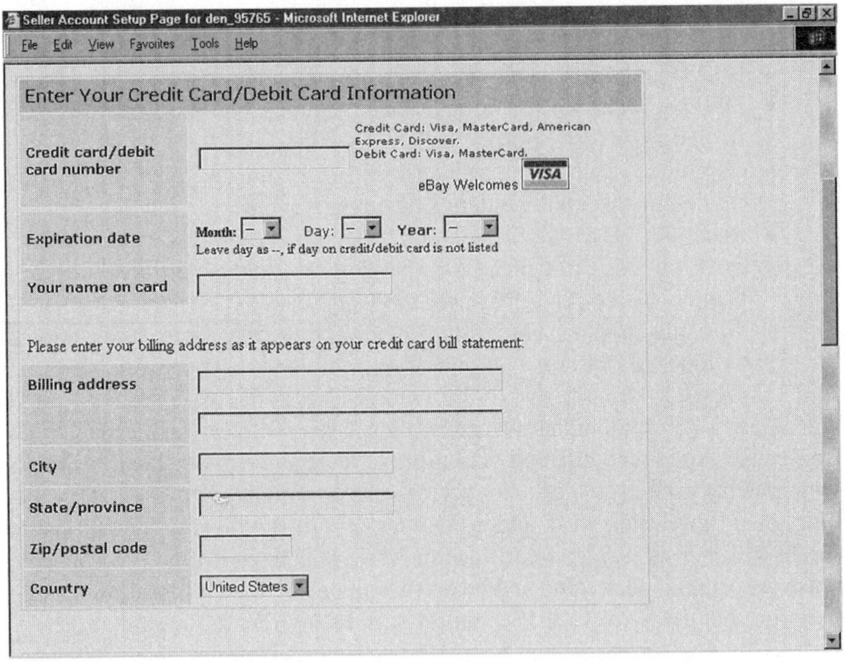

available. Practically all online transfers of this sort of data are handled via SSL transmission.

eBay TIP: Despite all the online security and privacy steps that have been taken over the years, providing sensitive account information such as this can be an uncomfortable proposition for many computer users. For maximum peace of mind, don't simply rely on what sites promise, but check with your credit card issuer and financial institution to determine what sort of privacy and fraud protection they offer. Seek out the sort of protection that provides for assisted dispute of charges and blocking of account activity, both of which are necessary if you ever believe your information has been compromised. With these extra protections in place, you can feel safe about proceeding through this step in setting up your seller's account.

Finally, select how you would like to pay your eBay fees.

Figure 11-3 illustrates the last part of the registration form. Here, you'll decide how you wish to pay your eBay fees. Whenever you list an item for

Enter Your Bank Account Information

Sample Check - U.S. Account (lower left corner)   View Non-U.S. Account Checks

⑈739811823⑈   632   0173136142⑈

The Bank Routing number   The check number should   The Checking Account number is usually
is 9 digits between the   match the number in the   to the left of ⑈. If check number is left of
⑈ ⑈ symbols   upper-right corner   account number, ignore check number

Note: These three sets of numbers may appear in a different order on your check.

| Account owner | | | |
| First name | MI | Last name |

Country of account   United States ▾

Bank name   You can find the Bank Routing # and the Checking
                       Account # on the bottom of your check, as shown
                       above.

Bank routing #

Checking account #

Retype Checking
account #

Figure 11-2 Next, enter your bank account information.

---

② **Choose how you'd like to pay for eBay seller fees**

⊙ Deduct eBay seller fees from my checking account at no extra charge (recommended)

- eBay Direct Pay is a secure, convenient way to pay eBay. Your personal information is encrypted, safe, and protected. Learn more.
- If you are a business owner, you can now use your business bank account

○ Charge any eBay seller fees to my credit card

Note: eBay only accepts US checking accounts for eBay Direct Pay

Continue ...
After clicking "Continue," please wait up to 30 seconds while we process your information

Announcements | Register | Safe Trading Tips | Policies | Feedback Forum | About eBay

Copyright © 1995-2003 eBay Inc. All Rights Reserved.
Designated trademarks and brands are the property of their respective owners.
Use of this Web site constitutes acceptance of the eBay User Agreement and
Privacy Policy.

TRUST**E**
site privacy statement

Figure 11-3 In this screen, select how you would like to pay your eBay fees.

sale, a fee will be assessed. When you select special selling features, additional fees may be assessed. When you sell an item, a sales commission (known as the *final value fee*) will be assessed. The fees aren't exorbitant by any means, but you will be charged for listing and selling your items in this worldwide marketplace. At the end of each month, you'll need to pay your outstanding balance for the month's accumulated fees, and this last part of the seller's account form is where you indicate whether you wish eBay to deduct the fees from your checking account automatically or whether you'd prefer to have your credit card charged instead.

eBay TIP: How you choose to manage payment is up to you, but remember that if you accumulate fees on your credit card and fail to pay off that credit card balance at the end of the billing cycle, your card issuer will charge interest on your unpaid balance. With respect to making your fortune, you'll want to be sure that the assessment of interest charges doesn't unnecessarily increase your cost of using eBay, thereby reducing your ultimate profit.

Complete the information on the form and click on the button labeled "Continue." Your account information will be encrypted and verified via VeriSign. After about 30 seconds or less, if everything checks out, you'll see a screen like the one in Figure 11-4, indicating that you've completed the setup of your seller's account. Good work!

LISTING YOUR ITEMS ON eBAY

With your seller's account established, now comes the fun part: creating listings—perhaps like those you shopped when you were planning your wedding—to tantalize and excite the next wave of eBay brides. In a nutshell, here's how easy it can be to pass your unneeded wedding items along to the next bride and groom.

First, click on the "Sell" button located at the top of the eBay home page (see Figure 11-5).

In the succeeding screen, you'll decide whether you want to list your item as a standard auction listing or as a Buy-It-Now fixed-price offering (see Figure 11-6). Then click on the "Sell Your Item" button and begin your listing.

From here, follow the screen-by-screen instructions as eBay guides you through the five steps in listing an item: (1) Category, (2) Title & Description, (3) Pictures & Details, (4) Payment and Shipping, and (5) Review and Submit. Here's a brief rundown of each step to help you in your first listings.

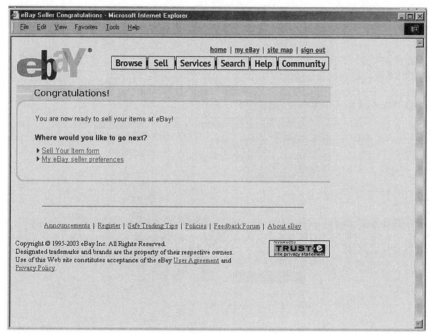

Figure 11-4 The simple yet effective confirmation screen indicating that your seller's account has been successfully set up.

LIST YOUR WEDDING ITEMS FOR AUCTION OR SALE ON eBAY

Now here comes the exciting part. The great thing is, once you get the hang of posting a few items, the rest are really easy. Here are some easy tips on how to post your wedding items on eBay:

- *Step 1: Category.* Select your category by using the easy pull-down tools. You can also enter item keywords in the search bar to let eBay suggest a category for you. You can also choose to list your item in a second category simultaneously (for greater exposure), but this will incur additional listing fees.
- *Step 2: Title & Description.* Enter your item title in the appropriate space. Make judicious use of the space provided (there is a maximum of 55 characters, including spaces), and avoid extraneous "noise" words such as *the, and,* or *a.* Be as specific as possible, and yet concise. For example, you can type in *WEDDING GOWN DRESS Like New White Sz 12 Vera Wang.* Use the search term discussions in Chapter 8 to

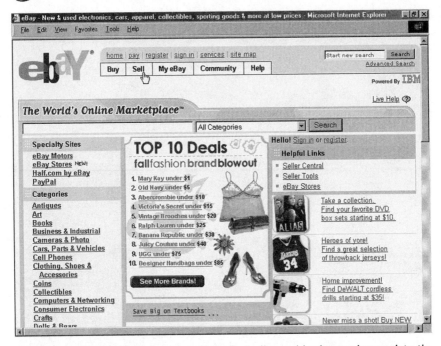

Figure 11-5 Click on "Sell" from the eBay main toolbar and begin your journey into the wonderful world of becoming an online auctioneer.

guide you in crafting your item title. For an additional fee, you can place more information in the available "Sub-Title" to help you catch an eBay bride's eye more easily. For example, you can type in *Retails $1,200 Get a steal now!!* Though this will cost an additional fee, some sellers say that the subtitle provides the right amount of encouragement to help shoppers stop in and take a closer look.

- *Step 3: Pictures & Details.* This is one of the busiest screens of the listing process, and there's a great deal of information to provide as you ready your listing. Begin by providing a full description of the item, making sure that all pertinent details are presented to help the bidder or buyer make an informed decision. Also within this space, provide clear instructions regarding your payment policy (how you'll accept payment and how soon you'll expect to receive it), your shipping policy (how you'll ship the item, the costs to be incurred, and the expected time for delivery), and your return and exchange policy (if you'll accept returns, if you'll offer refunds or exchanges, and under what circumstances).

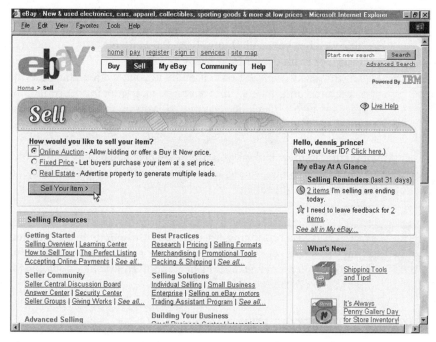

Figure 11-6 Let 'em bid or buy it now? You decide how you'll list your item for sale.

With that done, now enter your Starting Price, Buy-It-Now Price (if you want to offer that simultaneously), and Reserve Price (if you want to establish a lowest price at which you'll sell). Then it's on to deciding the duration of your listing (1, 3, 5, 7, or 10 days), the quantity you're offering, the geographic location of your item, and the all-important images (see the discussion of that later in this chapter).

There are many listing "features" that you can elect to use (listing designers, bold text, and so on), but few of them really make a difference to the success of your listing; most of them only cost you additional listing fees. The Gallery option, however, is very useful, and you should consider using it. Essentially, it places a small version of your item picture on an eBay search hit list, allowing shoppers to get an immediate look at your item within a results list of items that matched their query.

- *Step 4: Payment and Shipping.* Although you offered the details of this in your item description, this fourth step of the listing process allows you to further define your policy. Select the methods of payment you are willing to accept. Outline your shipping costs, and give specific payment instructions. Select the locations you are willing to ship to—specify whether you will ship only to the United States, to specific countries, or to all countries.

- *Step 5: Review & Submit.* Look carefully at your auction title, description, pictures and details, and payment and shipping information. Correct any errors. Click on "Submit" if everything looks good. Congratulations! Your wedding item is now for sale on eBay!

Although the first few listings you offer may take you a bit of extra time, you'll soon whip through the process quickly as you become an experienced wedding (and anything else) seller.

 eBay TIP: If you're looking for detailed instructions for listing and selling as well as some proven methods for getting the best prices for your goods, please see Dennis Prince's book *How to Sell Anything on eBay . . . and Make a Fortune!*

QUICK TIPS FOR BETTER ITEM IMAGES

Your pictures can truly be worth a thousand bucks if you take the time to manage your item images well when you list items at eBay. In fact, these days, your opportunity to sell an item is almost entirely dependent upon whether or not you've provided good images for prospective bidders to see. The good news is that imaging has gotten incredibly simple, with digital cameras and flatbed scanners having become highly affordable and image hosting being readily available at your nearest ISP as well as at eBay itself.

First, if you employ some simple photo-taking techniques, you will have put your item in the best position to sell:

- Unless your item is flat and will fit on a scanner bed, a digital camera is your best bet for capturing images from a variety of angles.
- Ensure that your item is placed against a neutral, contrasting background (nothing cluttered that will look sloppy or detract from the item itself).
- Whenever possible, photograph under natural light for best effect. Otherwise, use incandescent lights situated on either side of the item (as in a photo studio).
- Use a tripod for a steady and crisp image.
- Use an image-editing program to crop or enhance the photo as necessary.

- Capture images at a resolution that will result in a file size of 40 kB or less. If the image is larger than this, there may be a delay in display, forcing your potential bidders to wait (or not!). Use your image-editing software to reduce the size if necessary.
- Store your images on your PC or upload them to your personal Web space (often provided free by your ISP).

Recall that Step 4 of the listing process is where you select the images that will accompany your item. You have two choices for uploading images. First, in the eBay "Pictures & Item Details" listing form, designate images from your PC using eBay's Picture Services image hosting. The first image is free; additional images incur a small fee. eBay Picture Services will locate the image file on your PC and upload it for you.

If your images are stored elsewhere on the Web, use the URL address window to specify an image.

eBay TIP: If you're handy with HTML (HyperText Markup Language), you can elect to reference images directly within the description area of the eBay listing form. This way, you can list more images and not incur the fees for adding additional pictures.

Always be sure to review the item listing before submitting it to ensure that your images are being displayed properly.

Why do images matter? If your item has a great description, what more can an image provide? Consider these compelling reasons why bidders feel the need to see an image before they'll bid:

- Images provide a nearly indisputable reference for item identification and authentication.
- Images allow bidders to compare what they see with what's been written in the item description, calling attention to any potential discrepancies.
- Images offer close-up views and alternative angles (assuming that the seller has included these) to allow the bidder a more complete visual inspection.
- Images can relieve bidders of having to contact the seller and wait for a response, provided that there's enough time left before the auction ends.

While images are not 100 percent required in order to list an item or even make a sale, many bidders will flatly refuse to bid if an image of the item isn't available to view.

UNDERSTANDING eBAY FEES

We've mentioned the fees associated with listing and selling items on eBay, so, in a nutshell, here are the details of the fees we're talking about. When you list an item, always look for ways to reduce your insertion fees (such as avoiding needless upgrade fees) and thereby increase your final profit. Note also that eBay's fees are subject to change and may eventually differ from what you see here. For the most current eBay fees, visit eBay's fee page at http://pages.ebay.com/help/sell/fees.html.

Insertion Fees

Starting or Reserve Price	Insertion Fee
$0.01–$0.99	$0.30
$1.00–$9.99	$0.35
$10.00–$24.99	$0.60
$25.00–$49.99	$1.20
$50.00–$199.99	$2.40
$200.00–$499.99	$3.60
$500.00 or more	$4.80

Final Value Fees

Closing Price	Final Value Fee
Item not sold	No fee
$0.01–$25.00	5.25% of the closing value
$25.01–$1,000.00	5.25% of the initial $25.00 ($1.31), *plus* 2.75% of the remaining closing value balance ($25.01 to $1,000.00)
Over $1,000.01	5.25% of the initial $25.00 ($1.31), *plus* 2.75% of the initial $25.00–$1,000.00 ($26.81), *plus* 1.50% of the remaining closing value balance ($1,000.01–closing value)

Reserve Price	Fee
$0.01– $49.99	$1.00
$50.00–$199.99	$2.00
$200.00 and up	1% of reserve price (up to $100)

Feature	Fee	Feature	Fee
Gallery	$0.25	Border	$3.00
Listing Designer	$0.10	Highlight	$5.00
Item Subtitle	$0.50	Featured Plus!	$19.95
Bold	$1.00	Gallery Featured	$19.95
Buy It Now	$0.05	Home Page Featured	$39.95
Scheduled Listings	$0.10	Quantity of 2 or more	$79.95
10-Day Duration	$0.20	Gift Services	$0.25
		List in Two Categories	x2

COMPLETING A SUCCESSFUL TRANSACTION

When your listing ends with a winning bidder, it's time to complete the transaction. This is safe and fast, especially if you accept PayPal payments.

- Log on to "My eBay" with your eBay user name and password. Go over to "Items Sold" to look at your most current completed listings.
- From the "My eBay" page, you can easily manage your completed listings. You can contact your buyer, view his or her payment status, leave feedback, print a shipping label for your buyer (if your buyer paid with PayPal), relist the item (if you have duplicates or if the item didn't sell), look up your buyer's e-mail address and zip code, or send a payment reminder.
- If your buyer prefers to send you a check or money order, be prompt in e-mailing him or her as soon as you receive it in the mail. Send out your package promptly. Leave positive feedback for your buyer, and urge her or him via e-mail to do the same. Remind your buyer to leave you feedback by also including a packing slip with a simple note as a reminder. Congratulations! You have just completed a successful eBay transaction.
- If for some reason your buyer does not respond to your e-mails and invoice, you can send a Payment Reminder via your "My eBay" page. If you still don't receive a response within a reasonable amount of time, you can scroll down to the "Selling Links" on your "My eBay" page and click on "Report an Unpaid Item." Follow the easy steps to contact your buyer and/or get a refund of your listing fee if you have a strong feeling that your buyer isn't going to contact or pay you. Leave appropriate feedback for your Non-Paying Bidder. Then dust yourself off and relist your item (eBay will refund you the listing fee

if your item sells this time); 99.9 percent of the time, your next buyer will be a conscientious eBay member who is truly looking for a bridal bargain.

READY TO SELL MORE?

Now that you've mastered the basics of selling your wedding items on eBay, get ready to kick into high gear by reading the next chapter to find out even more advanced selling techniques straight from the experts themselves—eBay sellers (most of whom sell on eBay full-time!) who specialize in selling wedding items. Learn tips and tricks to get the most bids for your wedding items, and get a peek at how to start your own online wedding store on eBay. Also in the next chapter, learn how brick-and-mortar wedding shops have expanded their business by using eBay. Perhaps you'll be bitten by the eBay bug like they were and transform yourself from eBay bride to successful eBay seller! Read on to find out how.

12

How to Become an
eBay Wedding Seller

So you're thinking of becoming an eBay wedding seller. What a great idea! When you do, you'll join thousands of other eBay wedding sellers who not only enjoy a profitable business, but also love what they do. Luckily, since you've made your way through the exciting adventure of buying what you needed for your own wedding, you're well on your way to being an expert on the subject. Think about the lessons you learned, the sellers you worked with, and the transactions that, in your mind, were the true jewels of the bunch. With that experience, you're ready to take the best of the best from your own experiences and use them as your guide as you help other brides and grooms to have the best possible eBay wedding experience. Since you've learned so much from the sellers you've shopped with, you're ready to emulate their example and become a stellar eBay wedding seller yourself. If you're considering taking this next step (and why shouldn't you?), this chapter will give you a look at what it takes to step into the wonderful selling opportunity awaiting you at eBay.

FIRST THINGS FIRST:
ESTABLISHING YOUR INVENTORY

Many eager new eBay sellers begin by pondering just how large a business they'd like to launch and how soon they might be able to quit their day jobs after those auction dollars start pouring in. It's good to consider the potential scope of your selling enterprise, but you need to be sure you don't get too far ahead of yourself. Before considering the size of your dream enterprise, begin with the most rudimentary prerequisite of any eBay venture: What are you going to sell? Inventory matters are often a cause of concern, confusion, and sometimes retreat for would-be sellers, who realize that their business can grow only as far as their access to salable goods will take them. We're focused on weddings here, and, as you've just successfully celebrated your own wedding, the good news is that you probably have inventory readily at hand (although you may not realize it immediately). If you're considering becoming an eBay wedding seller, begin with the following points of consideration regarding what you'll sell and where you'll find it:

- Consider items you purchased for you own wedding that may have gone unused. Recall some of our previous discussion about items that ended up not being exactly what you wanted, but that might be exactly what another bride was seeking. Consider items that were only "gently" used during your ceremony and ensuing celebration. A savvy bride and groom realize that these sorts of items (those that would be unlikely to be kept as mementos) are the perfect beginning of an eBay seller's inventory.
- Now think of creative ways to find wedding items that you can purchase and then resell at a profit. Perhaps you found some incredible deals while you were scouring eBay for your own wedding and realized that, whether the items were miscategorized, misspelled, or missed by other eBay bidders and buyers for some other reason, those are perfect purchases for resale. All you need do is relist the goods in a more compelling and visible manner and, poof!, you've made a profit.
- Next, recall your visits to the various craft stores, home improvement stores, discount stores, department store clearance sales, dollar stores, and other such places on the Internet, and look for additional bargain purchases that, based on your previous research, can provide goods that will likewise yield a quick profit on eBay.
- As you consider the goods you'll sell, keep in mind that items that are in new and like-new condition generally sell better than items that show more wear and tear (recall how selective you were when you were shopping eBay for the same sort of affordable elegance).
- Enterprising brides tend to purchase items that they themselves can resell after their wedding. Keep this in mind when choosing to sell trendy items versus traditional goods.
- Think of unique items and services that other sellers do not offer. If you are proficient at flower arranging, sewing, personalization, or other wedding-related services, consider offering those services just as you saw others doing during your eBay shopping excursions.

On a non-wedding-related point, take the same approach to considering other goods that you could possibly sell on eBay and that could buoy your business venture. If you believe you have the expertise to specialize in another sort of commodity (or several), research the activity for such goods on eBay (always monitor the completed listings) and make it a point to familiarize yourself with eBay's own "Hot Items" report, which reveals what's hot and what's not in the online realm. To find it, visit the "Seller Central" area (use the eBay site map page to link to "Seller Central"), then choose the "What's Hot" link along the left-side column of links. In the next screen, select the "Hot Items by Category" text link to launch the Adobe Document Viewer (it's free from www.adobe.com if you don't already have it on your computer), where you can review the detailed statistics of what eBay itself has identified as being the most popular items recently sold on the site (see Figure 12-1).

Determining what you'll sell is probably the most important starting point for launching an eBay-based business. Be sure to give it plenty of thought. Then, when you've settled on an inventory plan (maybe wedding goods, right?), get ready to take the next steps into the exciting realm of eBay merchandising.

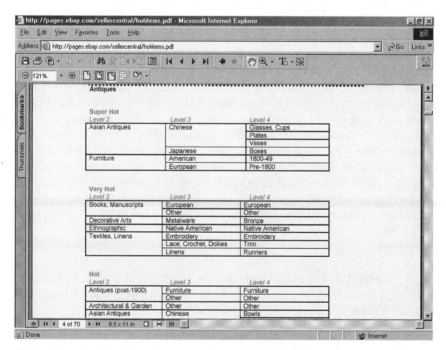

Figure 12-1 eBay's Hot Item list is an Adobe (.pdf) document that you can easily download and review from eBay's "Seller Central" area.

eBay TIP: Most folks start their eBay businesses by simply cleaning out their closets, attics, basements, and other such places and getting rid of all the things that clutter their lives. As you've likely seen from your buying activities, it seems that just about anything can be sold on eBay (and usually sells). Therefore, if you want to go beyond just wedding goods, take a look around your home to find things that you are ready to discard, then consider listing them on eBay instead of hauling them off to the trash. We maintain that everybody has a cache of unwanted items at his or her feet that can be sold for *at least* $3,000 to $5,000 total at eBay. Therefore, don't throw it away . . . throw it on eBay!

A-LISTING WE WILL GO

Now that you have a supply of items to sell, either wedding leftovers or anything else that you may have to offer, it is time to list your goods. You can start by listing items one at a time using eBay's "Sell Your Item" form; you'll find it by clicking on the "Sell" button seen in the main toolbar at the top of practically every eBay screen. From there, follow the on-screen directions to navigate through the five-step listing process, and before you know it, you'll be selling on eBay.

If you have quite a stockpile of goods that you want to sell or if you have a steady source of inventory that can support a large volume of concurrent and repeatable listings, turn to eBay's "Turbo Lister" tool to create and launch batches of listings quickly and easily. Visit the site map and find the "Turbo Lister" link. From there, follow the instructions for downloading the Turbo Lister program to your computer. Once you have downloaded this tool, you can use it to create listings off eBay in batches as large or as small as you want and with the same information and features that you give when you list items directly within the site. Then it's just a matter of determining when you want to upload your batch of listings to eBay, and, in one fell swoop, you can launch multiple items for sale with a single click of your mouse. If the items you're selling can be sold again and again (that is, if you have a steady inventory of such goods), you merely relaunch the listings whenever you like without having to re-create all of the listing information again.

eBay TIP: For the full rundown on the do's and don'ts of successful eBay listing, see Dennis L. Prince's best-selling book, *How to Sell Anything on eBay . . . and Make a Fortune!.*

Listing Tips to Boost Your Selling Success

Recall some of the previous discussions in this book regarding digging up great "hidden treasures" within eBay as a result of a seller's potential missteps in preparing the item for bid or sale, and take these useful tips into account to help make sure that *your* listings will always stand the best chance of getting seen and getting bought. To keep on topic, we'll steer these tips toward wedding-related items, but you should recognize their applicability to other goods that you may choose to sell.

- Most brides will search by typing the word *wedding* or the word *bridal* in the "Search" bar. Make sure you include these keywords in your titles so that brides can easily find your items.
- Always include clear and detailed photos of your items when you list them on eBay.
- Provide clear, thorough descriptions and important measurements or dimensions of the item to help brides visualize the goods you're offering.
- Let brides know that they can e-mail you at any time with questions about the items.
- Use the Gallery feature and other eBay picture options to maximize the appearance and appeal of your item to prospective buyers.

ESTABLISHING A SUCCESSFUL SALES POLICY

Another thing to consider as you delve into selling on eBay is your policy in offering your goods. More to the point, you'll need to be very clear about how you manage your sales, what customers can expect in terms of service and satisfaction, and how you'll address any potential problems that might arise. Take a proactive approach here, and develop a comprehensive sales policy that helps your potential bidders and buyers understand just how you'll do business and how they can best transact with you to a successful end.

No doubt you've read other sellers' sales policies—those you encountered when you were shopping for your wedding items. Now it's time for you to develop a policy of your own. In short order, here's what a good sales policy should address:

- *Payment terms.* State the forms of payment that you'll accept and when you'll expect payment to be received. It's a good idea to accept multiple forms of payment to allow your customers choices based on their experience and preferences (such as PayPal payments, money orders, and personal checks).
- *Shipping charges:* Describe what shipping methods you offer and whether any other related fees (handling, materials) will be charged. In addition, indicate the fees for insurance and tracking services. Again, it's a good idea to offer several different methods (such as standard delivery, priority delivery, or even overnight delivery) to help meet your customers' specific needs.

- *Shipping restrictions:* As eBay is a worldwide marketplace, you'll need to be clear about whether you'll ship internationally.
- *Guarantees and refunds:* Be extremely clear about whether you'll accept item returns and offer refunds. What conditions, if any, will you put on an item return? It's OK, incidentally, to list an item as "sold as is." Whatever your policy, state it up front to avoid confusion or potential confrontation later.

A final point about your sales policies: expect them to change. That is, as you do more business on eBay, you'll learn which policies work for you and which don't. More importantly, you'll learn whether your policies truly help you attract and retain satisfied customers or whether some stipulations fall short. Always be open about revising and refining your sales policy to the mutual benefit of you and your customers, and you'll be sure to take your eBay business far into the land of success.

A Brief Word about Customer Service

Remember how important finding a good seller that offered superb customer service was to you? You'll want to be sure you can provide the same to your bidders and your buyers, both through your sales policy and through your overall management of your listings. Here are some of the most important service tips to consider when you begin selling on eBay:

- Answer each e-mail promptly to encourage potential buyers to bid on your items confidently.
- Offer fair shipping prices. Use reputable shipping companies, such as FedEx, UPS, and the U.S. Postal Service.
- Avoid hidden fees, such as unstated "handling charges" or "packaging costs" that some sellers have used to artificially and unfairly inflate final sales prices. If you plan to charge such fees, be sure your sales policy states this in order to avoid unexpected surprises for your buyers.
- Ship each item promptly, using sound and sturdy packaging materials. Offer insurance for all goods (allow the buyer to decide whether or not to purchase the coverage), especially for expensive, rare, or breakable items.
- Follow up with your buyers to ensure that they have received their items safely and to confirm their satisfaction.
- Always offer to leave positive feedback for your buyers, and don't be bashful about asking that they do the same for you in return.
- Keep a list of your customers and offer them complimentary notifications of similar goods that may interest them. Always allow customers to "opt out" from receiving future notifications at their request.

GETTING YOUR BUSINESS SHIPSHAPE

One thing many new eBay sellers underestimate is the difficulty of packing and shipping the items they sell. Before you begin listing goods, be sure you're well prepared to properly pack and ship the goods that your buyer is so eagerly awaiting. If you have a shipping solution established up front, you'll be sure not to disappoint a buyer who is anxious to receive the goods she or he has paid for. Before receiving payment, then, ensure that you have the necessary supplies to properly pack the item. Here are the most common supplies you'll need:

- Sturdy shipping boxes or reinforced envelopes
- Box fill (packing peanuts or bubble pack), as needed
- Shipping tape
- Shipping labels
- Shipping forms (as needed, such as insurance forms, customs forms, and so on)

When it comes to packing an item, although this can be something of an art, it's a skill that is easily mastered if you have the right supplies and know how to use them. Here are some expert packing tips to consider:

- Think "lightweight" to save on shipping costs, but not at the expense of safe delivery.
- Pack items snugly in boxes, but don't overdo it lest you damage the item before it ever leaves your home.
- For fragile items, use the "box within a box" method to ensure extra cushioning and protection (still being mindful of total package weight).
- Use rigid mailers or padded envelopes, or insert cardboard stiffeners to protect flat items.
- Be considerate of the recipient and don't overtape or otherwise excessively seal a package; the item could be damaged as the buyer tries to wrest it free.

The good news is that most packaging supplies are available free of charge from the U.S. Postal Service, UPS, and other carriers. You can easily order supplies online for free home delivery or visit a local shipping center. Be sure to visit a carrier's Web site (such as www.usps.com or www.ups.com) for more details.

THE BUSINESS OF GOOD RECORD KEEPING

No doubt about it, record keeping requires discipline, but if you consider this aspect of your business venture at the same time as you plan what sorts of items you will list and where you will obtain your inventory, you'll stand the best chance of establishing an efficient operation. With a well-thought-out plan up front, you'll find it's easy to manage and grow a selling business while taking the pain out of keeping track of your eBay activity. Briefly, here are the sorts of activities and expenditures you'll need to monitor if you plan to launch an ongoing auction business:

- Inventory acquisition and storage costs
- Listing fees and other sales-related costs
- Capital equipment purchases used to support your selling activity (such as computer components, printers and supplies, postal scales, and so on)
- Payment receipt fees (if you use PayPal or other credit card processing services)
- Sales records (the final price of item sold)
- Customer records (most important for maintaining repeat business)

This seems like a lot to track but it's important to keep clear records of your selling activity, especially if you are trying to actually launch a bona fide business (and thousands of people do just that every year). To help ease your worries about establishing a record-keeping regimen and to ensure you can maintain it, consider these tips:

- Adopt a method that's easily repeatable and that can be useful for high-volume as well as low-volume selling.
- Be sure your method is efficient enough that *you* won't be tempted to abandon it in the near future. Record-keeping methods can be enhanced, but if you find yourself changing over to a new style every other month, you may have developed something that's too complex.
- Keep it as simple as possible. You don't have to keep every single bit of data. Decide on the most pertinent information that will serve you for one year's time and go with that.
- Make use of the numerous computer-based tools available today, such as spreadsheet programs, database applications, and even inventory management solutions.

LEARNING FROM THE BEST—SUCCESS STORIES FROM OTHER eBAY WEDDING SELLERS

Selling on eBay can be terrific fun and extremely profitable, but it takes some work. If you're not yet convinced that it can be a beneficial venture for you, or if you're just not certain how you might begin and where you might progress, consider these stories of excellent eBay wedding sellers who have found fun and fortune within the eBay space.

From Hobbies and Helping Others to Becoming Happily Employed on eBay

Many top eBay sellers started out by having craft hobbies or helping friends and family with their weddings. That's exactly what Barbara Dimoush (seller ID packageperfect) did; she's now a certified eBay PowerSeller.

> I actually got started on eBay in January of 2002 with silk flowers, party favors, and Christmas (ornaments and silk pieces) type items. During that time, I helped a few friends with their weddings (I made a lot of pew bows) and did some centerpieces, etc., for charity events. One thing led to another, and the next thing I knew I was selling pew bows on eBay and searching for unusual and very affordable wedding items to add to my existing inventory. I continue to offer silk flowers, party favors, and Christmas/seasonal items and have since added baby shower items in addition to wedding pew bows, flowers, decorations, accessories, and favors. My biggest seller is the lighted rose garland followed by the Holland rose ball. I also do very well w/ my wedding pew bows. I pride myself on designs that are a little different from everyone else's and am constantly looking for different types of flowers and deluxe (some wire edge) high-quality ribbons.

More Success Stories: eBay Self-Starters

Many budding entrepreneurs have discovered that eBay is a great place to start a small business without the fear and financial risk of starting a traditional brick-and-mortar shop.

Cindy Johnson (seller ID jcsm2003), also an eBay PowerSeller, explains how she launched her own enterprise:

> I started selling on eBay almost a year ago. I put up many auctions under many different categories. I began to look at the items I was selling under home decor and thought that many of my items would be a great deal for weddings, anniversary celebrations, bridal or baby showers, if I put them into groups that people could afford. At first I listed only what I thought were traditional things for a wedding, but I soon discovered that everyone has different ideas of what they want for a wedding. I now have topiaries, candleholders, unusual candles, spunglass cake toppers, candelabras, and gifts for bridesmaids. I am continually looking for new and unusual items to offer brides-to-be. Since I have expanded into mostly wedding items (although I still sell many other items in my store), my business has gone through the roof, and I am now an eBay PowerSeller. To pick my biggest seller is hard. It seems to go in waves. The ivy topiaries, rose topiaries, and silver candelabras are very big sellers. They are out of stock right now, but I have many customers on a wait list when they come back in, in June. Right now my biggest sellers are the bridesmaids' gifts I have in my store and up for auction. I have two different styles of unique bud vases, and the brides seem to love them.

From Casual Collector to Professional Proprietor

Many eBay sellers say that they were never interested in owning or operating a business; they were just avid collectors of goods. However, upon seeing the potential within the eBay marketplace, many have launched successful virtual establishments of their own. That's how Lola Tinney (seller ID lolasboutique) got started:

> It started with a fascination for old wedding photos. I was so intrigued by the people in the photos and what they wore. At first I shopped local antique shops, but the photos were few and far between. Then I discovered eBay in 1998. There were so many old photos! My collection grew rapidly. Then I started buying vintage wedding dresses from eBay. I bought one for a New Year's Eve costume party, one for a display at a wedding shower, another for Halloween. I was hooked. I moved from being a buyer to a seller in 2002 after being downsized from my job as a corporate training manager. I enjoyed it so much that I turned it into my full-time job this year. I now have a staff of three and sell over 100 gowns a month. I am continually amazed at the people I meet and their individual stories. I still collect old wedding photos, and I have a collection of vintage gowns. The destination wedding gown is by far my best-selling item. The destination wedding has become very popular, and I can see why. It allows the bride to have both the fairy-tale dress and a fairy-tale location. These dresses are easy to pack and easy to wear, yet still have very romantic touches, such as a sweep train and chiffon or lace overlays. We have also seen a trend toward the themed wedding. Brides are just having more fun these days.

From eBay Bride to eBay Wedding Seller

And, of course, there are the many sellers who began as eBay brides and grooms themselves. Couples like Shannon and Vance Kane (seller ID handykane) have successfully parlayed their positive eBay wedding experience into becoming eBay wedding sellers in their own right, now helping others enjoy a cost-effective eBay-based wedding:

> We are an eBay couple. My husband, Vance, and I have been together seven years, married four, and almost everything for our wedding I purchased off eBay. I also sold my wedding dress on eBay after our wedding for more than I paid for it. We have had a very solid and sought-after wedding business for three years now, and the referrals alone we get from the ecstatic brides would keep us in business. We also offer the most sought-after designs and custom designs that you cannot find anywhere else! We also cater to many high-dollar and pseudo-celebrity events as well. We have also had the mention of one of our brides on TLC's *A Wedding Story*, as she was so pleased that we are the wedding company to develop full lines of items to cater to brides of all races, colors, and ethnicities. We had a large, extravagant wedding four years ago when we ourselves wed, and many people asked us how we did everything on

such a tight budget; they were shocked to find out that we ourselves had single-handedly created the whole affair. Our invitations were a huge success: Everyone was taken aback by their originality, style, and quality. Soon we began receiving phone calls to see if we could do so-and-so's wedding, etc. It started off small; we began taking classes, learning how all of the top wedding designers worked, what the most sought-after items were, and what were the top celebrity wedding choices. We began incorporating everything and became freelance wedding planners/coordinators. Brides never ceased to be amazed at our prices! They always told us that we should raise our prices—we could get paid triple the amount. We always kindly refused: We know how difficult it is to get married on a tight budget, and there is no reason to spend a fortune when the work can all be done for a reasonable price. Since we'd purchased so many of our wedding items on eBay, we decided to try placing our line of invitations on the largest mall on the Net. Quickly our business began to grow and grow. Today we have our own full-time custom design shop and have a small staff. We feel so blessed for what the Lord has given us, being able to run our successful business, that we joyfully give back as much as possible, and our company HandyKane sponsors many charities and families in Third World countries. Our charities are all outlined on our Web site, and also information on how you can become involved! Our best-selling auction/item would have to be our Cinderella line of items, more specifically, our Ancient Royal Scroll invitations. We're the only place you can find them, and they are definitely our most in demand invitations, with the most amazing reviews. Our Cinderella "Royal Reception" Ball tickets perfectly compliment them, making a bride's wedding the event of the year. We have the perfect tailored package for this on our Web site, www.handykane.com.

eBAY AND YOU: LOOKING AHEAD TO YOUR FUTURE

Now that you've read all about how to become an eBay wedding seller, you can read on to find out how to use eBay to start your married life with fun and savings. The next few chapters will address how to use eBay to supplement your wedding registry, deal with duplicate gifts, keep your new home running happily and cost-effectively, and consolidate your belongings and sell the rest. Start your married life with eBay!

13

Supplementing Your Wedding Registry

Congratulations, you're newlyweds! Take a moment to congratulate each other for having successfully planned your budget-conscious yet elegant wedding on eBay. You can now stand alongside other couples like you who have begun their new life together on the right path, one that incorporates a new way of thinking and a breakthrough way of shopping for the things they, and you, want, need, and deserve as a married couple.

Now, as you settle into your new home together and look through the wedding gifts your guests gave you, it's appropriate for you to take stock of what you received and compare it to your wedding registry selections. Once you've finished handwriting your personal thank-you notes to your guests (etiquette says that you should send your thank-you's within two months after receiving your gifts), it's time to see if there are still some items that you need to run your new household, items that perhaps you didn't find in the gift pile. Don't worry, you're not acting spoiled or ungrateful when you sift through all the thoughtful gifts to see if there's something that is still needed. Instead, you are simply determining what you need in order to enjoy your life together. As a seasoned, savvy eBay shopper, it's time for you to return to the auction site to supplement your wedding registry the eBay way.

HOME AND GARDEN GOODS ON EBAY

The best place to start browsing for home and garden items on eBay is the site map. As you've learned in earlier chapters, the "Site Map" link is at the top of every eBay page, so it's hard to miss. It also places you at the very heart of eBay categories and gets you on the ground and running (well, shopping) from day one. Here's how to get to the Home & Garden categories:

Site Map > Browse > Categories > Home & Garden

A quick shortcut to the Home & Garden categories is to go to http://home. ebay.com/. Here you can find virtually anything you can think of for your home, indoor or outdoor (see Figure 13-1). The subcategories are

- Baby
- Bath
- Bedding
- Building & Hardware
- Dining & Bar
- Electrical & Solar
- Food & Wine
- Furniture
- Gardening & Plants

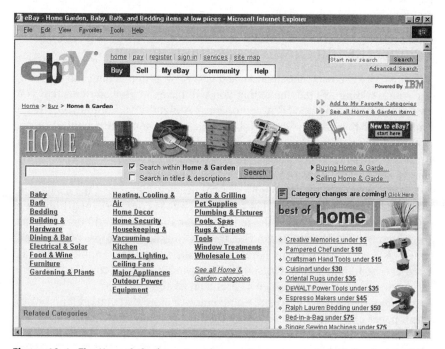

Figure 13-1 The Home & Garden categories on eBay are a great place for newlyweds to supplement their wedding registry.

- Heating, Cooling & Air
- Home Décor
- Home Security
- Housekeeping & Vacuuming
- Kitchen
- Lamps, Lighting, Ceiling Fans
- Major Appliances
- Outdoor Power Equipment
- Patio & Grilling
- Pet Supplies
- Plumbing & Fixtures
- Pools, Spas
- Rugs & Carpets
- Tools
- Window Treatments
- Wholesale Lots

Just as you diligently shopped for all your wedding goods on eBay, you can now turn your attention to outfitting your new home, finding just about anything you want or need.

FINDING THE THINGS YOU NEVER THOUGHT ABOUT

With all the excitement, anticipation, and nervousness of planning and preparing for your wedding, it's inevitable that you will have overlooked items that you, as a new couple, will need ("A can opener? A blender? I thought *you* already had those."). Inevitably, there will be items, big or small, that neither of you previously owned and that neither of you thought to add to your registry. No problem—eBay can once again help you with the items you forgot about (and maybe still haven't considered).

To determine how thorough your gift needs list was, visit the eBay Wedding Gift Blowout page (found at http://pages.ebay.com/weddinggiftblowout, an area on the site devoted to the most popular and useful wedding gift ideas) (see Figure 13-2). There you can find the top 10 gifts that people buy for weddings, as well as categories where many of the things new couples want and need can be found: China, Crystal & Glassware, Home Decor, Kitchenware, Bridesmaids' Gifts, Groomsmen's Gifts, and more.

Next, if you have a favorite brand name or store that you prefer, click on http://pages.ebay.com/homebrandsavings/, where you can access thousands of listings of brand-name furnishings, home decor, appliances, linens, and almost everything else for your home. You can look at the "Hot Deals" section and find out what is popular with buyers like yourself. Or you can easily click on "Favorite Brands," which will take you to the most popular home brands

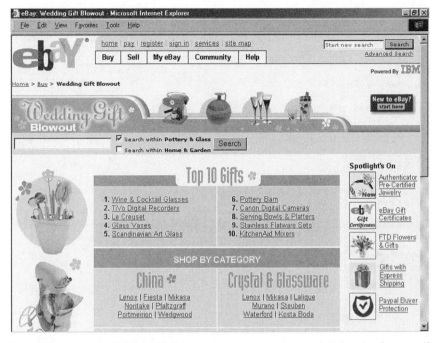

Figure 13-2 The eBay Wedding Gift Blowout page is a great place to start shopping for yourself and your new home (or to give ideas to your wedding guests).

around, such as IKEA, Pottery Barn, KitchenAid, Williams Sonoma, Pier 1,Tupperware, and many more (see Figure 13-3).

USING eBAY TO FULFILL ANOTHER BRIDE AND GROOM'S WISH LIST

It seems that brides- and grooms-to-be run in packs, doesn't it? No sooner have you returned from your honeymoon and begun eagerly setting up your new home than you receive one, two, or several invitations to *other* weddings. Whether it's family, friends, work acquaintances, or whoever, you're likely to find that you're invited to a wedding. So, with all you know about eBay, where will you consider shopping for a gift for that other lucky couple? eBay, of course.

While eBay doesn't currently have a wedding registry area, you can provide the eBay-inclined bride and groom with the next best thing: an eBay gift certificate (see Figure 13-4). How does this program work? First, visit the eBay home page, then scroll down to the "Gift Certificates" link or go directly to https://certificates.ebay.com (the extra "s" in "https" means that the page you are being taken to is a secure one and you are able to engage in secure

Figure 13-3 Hot deals and great items can be found quickly on the eBay Home Brands Savings page.

financial transactions like making payments). Direct from eBay, here's a brief description of how the gift certificate program works:

> eBay Gift Certificates let you share the fun and excitement of bidding and buying on eBay—the world's online marketplace. There's something for everyone on eBay, so take the guesswork out of gift giving and give the gift of eBay!
>
> eBay Gift Certificates are easy to buy, safe and convenient. Here are some highlights:
>
> - Anyone can buy an eBay Gift Certificate, you don't need to be a registered eBay user.
> - Pay for Gift Certificates securely with PayPal (an eBay Company).
> - Send your eBay Gift Certificate via email, or print it out to deliver yourself. It's your choice.
> - Add a personal greeting that will appear on the Gift Certificate.
> - Recipients can redeem eBay Gift Certificates using PayPal for any of the millions of eBay items that accept PayPal.

Gift certificates can be purchased in increments from as little as $5 to as much as $200. eBay gift certificates are a fun way for wedding guests to help

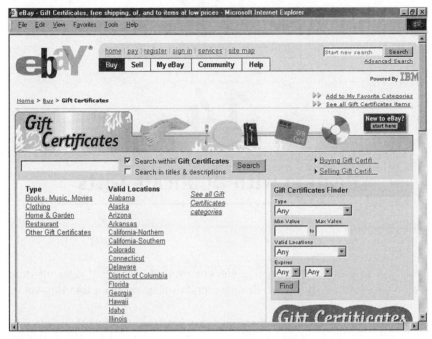

Figure 13-4 Wedding guests can purchase eBay gift certificates for your wedding via the "Gift Certificates" link.

you fulfill your wish list. They're the perfect complement to your affordable, elegant eBay wedding!

Now that you've read about how to use eBay to supplement your wedding registry and to offer a unique gift to another bride and groom, what about those duplicate gifts you've received that are difficult to return or exchange at the store? Never fear, eBay comes to the rescue once again, as you'll learn in the next chapter.

14

Dealing with Duplicate Gifts

Do you have duplicate gifts that you can't return because of difficult store policies? As you'll learn in this chapter, this is no problem for eBay-savvy newlyweds.

While retail and online stores that provide wedding registry services do their best to update a couple's wedding registry when a guest makes a purchase, sometimes an item from your registry list will show up twice when you're opening gifts. And some stores and online sales sites simply do not allow returns or exchanges (yes, that's more the exception than the norm, but it *does* still occur). If you find you have a duplicate item and you can't return it, you can always consider keeping it as a sort of "spare on hand." However, if there's just no room for two of the same gift in your life, then look to eBay again for an answer to your problem.

A DIFFERENT SORT OF "EXCHANGE"

You guessed it: You can sell your duplicate gifts on eBay without your guests being any the wiser. (Of course, receiving a duplicate gift is no excuse for not sending a thank-you note to the gift giver.) Now, as you consider off-loading duplicate items, here are some things to consider as you prepare to list the unwanted goods on eBay. Review Chapter 11 on the basics of how to list your items for sale on eBay.

- If you have a duplicate item, try to keep the original packaging intact. This increases the item's appeal to a buyer. Open one gift and keep the other one untouched—this is the one to sell. Sealed and new items are likely to bring in more bids (and higher final prices) than opened packages.

- Consider adding a subtitle to your item, such as "Perfect for wedding gift!" to attract buyers.
- Try listing the item under the "Wedding Supplies" category as well as the "Home & Garden" subcategory to reach more brides and wedding guests who are shopping on eBay.
- If your item has a popular brand name, such as Calphalon, Pottery Barn, or KitchenAid, be sure to mention that in the title for more visibility and recognition.
- Emphasize that the item is in brand-new, never used condition. Use abbreviations such as NWT (new with tag), NIP (new in package), NIB (new in box), or NRFB (never removed from box), or simply say *NEW* in your item title.
- Place the money earned from your eBay listings in a savings account for a rainy day, or use it to go shopping on eBay to supplement your wedding registry (look back at Chapter 13 for more details).
- If you are somehow unable to sell your duplicate gift on eBay, relax and just hang on to it for a while. If a gift-giving occasion arises in the future (such as a wedding, housewarming, or bridal shower), you can give your gift to someone else to enjoy (with no one the wiser). Just make sure that the gift is in brand-new and unopened condition, and that you've taken off any previous "To/From" tags with your names on it.

THE ETIQUETTE OF AUCTIONING UNNEEDED WEDDING GIFTS

It's inevitable that you and your new spouse will receive gifts that aren't on your wish list and don't necessarily fall within your spectrum of personal taste. Whether it's a large, gaudily colored vase from Grandma Martha, a tacky orange lamp from your cousin Buddy, or a sushi dish set from your college friend Matt (you don't eat sushi), some gifts, thoughtful though they are, simply don't have a place in your life or your lifestyle. Now, here comes the tricky part. According to the *Seinfeld Primer*, *re-gifting* is the practice of giving a gift you've received from someone else. By some, this is considered to be bad form, yet re-gifting of unwanted items is reportedly practiced by 53 percent of Americans, according to those analytical tattletales at the United Mileage Plus Visa Card Shopping Index.

More in keeping with what we're discussing here, the newest twist on the recycling of all manner of garish gifts (from weddings, birthdays, Christmas, or whatever occasion) is the opportunity eBay provides for summarily *de-gifting* such items: offering them outright for sale or bid to the worldwide marketplace. There is a bit of ethics and method needed here, to ensure that your Great Aunt Pat isn't crushed and dismayed when she doesn't find the hideous metal sculpture she gave you the next time she pays you a visit.

Is It Right to De-Gift?

Of course, the matter of ethics will be your first hurdle to clear: Is it proper to even consider selling a gift that was recently given to you? Well, as re-gifting has found something of a humorous acceptance in our current-day society, de-gifting seems poised for equal acceptance for the frugal, fiscally minded, and Internet-enlightened among us. Besides, there may be someone out there in cyberspace who can truly appreciate the gift that you and your spouse simply cannot warm up to.

"For every unwanted present we throw into the back of our [closet] there is someone out there who wants it," offered Jonathan Attwood, CEO of UK-based Webswappers.com. "[Equally], there will be other people who have the things you hoped for but [you] didn't get."

But with ethics being the crux of this question of whether it's right to de-gift, why not take it direct from an ethics expert? According to Judith Martin, aka "Miss Manners," re-gifting is fine provided you don't get caught doing it.

"If you're going to recycle a gift, you must cover all traces that it's been given before," Martin warns. Again, that means removing all tags and other markings, as far as possible, to prevent its being detected as being a re-gift or de-gift. Realistically, getting caught *de*-gifting an item online is much less risky than actually re-gifting it at next year's gift exchange. Then again, de-gifting involves receiving cash in exchange for the item given you—is that an ethical taboo? Ethics columnist Randy Cohen sees nothing wrong with selling an unwanted gift. "If you accept the idea that [re-gifting] is okay, then I think a sale is okay unless you believe touching money taints you."

Ultimately, it comes down to your personal value system and how much of a beating your conscience might take if you sell a former gift. Of course, returning the item to where it was originally purchased and receiving cash back doesn't seem to yield a very different result—only the method has changed.

Marketing Your De-Gifted Goods

Assuming you've decided that it's okay to offer your unwanted wedding gifts online, you need to decide where you'll put them up for sale. Naturally, eBay is the place to begin your recycling efforts. In fact, analyst Daniel Mackeigan has noted that auction sites like eBay tend to triple their gross sales after the holidays, probably the most prevalent source of unwanted gifts, so relax—you're in good company.

eBay is probably the best venue for finding an appreciative owner for your wayward gifts, given that millions of shoppers continue to scour the on-line offerings year round. But the nagging question you might encounter could be, "Should I actually *admit* that this is an unwanted gift?" Depending upon the item, you might not need to divulge anything—garish holiday ties and Chia Pets seem to shout out their Yuletide provenance, and partial drinking goblet sets and standout serving platters might likewise announce their origin. But if you want to have a bit of fun, you might explain that you're de-gifting an item that either didn't fit you or is something you already possess or just don't want. If you do this with a wink and a smile, you are likely to add a bit of charm to the item in the bidders' eyes.

Then again, if the item is more akin to being a collectible, there's really no disclosure required—it's just another item that you're offering up for bid in a marketplace that regularly accommodates such goods. In fact, if these goods are outside your usual style of inventoried offerings, you may find that offering them leads you to new customers, and vice versa. Many sellers have claimed that selling such a "one-off" item has ultimately helped them branch out into a new commodity.

Then there's the handmade gift that can't be bought in stores (and sometimes for good reason). If you've received a spotted, speckled, sculpted bird—the one purported to embody the spirit of oneness for a new couple—and it's likely that you'll never encounter one again (if you're lucky), market it on eBay as a "one-of-a-kind" piece. Handmade goods are quite popular in the online marketplace, and even if the ceramic gooney won't enhance your current decorating scheme, it might be just the ticket for a customer out there seeking a truly unique item.

And while you may elect to post a de-gifted item to your online fixed-price store (your eBay store or perhaps your own Web site), you should remember the original caveat of re-gifting: Ensure that the original gift giver will not learn of your activity. Therefore, if your friend Susie likes to frequent your eBay store or Web space to see what you're selling, make sure the purple-and-orange ceramic frog she gave you isn't prominently priced to sell. Oops!

Guilty Conscience?

If you're still struggling with the moral issue of whether you should sell a gift that just didn't strike your fancy, avoid the guilt and hang on to the item for six to twelve months. If, after that time, you're still no closer to embracing the wedding whatchamacallit, consider again whether it's time to set it free in the online wilderness . . . then don't look back.

15

Consolidate Your Belongings . . . and Sell the Rest on eBay

And now, as you settle into your new home with your spouse, it's time to take stock of your joint belongings and how the two of you are going to arrange them in your shared space. If you are lucky, your new home will have enough space for everything you both own. But if space is at a premium, consider consolidating your belongings and selling off the extras, especially any duplicates, on eBay—you can sell items as small as a coffee cup or as a large as a king-sized bed. You can then put the money you earn on eBay away for a rainy day, or use it to buy items you really need.

Imagine holding a yard sale and having millions of people drop by to see what you have to offer. Imagine receiving multiple offers for a single item. That's what eBay does for you and your belongings. If you're not already convinced, here are some items to look at as you sort through your stuff and your spouse's:

- You have books, CDs, clothes, tools, and other such items that you no longer want or need—and these items are still in good condition.
- Your childhood collection of vintage Barbie dolls or baseball cards may now be worth a fortune—and you *can* see yourself parting with them (for the right price, of course).
- You and your spouse each own a copy of *The Sound of Music*, and you really need only one.
- You'd like to change or update your furniture, but you don't want to throw out your perfectly good La-Z-Boy recliner or your sturdy coffee table from IKEA.

The list can go on and on, but you get the picture. Why not turn all that extra stuff into extra cash? Read on to find out the best ways how.

THE BEST MARKETS FOR YOUR GREAT GOODS

Sure, you'll be selling your items on eBay, but there are a few nuances to listing goods in particular "niche" areas that will help you sell the most goods at the best possible prices. Specifically, there are a couple of ways to go with eBay now, as follows:

- *www.eBay.com.* You already know that there are millions of registered eBay users just like you out there. There are tons of specific categories on eBay that make listing your item very easy. Review Chapter 11 for tips on how to list items for sale on eBay or look at Dennis Prince's book, *How to Sell Anything on eBay . . . and Make a Fortune!*
- *www.half.com.* This is an eBay-owned site, and therefore your eBay user name and password work here, too. Here you can list books, movies, music, computers, and electronics very easily (see Figure 15-1). The site

Figure 15-1 Half.com by eBay—a great place to sell your books, music, movies, and more.

is not an auction site. It's basically an online "store" that lets you list your item for free for an indefinite duration of time. Buyers find your item by typing in the title or typing in a code (such as the ISBN for a book or a UPC for a CD or DVD movie). Half.com will take a small commission fee *only if your item sells.* When buyers purchase your items, they pay Half.com directly with a credit card. As the seller, you receive an official e-mail notification from Half.com stating that a buyer has paid for your item, and that you should send it off right away. The e-mail notification will include a packing slip ready for you to print out and include in your package. In return, Half.com will send you your earnings (minus the commission fee) via direct deposit into your designated bank account. How simple is that?

TURN YOUR EXTRA STUFF INTO CASH

To give you a head start, here are some quick and easy tips regarding the best way to categorize and list your excess goods.

Accessories

Accessories can include handbags, scarves, sunglasses, shawls, gloves, shoes, and any other item that helps complete an outfit. Jewelry is addressed in its own section in this chapter.

- Designer names usually sell well. If you have a Louis Vuitton, Coach, Prada, Kate Spade, Gucci, or other high-end designer bag or item that is gently used, like new, or brand-new, you can auction it off on eBay for a good price. Just make sure you are selling the real thing and not a fake or "designer-inspired" item, since these are prohibited on eBay. Include a store receipt if you still have it in your possession.
- If you still have the original packaging (e.g., store bag, tissue paper, box, sunglasses' case, original shoebox, and so on), include it in the listing to attract more buyers.
- Watch for fashion trends and capitalize on whatever is the most "in" thing or "hot" item in the news and in the fashion magazines. An example is the trendy "poncho" or "pashmina" shawl or scarf. Once your item becomes popular again, it's time to list it on eBay.
- Accessories tend to be seasonal. Hence, list your wool scarves during the winter and your straw handbag in the summer.
- When listing shoes for sale on eBay, list the shoe size and whether the shoes are for men or women. Specify color, heel height, material, and condition (brand new, like new, gently used, and so on) Brand names

usually sell well (Nike, New Balance, Nine West, Aerosoles, Aldo, Adidas, Reebok, and so on).

Books

- Make sure to list the title of the book and the author's name in your listing title so that fans of that author will be able to locate your listing.
- List the format in which your book was published: hardcover, trade paperback, or mass-market paperback. Common abbreviations are HC (hardcover), HC/DJ or HCDJ (hardcover with dust jacket), and PB (paperback). Trade paperbacks are larger than mass-market paperbacks and are typically priced in double digits (generally around $11.95 to $24.95). Mass-market paperbacks (usually fiction, romance, or mystery novels) are smaller, and the most expensive ones cost less than $10.
- It is important to list the condition of the book in your title and in your auction description. Examples are "new," "like new," "mint," "gently used," "normal shelf wear," "creased spine," and so on. Emphasize the positive and downplay the negative, but be sure to mention both. For example, you can describe a book that has "normal shelf wear for the cover" but the "pages are clean, intact, and free of writing and high-lighter marks."
- Books that are "first editions" or "signed by the author" can be rare and can fetch high prices on eBay. If you do happen to have a first edition or signed book, consider hanging on to it a bit longer to see whether the going rate will rise. You can always take it to a used-and-rare-book dealer to see how much you should expect to receive from other bidders.
- Consider listing your books in "lots" or groups, especially if you have several books by the same author. Fans of that author will be more likely to bid on your listing if they can get several books at once—a great bargain for them and an easy sale for you. Include the word *lot* in your item title next to the author's name. For example, you can type *Stephen King Lot of 5 PB NEW*.
- If you decide to sell your books in lots or groups, you can group authors of a similar genre together in one auction listing. For example, you can type *Julia Quinn Lisa Kleypas Brenda Joyce lot of 8 pb books* or something to that effect.
- Offer Media Mail shipping as an alternative method for shipping books to your bidders—it is slower, but it is more cost-efficient for your buyer. Also, the heavier the package (as when several books are being shipped to the same address), the bigger the savings on shipping for your high bidder. Go to www.usps.gov (the official Web site of the U.S. Postal Service) for more information.

Clothes

- Designer names and popular brands generally sell well on eBay. Brands like Gap, Abercrombie & Fitch, Victoria's Secret, J. Crew, Banana Republic, Juicy Couture, Bebe, Diesel, Tommy Hilfiger, Urban Out-fitters, Old Navy, and Express are popular among the teen and young adult crowd. Ralph Lauren, BCBG, Liz Claiborne, Burberry, Esprit, Ann Taylor, United Colors of Benetton, and similar brands are favorites of the adult and older crowd. If you have these brand names hanging in your closet, consider putting them up on eBay to earn extra cash (and help you with spring cleaning).

- Details to include in the title of your listing: brand name, size, condition, material, and color(s). Use the care instructions label on your clothing item as a guide, since it usually includes most of the information you need to describe your item.

- New and like-new clothing sells well on eBay. There is more appeal to your item if it is NWT (new with tags), has never been worn, and is in great condition, or if it was seldom used. If your home is smoke-free, list that in your auction as well: *Item comes from a smoke-free home*.

- Be specific about the size. Mention the size on the label and/or price tag, and also mention how it really fits. For example: *Abercrombie T-shirt Size Large—but really fits like a medium*. This will give your buyer a better sense of the item's size. If possible, measure the dimensions of the item. For example: *Shirt measures 22" at widest point and 45" from neckline to bottom hem*.

- Be descriptive about the color and the material—100% silk is quite different from 100% polyester. Savvy bidders know how to spot a good deal when they see one. Specify care instructions, especially if the item is "hand wash only" or "dry clean only."

- Mention the retail price so that buyers will know that they are getting a great deal.

- Consider selling your clothing in lots, especially if they are about the same size and from the same or similar designer. For example, you can give the title as *Lot of 8 Tops Bebe Express Juicy Couture Abercrombie Size Med*.

- Use size abbreviations such as S, M, L, XL or Small, Med, Lg so that it is easy for your buyer to shop by size.

- If you are selling a used clothing item, wash and press it yourself, or have it professionally cleaned. Specify this in the listing description to attract more buyers.

- Review past listings of other sellers to see what sells and what is popular with eBay buyers.

Entertainment Memorabilia

- Go to http://entertainment-memorabilia.ebay.com to browse through the categories on eBay that are available for your items (see Figure 15-2). Or you can go through the "Site Map" link and look through the categories to arrive at the same site:

Site Map > Categories > Entertainment Memorabilia

- Search completed listings of items similar to yours to research how much buyers are willing to pay for the same or a similar item.
- In your listing title, always include the name of the musician(s)/movie/ musical/Broadway play that your memorabilia is from.
- Offer insured shipping if your item is rare, expensive, or one-of-a-kind (for example, a rare autographed photo hand-signed by all the members of the Beatles band).
- Consider setting a reserve price on your auction to protect your investment.

Figure 15-2 The Entertainment Memorabilia categories page on eBay is a great place to auction off your hard-to-find treasures.

Furniture

- Take accurate measurements of the dimensions of the piece of furniture you want to sell on eBay. Buyers want to know whether they can fit your 72-inch-long, 56-inch-wide sofa sleeper in their home before they consider placing a bid.
- Assess any flaws like scratches or normal wear and tear on your piece of furniture, but emphasize the positive. For example: *Minor scratches on top of coffee table, but will look great after a quick spritz of Pledge. Very sturdy and classy, perfect for your living room or den.*
- Be descriptive as to the colors and materials used in your piece of furniture. If a picture of the item is available on the Internet, refer buyers to the official Web site for more detailed information to supplement your listing. For example: *As seen on the IKEA 2004-2005 Catalog on www.ikea.com.*
- If your item is too heavy to ship, specify that the winning bidder must pick up the item locally. Buyers won't think your $20 La-Z-Boy recliner is such a bargain if it costs $100 to ship it to them.
- Throw in a bonus item if your buyer does a Buy-It-Now purchase, or sell your items together as a set. For example: *Free lamp with a Buy-It-Now purchase!* This will attract more buyers who are willing to consider purchasing your item immediately.
- Know the furniture and household décor brand names that are most popular on eBay, such as IKEA, Pottery Barn, Pier 1, Ethan Allen, and so on. (Look up the brand names on http://pages.ebay.com/homebrand-savings—see Figure 15-3.) If your furniture item is from one of these stores, or is of a similar design, mention this in your title and description.
- Take a good detailed photo of your furniture item with the best possible lighting and in the room that will showcase it the best. Take close-up photos of any fine details (such as the pattern on the upholstery or the hand-carved details of a chair or table).
- Everyone loves a bargain. Don't set your starting bid too high. If your item doesn't sell, consider relisting it at a lower starting bid amount.

Jewelry

- You can list fine jewelry or costume jewelry on eBay. There are specific categories for each, so it is easy to list your items once you figure out which ones you can part with. Check out http://jewelry.ebay.com to see the plethora of categories for jewelry on eBay (see Figure 15-4).
- Good pictures are key to listing jewelry items for sale. If you have a good digital camera, make full use of its zoom and editing features to take detailed images of jewelry. Take a photo of the jewelry item displayed both in and out of its case.

Figure 15-3 The Home Brand Savings page on eBay—great deals on your favorite brands.

- List your item's attributes in the listing: the precious metal it's made of (usually yellow gold, white gold, silver, or platinum) and the karat weight (usually 10K, 14K, or 18K for gold items, "925" for sterling silver, and "PT 950" for platinum). Specify whether the item is solid metal, gold-plated, or silver-plated.
- Specify where you got the jewelry item (from a retail store, your grandmother's vault, or a gift from an ex-boyfriend or girlfriend, for example) and its condition (brand new, like new, rarely worn, minor scratches, and so on).
- Describe any gemstones by carat weight, cut, color, and (if applicable) clarity. If your piece is a high-end item like an engagement ring or wedding band, consider paying for a certificate of appraisal and including this in your listing to attract more buyers.
- If you still have the original packaging (ring box, bracelet box, gift bag) and certification papers, include these in the listing as well.

Movies

- Movies are great-selling items on eBay, whether they're on VHS or DVD. If you own movies that you no longer watch, or if you have duplicates with your spouse, sell them on eBay or half.com.

Figure 15-4 The jewelry categories on eBay offer a great way to specify what kind of jewelry item you are selling.

- Consider selling lots or groups of movies that have a common theme, actor, or director. For example, you can a list a *Lot of 7 Julia Roberts movies VHS DVD* or a *Lot of 3 Martin Scorsese movies VHS DVD*.
- If you have the UPC code (the bar code number on most items), the title, or the director, you can type it in and use the "List with Pre-filled Item Information" option that you will encounter when you are creating a listing to sell a VHS or DVD movie. eBay and half.com will provide the information (year released, format, genre, and more) as well as a stock photo of your item.
- Offer inexpensive shipping for small items such as DVDs and VHS movies. Buyers will shy away from your listing if you are charging $5 or $10 to ship an item that may cost less than the shipping you are charging. First-class mail, Priority Mail flat rate, or Media Mail shipping is fine. Offer your buyers choices whenever possible.

Music

- Music CDs and cassettes are great-selling items on eBay. If you own CDs that you no longer listen to, or if you have duplicates with your spouse, sell them on eBay.

- Consider selling lots or groups of CDs that have a common genre, singer/band, or music era (for example, the 1970s, 1980s). For example, you can a list a *Lot of 6 Dance Music CD Erasure La Bouche* or a *Lot of 8 Celine Dion CDs*.
- If you have the UPC code (the bar code number on most items), the title of the album, or the artist, you can type it in and use the "List with Pre-filled Item Information" option that you will encounter when you are creating a listing to sell a music CD or audio cassette.
- You can also list CD singles, box sets, or vinyl LPs and 45s on eBay and half.com.
- As with movies, offer inexpensive shipping for small items such as CDs and cassettes. Again as with movies, buyers don't want to pay more for shipping than the item costs, and first-class mail, Priority Mail flat rate, or Media Mail shipping is fine here as well. Offer your buyers choices if at all possible.

Toys

- Visit your attic and basement and see what kinds of toys and fun stuff you can sell off on eBay. Comb through your current collection and set aside the stuff you no longer want so that you can sell it on eBay.
- You can sell in either the "Dolls and Bears," "Toys and Hobbies," or "Video Games" category depending on the item you are listing for sale. Popular items include video games, Lego, Barbie dolls, GI Joe figures, stuffed animals, cartoon characters, and action figures from TV shows and movies (Spiderman, Superman, Batman). You can also sell your old board games like Monopoly, Scrabble, chess, and other classic games (vintage items sell extremely well).
- Include the original packaging if you have it. Most buyers who shop the Toys categories are collectors or parents who want to get a good deal on a toy for their children.
- If there is a toy craze during the holidays, eBay is a great place to find and sell the hottest toys. (Remember the Beanie Baby, Furby, and Tickle-Me-Elmo fads?) Sellers who get a bunch of these hot toys can make a lot of money selling them on eBay.

Trading Cards

- If you collected trading cards as a kid, hoping to make big bucks later on, eBay can offer you that chance. Go to http://sports-cards.ebay.com and look at other sellers' listings to get a feel of what trading cards are in demand (see Figure 15-5).
- For tips on selling in this category, check out http://pages.ebay.com/ sportscards/selling_tips.html. The information is detailed and up to date, so make sure to take advantage of your eBay resources.

Figure 15-5 The "Sport Cards" categories on eBay—there's something for everyone.

- Check out http://pages.ebay.com/sportscards/faq.html for answers to your FAQs (frequently asked questions).

Other Items

- There are tons more items that you wouldn't normally think you could sell on eBay, but almost anything is possible if you use your imagination. Here are a few examples: new and used sporting goods, appliances, cameras, coins, computers and computer parts, TVs, DVD players, CD players, musical instruments—in fact, almost everything, including the kitchen sink (try searching for *kitchen sink* and you will find a whole bunch!).

Most importantly, don't forget to have fun when you sell your stuff on eBay. There's nothing like the thrill of a successful sale. Selling on eBay gives you two advantages: It can earn you some cash, and it can help you consolidate your belongings. What a great way to use eBay to start your married life together!

Afterword

---

55 Fun Ways to Enjoy
Your eBay Wedding

We've covered quite a bit here, and we hope you've seen the sense and value of using eBay to plan and prepare your wedding and to guide you into your married life. We've shown you how taking a very deliberate and decisive approach to planning an eBay wedding will help you save a fortune compared with going the more traditional retail route. And, since we've scrubbed and scoured the site with vigor to wrest free the best values, we hope you'll also be sure to enjoy the entire experience. Yes, saving money does take effort and can even be hard work, but this is, after all, your wedding, and you should cherish every moment of it. Therefore, before wrapping up, we'd like to remind you to have a good time throughout your eBay adventure, offering you these 55 ways to enjoy your eBay wedding.

BEFORE YOUR BIG DAY

1. Make your own wedding Web site from www.theknot.com, www.weddingchannel.com, or a similar wedding Web site. Place a link to eBay from your wedding site.
2. Consider becoming an eBay affiliate (see "eBay Affiliate Program" for more details). If a relative or friend joins eBay through your referral, you earn some cool cash!

Site Map > Services > eBay Affiliate Program

3. Support eBay wedding sellers (such as handykane) who support worthy charities. Make other people's dreams come true as well as your own. You can also try shopping via eBay's Giving Works Program: "the

dedicated program for charity listings on eBay, offering a marketplace for compassionate commerce—buy items and support worthy causes at the same time!" Shop for a good cause at http://pages.ebay.com/givingworks/index.html.

4. Specifically request (from your photographer and/or a trusted friend or family member) digital pictures of you on your wedding day, as well as your eBay purchases. Store these images for future use (e.g., in reselling your wedding items on eBay after your big day).

5. Shop for a "wedding time capsule" that you and your fiancé can fill together. Open the capsule on your fifth, tenth, or twentieth wedding anniversary. Keywords: *wedding time capsule*.

6. Transform your pictures into creative wedding invitations or wedding programs for a truly unique souvenir. Keywords: *wedding invitation* photo**.

7. Put eBay gift certificates on your wish list, and let your mom or your maid of honor spread the word that eBay gift certificates are part of your wedding registry.

8. If you anticipate going to additional formal weddings and events in the future, consider purchasing a complete tuxedo outfit on eBay for about the cost of a rental. (Try the seller monkeysuits.)

9. Use a fairy-tale or medieval theme for your wedding and become a prince and princess for a day. Keywords: *Cinderella (wedding,bridal) or (fairytale,fairy tale) (wedding,bridal) or (Lord of the Rings,LOTR, medieval) (wedding,bridal)*.

10. Crave comfort in your bridal footwear? Search for bridal sneakers on eBay like those in the movie *Father of the Bride*. Keywords: *(wedding,bridal) (sneaker*,ballet,slipper*)* or try the seller daddyskiki.

11. Surprise your fiancé by shopping for a T-shirt or sweatshirt hoodie with "Soon to be Mrs. Future Last Name" embroidered on it. Wear it during your engagement and watch as strangers come up to you to give you their best wishes. Keywords: *soon to be,* or try the sellers spoolofdesign or queblessed3x.

12. Search for a bridal name-change kit on eBay and get your paperwork for your name and address changes in order. Keywords: *name change kit*.

eBAY FUN FOR YOUR CEREMONY

13. Thank your officiating celebrant with a personalized "Thank You" plaque.

14. Shop for wedding roses in bulk on eBay and save money on decorations for the church. (Try the sellers bigrose_roses and www*rosesource*com.)

15. If you or your friends or family members have the artistic talent to create favors, invitations, and decorations, purchase your materials at wholesale cost on eBay and save. (Try the sellers efavormart, nyardor0217, pcmailer, and abyersmkt.)

16. Go gourmet with your wedding favors without going broke. eBay offers gourmet treats without the hefty price tag. Chocolate truffles can be found for about $1 a piece. (Try the seller mema-pops.)

17. Wow your guests with amazing (yet affordable) silk floral centerpieces from eBay. Place a "Take Me Home" gift tag on each one so that a lucky guest or couple from each table can bring the centerpiece home as a gift.

18. Give personalized bookmarks (with your favorite photo and verse) as great wedding keepsake favors.

19. Save-the-date magnets make awesome wedding favors that are also useful.

20. Shop for additional flowers in bulk on eBay and save money to decorate your reception site.

21. Try personalized wedding CDs as wonderful favors that your guests will truly keep and use. Keywords: *wedding CD* favor**.

22. Shop for a balloon archway as a spectacular yet affordable entrance or backdrop to your reception hall. Keywords: *wedding balloon arch*.

23. Get a personalized wedding cake topper that will surely be a conversation starter. Keywords: *wedding cake top* (personal*,custom*)*.

24. Order personalized candy wrappers for gift favors. Some popular phrases are "Mint to Be Together," "LoveSavers," for LifeSavers candies, and "HereTheyAre" for Hershey bars.

25. Search for custom-made wedding fortune cookies that will entertain your wedding guests after dinner. They will surely get everyone talking. Try the seller mstnggt66 or the keywords *wedding fortune cookie**.

26. Have great fun during your reception by giving out glow sticks to your wedding guests during the dancing. They will surely be the hit of the party. Keywords: *(glowstick*, glow stick*)*.

27. Shop eBay for disposable cameras and pay less than retail for them. Ask guests to take candid photos and leave the film developing to you. Use an online film developing service such as www.snapfish.com or www.shutterfly.com and enable your guests to view the pictures and even order whatever pictures they would like for themselves.

eBAY FUN FOR YOUR WEDDING GUESTS

28. Send more than a thank-you card to select individuals who have been extra helpful to you in planning your wedding. Shop for affordable gift baskets on eBay and have the gifts sent directly to the lucky

recipient(s). Or have the gift baskets ready and waiting in the hotel rooms of your out-of-town guests to give them a welcoming feeling.

Site Map > Browse > Categories > Everything Else
> Gifts & Occasions > Gift Baskets

29. For wedding party attendants, send a personalized thank-you gift from eBay. Research their favorite music artists or book authors and shop eBay or www.half.com for new books and CDs at affordable prices.

30. Personalize, personalize, personalize! Nothing says "thoughtfulness" like a gift with the recipient's name or initials engraved or embroidered on it. The cost is minimal on eBay, and the "wow factor" is more than worth it. (Try the sellers queblessed3x and ds_decals.)

31. For shower gifts, suggest an "eBay shower" to your mom or maid of honor. Have her spread the word that shower guests are invited to share their innate creativity by shopping for your shower gift on eBay.

32. For your bridesmaids, order monogrammed or personalized brides- maids' tote bags on eBay. Fill each one with goodies hand-picked for that bridesmaid's personality. Keywords: *bridesmaid* tote**.

33. Organize and distribute personalized wedding shower crossword puzzles and games using the bride and groom's information, e.g., the bride's hometown, the groom's favorite drink, and so on. Hand out goofy prizes to the winners who successfully complete the games. Keywords: *(wedding, bridal) shower game**.

34. Help members of your bridal party go eBay shopping. Make it a joint, fun adventure, and help them save money.

35. Break the tradition of the dreaded bridesmaid's dress that will never be worn again. Make your bridesmaids feel special by selecting a main color and asking them to make a choice from a variety of dresses available on eBay. [Try the sellers jennieqxw, humbride, newgowns (formerly cdabridal), and cyberexotic.]

36. Don't send regular thank-you cards to guests. Have some cards made up with your favorite wedding photo for a keepsake they will treasure. (Try the seller handykane or the eBay keywords *wedding photo thank you*.)

37. Search for personalized T-shirts with phrases like "Father of the Bride," "Mother of the Groom," and so on, and have your special wedding guests wear them proudly at your wedding rehearsal. (Try the seller queblessed3x.)

38. Shop for fun T-shirts for you and your fiancé to wear to wedding showers or the wedding rehearsal. Fun phrases include "Property of the Bride" for the groom to wear, and "Property of the Groom" for the bride to wear.

39. Don't forget your ring bearer and flower girl(s). Get them personalized T-shirts and gifts that they can keep long after the event.
40. Have your parents' and your fiancé's parents' wedding photographs transformed into handmade drawings. Display them prominently on your guestbook table, and then give them to your parents afterwards as a thank-you gift. Or place the drawings in your home in a place of honor.

Site Map > Browse > Categories > Everything Else > Specialty Services > Artistic Services >Painting & Drawing

41. Have your wedding video converted to DVD. Order extra copies to give to loved ones, especially those who couldn't come to your wedding.

Site Map > Browse > Categories > Everything Else > Specialty Services > Media Editing & Duplication

42. Consider a "To My _____ on My Wedding Day" framed picture or poem as a thank-you gift to loved ones. Keywords: *to my on my wedding day.*
43. Create a montage of pictures set to music on VHS or DVD. Show the montage to your guests during the reception and then give copies to close friends as gifts.

Site Map > Browse > Categories > Everything Else > Specialty Services > Media Editing & Duplication

44. Give restaurant gift certificates to friends and family as thank-you gifts. You can specify their zip code or city. (Try the seller restaurant.com.)
45. Surprise your parents (or your new spouse's parents) with an affordable three-day vacation through eBay's travel sellers. Let them know how much you appreciate them.
46. Give gift certificates to loved ones to show your appreciation for their participation in your big day.

Site Map > Categories > Gift Certificates

47. Shop for designer handbags and accessories for important female wedding party members (like your mom and his mom) and get huge savings off retail.

eBAY FUN FOR YOUR HONEYMOON

48. Shop for fun "Just Married" items (clothing, hats, tote bags, flip-flops) that you can take with you on your honeymoon. Watch well-wishers

and airline and resort employees give you their best wishes, along with some great bonus perks (airline upgrades, room upgrades, free champagne, complimentary fruit baskets)! (Try the sellers designsbyheidi and dnsmartshop.)

49. Have a great honeymoon, eBay-style, and don't forget to tell your friends and family all about it. (Review Chapter 9 for more details.)

eBAY FUN IN YOUR NEW LIFE TOGETHER

50. Get your favorite wedding photo turned into a portrait painted on canvas. Give it to your new spouse as an anniversary gift, or to either set of parents as a thank-you gift. (Try the seller veradi.) Or build your own wedding photo album or scrapbook for a more personalized touch, making your wedding memories last forever. Keywords: *wedding scrapbook*.

51. After the wedding, collect your bridesmaids' gowns and any other wedding items. Auction them off on eBay and donate the proceeds to your favorite charity.

52. For your anniversary, surprise your spouse with a quick three- or four-day vacation from one of eBay's authorized travel sellers. Consider it a second honeymoon.

53. Gather up wedding magazines and books that you've used and no longer need. List them for sale on eBay and let another bride share in the wealth of wedding information.

54. Order a "Mrs. New Last Name, Established MM.DD.YY" embroidered T-shirt or sweatshirt on eBay and wear it proudly after your wedding day. Your new spouse will be thrilled, and you will inspire other brides with this creative idea.

55. Share your eBay knowledge with friends and family members who you know are getting married. Share this book with them and have fun helping them to have their very own elegant yet affordable eBay wedding.

INDEX

About the Authors

Dennis L. Prince is a well-recognized and long-trusted advocate for online auction-goers who continues his tireless efforts to instruct, enlighten, and enable auction enthusiasts and business owners, assuring his readers' success every step of the way. His perpetual passion for online auctions and his adherence to good business practices have earned him recognition as one of the Top Ten Online Auction Movers and Shakers by Vendio.com (formerly AuctionWatch.com). His insight and perspectives are regularly sought out by others covering the online auction industry. He has been featured in the nationally distributed *Entrepreneur Magazine* (2003) and *Access Magazine* (2000), and he has been a guest of highly rated television and radio programs such as TechTV, BBC-Radio, and C/Net Radio.

Besides his previous books about eBay and Internet commerce, his vast editorial contributions to industry stalwarts like Vendio.com (formerly AuctionWatch), Krause Publications, Collector Online, and Auctiva have earned him a well-regarded reputation for his ongoing analysis of the online auction industry. He likewise maintains active interaction with his ever-expanding personal network of auction enthusiasts, power sellers, and passionate collectors, online and off-line.

He married his true love in 1987 and has been smiling ever since. He is likewise enjoying raising his two boys, Eric and Alex.

Sarah Manongdo and Dan Joya celebrated their engagement on Valentine's Day, 2004. Dan graduated from the University of Illinois with a B.S. in finance and is currently working for a consulting firm. Sarah graduated from Loyola University Chicago with a B.S. in biology and is pursuing a doctoral degree at the Illinois College of Optometry. She has supplemented her practically non-existent student stipend by buying and selling on eBay since 1998. Dan and Sarah, faced with the challenge of paying for their wedding, have teamed up to plan an elegant yet affordable "eBay wedding." Prompted by friends and family to expand their shared hobby of writing, this is Dan and Sarah's first joint writing effort. After their wedding (set for Memorial Day weekend 2005), the couple will reside in Chicago.